OXFORD STUDIES IN AFRICAN AFFAIRS

General Editors

John D. Hargreaves, Michael Twaddle,
Terence Ranger

MOMBASA, THE SWAHILI, AND THE MAKING OF THE MIJIKENDA

Mombasa, the Swahili, and the Making of the Mijikenda

Justin Willis

CLARENDON PRESS · OXFORD
1993

HOUSTON PUBLIC LIBRARY

Oxford University Press, Walton Street, Oxford OX2 6DP

Oxford New York Toronto
Delhi Bombay Calcutta Madras Karachi
Kuala Lumpur Singapore Hong Kong Tokyo
Nairobi Dar es Salaam Cape Town
Melbourne Auckland Madrid

and associated companies in
Berlin Ibadan

Oxford is a trade mark of Oxford University Press

Published in the United States
by Oxford University Press Inc., New York

© Justin Willis, 1993

British Library Cataloguing in Publication Data
Data available
ISBN 0-19-820320-9

Library of Congress Cataloging in Publication Data
Willis, Justin.
Mombasa, the Swahili, and the making of the Mijikenda / Justin
Willis.
(Oxford studies in African affairs)
Includes bibliographical references.
1. Mombasa (Kenya)—History. 2. Nika (African people)—History.
3. Kenya—Politics and government—To 1963. 4. Mombasa (Kenya)—
Ethnic relations. I. Title. II. Series.
DT434.M7W55 1992   967.62'3—dc20   92-23255
ISBN 0-19-820320-9

Set by Graphicraft Typesetters Ltd., Hong Kong
Printed and bound in Great Britain by
Biddles Ltd, Guildford and King's Lynn

For Susan

Acknowledgements

T H I S book has been made possible by the help, kindness, and patience of many people; it is impossible to name here all those who made my research possible, and who helped me to write up the research and to turn the unwieldy results into a book. I would like first to express my humble gratitude to the many whom I do not mention here. There are, however, some whose help and influence has been such that they must be named, both from courtesy and from a desire to help future researchers into academic networks.

At the School of Oriental and African Studies, I would like to thank Andrew Roberts and David Anderson for invaluable advice and patient reading of manuscripts, and Richard Gray for his encouragement. Particular thanks must go to Roland Oliver for many years of support and advice.

My fieldwork in Kenya would have been impossible without the help of Ahmed Salim, Godfrey Muriuki, and Karim Janmohamed. Equally invaluable was the assistance provided by Mr Musembi, Nathan Mnjama, and Richard Ambani, of the Kenya National Archives in Nairobi. I gratefully acknowledge the co-operation of the Office of the President in Nairobi, and of the many administrative officers in Mombasa, Kilifi, and Kwale Districts who assisted me in my fieldwork.

Fort Jesus Museum, the Municipality of Mombasa, and the Mombasa Lands Registry were most generous in allowing me access to their records, and Abdurrahman Mwinzagu of the National Museums of Kenya took great interest in my work and helped introduce me to a number of informants. I was greatly helped in my research by the patience and kindness of Justus Mweni Mramba and Johnson Ruwa. I must also thank Thomas Spear, whose commendable decision to publish some of his interview material has been enormously helpful to me and to other researchers. The staff of the British Institute in Eastern Africa were endlessly kind to me, and I would like to thank the Council of the British Institute for allowing me the time to complete this manuscript.

While I was conducting research in Kenya, I benefited very greatly from the help, friendship, and advice of other researchers, particularly Mary Porter, Jeanne Bergman, Bill Bravmann, and David Sperling. My thanks also go to Martin Walsh for his help.

The tolerance, and love of my parents supported me through the research and writing of my thesis. I thank them, once again. In Mombasa, the family of the late Shihabuddin Chiraghdin has shown me enormous kindness and hospitality over the years since my first visit to Mombasa.

The research for, and writing of, my thesis was supported by a grant from the British Academy.

J.W.

British Institute, Nairobi
December 1991

Contents

List of Maps

Abbreviations

Ag.	Acting
ADC	Assistant District Commissioner
APC	Assistant Provincial Commissioner
BISN	British India Steam Navigation Company Limited
CMS	Church Missionary Society
CNC	Chief Native Commissioner
DC	District Commissioner
EAS (D)	*East African Standard* (daily edition)
EAS (W)	*East African Standard* (weekly edition)
HIA	*History in Africa*
IBEA	Imperial British East Africa Company papers, in the Mackinnon Papers, at SOAS library, University of London
IJAHS	*International Journal of African Historical Studies*
Int.	Interview conducted by the author: see Appendix. Following fig. is the Informant's number, and following letter indicates which interview, e.g. Int. 3*a* is the first interview with Informant 3
JAH	*Journal of African History*
JAS	*Journal of African Studies*
JRAI	*Journal of the Royal Anthropological Institute*
JRGS	*Journal of the Royal Geographical Society*
KNA	Kenya National Archives, Nairobi
	AG Attorney-General deposit
	KFI Kilifi District deposit
	KWL Kwale District deposit
	MOH Ministry of Health deposit
	MSA Mombasa District deposit
LNC	Local Native Council
MHT	Mijikenda Historical Traditions, published in T. T. Spear, *Traditions of Origin and their Interpretation* (Athens, Ohio, 1982)
MOH	Medical Officer of Health
PC	Provincial Commissioner (unless otherwise indic-

	ated, this refers to the Provincial Commissioner of Seyyidieh or Coast Province)
PRO	Public Records Office, London
	CO Colonial Office series
	FO Foreign Office series
PWD	Public Works Department
SC	Senior Commissioner (unless otherwise indicated, this refers to the Senior Commissioner, Coast Province)
SNA	Secretary for Native Affairs
SOAS	School of Oriental and African Studies
SoS	Secretary of State for the Colonies
TNR	*Tanganyika Notes and Records*

Explanatory Notes

OFFICIAL TITLES

Until 1907, the senior official in British East Africa was His Majesty's Commissioner. Beneath him, there was a Sub-Commissioner in charge of each province, and a Collector in charge of each district of each province. After 1907, the senior official was the Governor, under whom there was a Provincial Commissioner in each province and a District Commissioner in each district. On the coast, there were also Assistant District Commissioners in Malindi and Mombasa Districts. In 1921 the Provincial Commissioners became Senior Commissioners, and the District Commissioner of Mombasa became known as the Resident Commissioner. In 1927 they reverted to their previous titles.

CURRENCY

The principal circulating coin on the East African coast in the later nineteenth century was the Maria Theresa dollar. In the mid-nineteenth century Seyyid Said imported a consignment of copper pice from India to serve as small change, which had until then been lacking. The Maria Theresa dollar was generally valued at about 2 Indian rupees, which was 32 annas, or 128 pice.

The Imperial British East Africa Company introduced the rupee, divided into pice and annas, as the currency of their territory, and this currency was maintained under the British Protectorate. However the authorities discovered that the number of pice to the rupee varied. They therefore ended the circulation of pice in 1906, and established the East African rupee as a separate currency, divided into 100 cents.

In 1920, the rupee was replaced, first by the florin, and then shortly afterwards by the shilling. Two shillings were equivalent to 1 rupee, and there were 100 cents to the shilling.

Introduction

Struggles for the City

The research on which this book is based was first conceived as a study of the relationships between two distinct groups, the Swahili and other inhabitants of the town of Mombasa and the Mijikenda who live in the immediate hinterland of that town. In the course of time it has become something rather different, a study of changing concepts of ethnicity, but even more, a study of the development in the early colonial period of the complex of institutions which constituted a town.

The efforts of colonial administrations to assert control over urban space in Africa have formed the subject of other studies. One of these has dealt specifically with Mombasa in the years after 1930, when the concerns of the administration were in some ways the obverse of those which had guided policy in the first forty years of British rule in Kenya:[1] in a sense, I seek in this book to explain how the colonial state and capital participated in the creation of certain institutions which, from the 1930s, the state was anxious to demolish. These other studies, while they have moved beyond the statistical emphasis of some writing on the African city,[2] have tended to concentrate on the role of the capital and the state, and the attitudes of officials, rather than on the complex of institutions which make up the

---

[1] C. van Onselen, *Studies in the Economic and Social History of the Witwatersrand*, i and ii (Harlow and New York, 1982); A. Proctor, 'Class Struggle, Segregation and the City: A History of Sophiatown, 1905–1940', in B. Bozzoli (ed.), *Labour, Townships and Protest* (Johannesburg, 1979); F. Cooper, *On the African Waterfront: Urban Disorder and the Transformation of Work in Colonial Mombasa* (New Haven, Conn., 1987).

[2] A prime example of this approach is A. O'Connor, *The African City* (London, Melbourne, Sydney, Johannesburg, 1983); see e.g. the discussion of migration, 57–72. A recent collection on urban food supplies has criticized the concentration on prices and statistics of other works; J. Guyer (ed.), *Feeding African Cities: Studies in Regional Social History* (Manchester, 1987), 8–14. Despite this, some of the contributors to this volume still avoid any historical analysis of social relationships; see D. F. Bryceson, 'A Century of Food Supply in Dar es Salaam: From Sumptuous Suppers for the Sultan to Maize Meal for a Million', in Guyer (ed.), *Feeding African Cities*, 155–97.

town. Cooper's edited volume has attempted to redress this imbalance, beginning as it does with the bold declaration that it is a book about 'daily struggles over the details of life in the workplace, the marketplace and the residence':[3] but not all the contributors are successful in laying open the daily life of the city. The task is not an easy one: a concentration on official attitudes is to some extent dictated by reliance on archival sources, whose information on the society of the town is generally limited and structured by the preconceptions of officials. As a result, whether the author's approach is informed by liberal or structuralist-Marxist ideas, in these studies the populations of the colonial urban spaces often remain an indistinct mass, without structure—a disorganized rabble, just as the administrators of the time were wont to perceive them.[4]

Yet beneath this appearance of indiscipline the daily lives of urban populations in colonial Africa were structured, through many different and sometimes conflicting institutions. Where the formal institutions of the town were minimal, the daily reproduction of an urban population relied on other, informal, arrangements, and this book follows history through these. In doing so it attempts to show, as the above quotation from Cooper suggests, that the struggle over the institutions of the town was, in truth, *many* struggles. Daily life in Mombasa in this period cannot be understood simply as the history of a conflict between capital and actual or potential workers: for though the academic today may see this as the dominant theme of history, this was not the perception which informed the actions of people in Mombasa at the time.

To be sure, the people of Mombasa and its local hinterland did resist the demands made upon them by capital and the colonial state. Yet they were involved in other struggles too: against creditors, and homestead heads; against husbands and uncles. It can be argued (and will be, here) that these struggles became increasingly involved with the struggle against capital, as the state sought to commandeer local institutions of power and use them in pursuit of its own ends. Yet this was not necessarily how people at the time saw it: in some ways, the

[3] F. Cooper (ed.), *Struggle for the City: Migrant Labor, Capital and the State in Africa* (Beverly Hills, Calif., 1982), 10.
[4] Ibid. 22. A survey of literature on the city can be found ibid. 7–45.

penetration of capital offered them welcome alternatives. Capital intensified exploitation and conflict within the hinterland homestead, but it also offered new options to those involved in existing conflicts over resource allocation within the homestead. Resistance to the colonial state was not whole-hearted or unified, because of this multiplicity of struggles. Moreover, accommodation with, and exploitation of, the opportunities which colonialism offered could in the long run be far more subversive of the state's intentions than was open resistance. It could be argued that the movement of women to Mombasa, and the diminished control which the state and men generally had over them there, was a much more enduring problem for the administration than was the brief outbreak of the Giriama revolt—even though these women were, in one sense, serving capital by helping reproduce an urban labour force.[5]

It will be argued here that the state's attempt to assert control of urban space led to fundamental changes in the institutions of town life; for official intervention changed the relative attractiveness of the options which these institutions offered. But while the power of the state was considerable, it was not overwhelming: in Mombasa, as elsewhere in Africa, the state was unwilling to bear, or to force capital to bear, the cost of formalizing the provision of food, housing, and other services to the urban populace, and so was forced into a continued tolerance of urban institutions which were beyond its control, and which could be used to subvert or evade its dominance.[6]

Moreover, while the colonial state did seek to work in the interests of capital, it was far from being a simple servant of business interests. By this I mean not simply that the state had to 'cope with the contradictions',[7] but also that the state was not monolithic and that official perceptions of the collective interest of capital were varied and not always very accurate. To borrow Cooper's image, the troops of capital's army were not disciplined or co-ordinated.[8] Much of this book deals with the period when the administration of Mombasa was dominated by C. W. Hobley, who conceived a number of

---

[5] Ibid. 8.   [6] Ibid. 29.
[7] J. Lonsdale and B. Berman, 'Coping with the Contradictions: The Development of the Colonial State in Kenya, 1895–1914', *JAH* 20 (1979), 487–505.
[8] Cooper (ed.), *Struggle for the City*, 18.

far-reaching measures to deal with what he saw as the problems affecting the coast. Yet Hobley's ability to implement these measures was limited, and his successors did not take up all his ideas with enthusiasm. Even where there was agreement within the state that a certain policy should be adopted, different officials and departments often sought to pass the costly and time-consuming responsibility of implementation on to one another.

The role of metaphor in the formulation of policy further suggests that the colonial state was often far from clear-sighted or efficient in the service of capital. That disease and contamination served as metaphors in colonial Africa is now well documented: social arrangements deemed inimical to good order or the interests of capital were condemned as pathological and contagious.[9] This was most certainly true of official discourse concerning the nature of society in Mombasa. Yet the image of contamination was not one simply called up by men who saw clearly their real economic interests and worked for the creation of social formations that would favour them; it was an analysis whose accuracy they accepted. In attempting to implement administrative measures conceived within this analysis, officials in Mombasa sowed the seeds of one of capital's major problems in the 1930s and 1940s: the vexed question of migrant labour.

Networks and Institutions

This is not a book about class. Neither the nature of social reproduction, nor the ways in which people perceived their interests and located their allegiances support a class analysis of Mombasa in the period of this study. This is, rather, a history of the struggles of many people *not* to be a class.[10] The concept of network is central to an understanding of these struggles, and of how Mombasa worked from day to day. Through this idea, this book seeks to explain the economic options for people living in and around Mombasa, why some

[9] M. W. Swanson, 'The Sanitation Syndrome: Bubonic Plague and Urban Native Policy in the Cape Colony, 1900–1909', *JAH* 18(1977), 377–410.

[10] Cooper, *On the African Waterfront*, 8.

were more attractive than others, and why some were mutually exclusive. That people had *some* options is a fundamental proposition of this analysis.[11] Tightly constrained as individuals were in the pre-colonial and colonial periods, they could none the less exercise choice, could manipulate the available options to secure for themselves some little space.

The idea of network, of which casual use has been made in some recent studies, was taken up by sociologists studying Africa in the 1960s, in an attempt to develop some analysis more appropriate for urban Africa than were the models used for rural societies.[12] It was adopted from European sociology, where it had been seen as one of several alternative ways in which people ordered relationships. As such it was ranked alongside structural order, which explained social behaviour in terms of position in a structure such as the family or the workplace, and categorical order, which explained behaviour in terms of a social stereotype such as ethnicity or class. An individual's network was, in this analysis, the sum total of all those people with whom they claimed some relationship not defined by structure or category.

This definition seems both too wide *and* too narrow for urban Africa, as Mitchell suggested by including ethnicity as one way in which people were recruited to networks.[13] In Mombasa, ethnicity and family were negotiable, and could easily be reconstructed; as, for example, when people claimed kinship with their creditors or other patrons. Family and ethnicity could be manipulated as ways of constructing networks, as this book will show: networks were not a separate order of relationship to family or ethnicity. At the same time, to call all of an individual's acquaintanceship their network blunts this analytical tool.[14] It was of the essence of the urban networks of

---

[11] See D. Parkin (ed.), *Town and Country in East and Central Africa* (Oxford, 1975), 9–14.

[12] J. C. Mitchell, 'The Concept and Use of Social Networks', in id. (ed.), *Social Networks in Urban Situations* (Manchester, 1969), 1–50. For a casual use of the term, see Cooper, *Struggle for the City*. I am deeply indebted to Mary Porter, then a doctoral student at Washington State University, for first mentioning to me the appropriateness of networks as a tool for analysing Mombasan society.

[13] Mitchell, 'The Concept and Use of Social Networks', 41.

[14] A. L. Epstein, 'The Network and Urban Social Organisation', in Mitchell (ed.), *Social Networks*, 77–116.

Mombasa that people did not make claims on everybody on whom they could potentially make claims, nor did they acknowledge the claims of all to whom they were potentially obligated—for there are choices and conflicts involved, and claims of one kind excluded those of another kind. Networks did not endure, and people could create entirely new ones. This book treats network as an 'action-set', a temporary coming together of people in particular circumstances—a definition also suggested by Mitchell, and one which has been taken up in a recent study of the creation of political communities in Lagos.[15]

These networks were ephemeral and situational—used to make or acknowledge claims, to obtain food, work, or accommodation. Having served their purpose, they might continually be recreated to maintain a relationship, or they might change their nature, or simply cease to be. More enduring were the many different institutions through which such networks were created, what Mitchell would call the 'content' of network.[16] Kinship, debt, religious affiliation, and dance societies were all institutions through which such networks could be constructed. It is argued here that ethnicity, which was initially a category defined largely through people's position in other institutions, became an increasingly important institution in the networks of Mombasa in the twentieth century.[17] It is for this reason that the ethnonym Mijikenda is not used for the period before 1930 in this book. By using Nyika as an ethnonym for the earlier period, I do not intend to offer gratuitous offence to those who feel that this is a pejorative term. Rather, this usage is intended to avoid a misleading anachronism, and to emphasize a fundamental point of analysis: that the unity of the peoples of the Mombasan hinterland was, until the 1930s, established only in terms of their common positions in the institutions which linked them to the population of Mombasa and other coastal settlements. As I argue below, they were not otherwise a distinct and unified group, in terms of history or cultural practice. The term Mijikenda, claiming a unified

---

[15] Mitchell, 'The Concept and Use of Social Networks', 41–3; S. Barnes, *Patrons and Power: Creating a Political Community in Metropolitan Lagos* (London, 1986), 9–11.
[16] Mitchell, 'The Concept and Use of Social Networks', 20–2.
[17] A. L. Epstein, *Politics in an Urban African Community* (Manchester, 1958), 231–3, writes on the importance of tribalism as an organizing institution of urban life.

identity which could itself act as an institution through which networks were constructed, was an innovation of the 1930s: this identity developed initially as a result of changing relationships with Mombasa, but it served as an expression of, and a mechanism for, a sense of unity in a way that Nyika identity never had. Ethnicity in Mombasa became a dynamic and negotiable feature of urban life, not a vestigial remnant of rural life.[18]

Individuals could use a network created through one institution to break into another institution, and through this create new networks. So a migrant to Mombasa might seek out and stay with a family member already living in the town, and through them join one of the urban dance societies. Through this, in turn, they might acquire a new patron, and find work and other housing. Life in Mombasa was a question not just of who you knew, but also of how you knew them. Involvement in the networks created through some institutions might not be compatible with involvement in other institutions—as I will argue, an active member of a Giriama clan would not dance in a *beni* dance society. Because these institutions were thus involved in daily life and survival, it is impossible to discuss ethnicity, or dance, without considering the daily exigencies of life in and around Mombasa. Conversely, it is an incomplete analysis which seeks to understand life in Mombasa without looking at these institutions.

It is through the analysis of these institutions that this becomes the history of the town of Mombasa itself; for the institutions which linked town and hinterland articulated with those which constitute the town itself, and they were constructed on similar bases. The relationships between these populations can, in the most basic way, be explained through Mombasa's position on what was, in effect, an ecological boundary. As with the inhabitants of other ports, and other kinds of border, the population of Mombasa controlled the access of hinterland people to the product of neighbouring zones.[19] Since food

---

[18] O'Connor, *The African City*, 99–111, gives the impression that tribalism is somehow vestigial and non-urban.

[19] Cf. R. A. Austen, 'The Metamorphoses of Middlemen: The Duala, Europeans, and the Cameroon Hinterland, *c.*1800–*c.*1960', *IJAHS* 16 (1983), 1–25; also M. Watts, 'Brittle Trade: A Political Economy of Food Supply in Kano', in Guyer (ed.), *Feeding African Cities*, 55–111.

shortages periodically affected parts or all of Mombasa's hinterland, the people, like those of other hinterlands elsewhere,
sometimes relied on imports of food. The people of Mombasa
themselves, like those of other ports and borders, needed access to the products of the hinterland: both because the coast
was not particularly productive of foodstuffs and in order to
realize their potential as traders. The viability of the domestic
economy in the hinterland was intimately involved with the
control of access to the coast, and therefore to the products
of other zones; and wealth and authority on the coast were
similarly bound up with access to the hinterland. Those who
sought wealth or power in either coast or hinterland were,
therefore, reliant to some extent on accommodation with their
neighbours.

In pre-colonial Mombasa and its local hinterland, people
were the fundamental determinants of wealth and status, and
fugitives were often welcomed by wealthy men as new clients
and dependants.[20] In the hinterland the control of people's
movement to and from the coast was essential to authority; for
patrons in the hinterland were always in danger of losing their
children, clients, slaves, or other dependants to patrons on the
coast who had superior access to goods and capital. The accommodation between coast and hinterland was always threatened by the possibility of conflict over dependants; yet these
dependants were also the currency of this accommodation.

Food imported through Mombasa, from elsewhere on the
coast or from the Indian Ocean islands, was in many cases not
paid for, but borrowed, the debt secured by a human pledge;
a pawned person, who might or might not one day be redeemed
through repayment of the debt. Debt, and clientship, were the
basis of the innumerable little networks, which linked the
people of Mombasa and those of its hinterland. Many of the
social networks of the town were similarly built around
clientship, producing a subtle hierarchy of dependency which
defined the claims and obligations of a population of slaves,
debtors, pawns, and patrons. Many occupied dual roles, both
debtor and creditor, client and patron.

[20] A common factor in African history; see S. Miers and I. Kopytoff, *Slavery in Africa: Historical and Anthropological Perspectives* (Madison, Wis., 1977), 14.

I do not seek to idealize these networks. Relationships of debt and clientage were conflictual, for patron and client each sought their own advantage, and tried to better the terms of the relationship. As well as conflict between patron and client, there was always the potential for conflict between patron and patron, for the possibility always existed of clients seeking to better their position by finding new patrons. In such conflicts, access to credit gave those within Mombasa the edge.

The uniqueness of Mombasa's history as a late pre-colonial and colonial town can be attributed to the institutions which developed due to a particular conjunction of economic and political circumstances. The great nineteenth-century expansion in East African trade was one of these circumstances. The significance of this expansion was not simply that increased demand for goods increased participation in trade. Even more importantly, the growth in trade was accompanied by a growth in the availability of credit, and thus a steady widening of existing networks of debt and dependence, to encompass larger geographical areas and populations.[21] As providers of food security, patrons in Mombasa had always had the advantage of access to the produce of a much wider area than that on which hinterland patrons could draw. The expansion of credit gave them even greater advantages. There were other African towns on coasts, and on ecological borders of other kinds, but Mombasa was unusual because of its position in the extensive credit networks of the Indian Ocean.[22]

Comparison with other towns of the East African coast reveals how important the particular conjuncture of economic circumstances in Mombasa was in determining the history of the town. While Dar es Salaam was on the Indian Ocean coast, and became an important city in the colonial period, it had no significant involvement in nineteenth-century trade.[23] Kinship and pawning relationships between the Zaramo of the

---

[21] A. Sheriff, *Slaves, Spices and Ivory in Zanzibar: Integration of an East African Commercial Empire into the World Economy, 1770–1873* (London, Nairobi, Dar, 1987), 155–200, plays down Mombasa's role in trade under the Busaidi, but the emphasis here is on the ivory trade. F. Cooper, *Plantation Slavery on the East African Coast* (New Haven, Conn., 1977), 100–5, shows the growing importance of Mombasa's grain trade in the later 19th c.   [22] Cf. the description of Kano, in Watts, 'Brittle Trade'.
[23] J. E. G. Sutton, 'Dar es Salaam: A Sketch of a Hundred Years', *TNR* 71 (1970), 1–19.

hinterland and the small Shomvi settlements of the Dar area
were in some ways similar to those found around Mombasa,
but since Dar was not involved in the coasting grain trade, and
the coast people had little role in the credit networks of the
Indian Ocean, these relationships involved far fewer people
than did those around Mombasa.[24] When Dar es Salaam became a colonial port and city, the administration could exert
a degree of control, for example over land, which was crucially
lacking in Mombasa, and no large 'Swahili' population developed in Dar to challenge the state's ideas on ethnicity and the
organization of work.[25] Bagamoyo and Pangani played important roles in nineteenth-century trade and developed much
wider networks of patronage than did Dar es Salaam.[26] There
were, though, significant differences between their pre-colonial
economies and that of Mombasa; which meant that in these
towns the institutions which linked town and hinterland developed rather differently. Bagamoyo relied much more on up-
country porters for the caravan trade than did Mombasa,
so that patronage relationships were less concentrated on the
local hinterland.[27] In Pangani, the great expansion in late
nineteenth-century agriculture was in sugar-cane, not grain.
Sugar-cane was not a staple crop, and it needed to be collected
and processed immediately after harvesting. This made it a
plantation crop, not one for small producers who controlled
their own time, and so the overlap between the statuses of
client agriculturalist and slave agriculturalist which was a feature of Mombasa farming in the later nineteenth century was
not so evident here.[28] In the colonial period, both Pangani and
Bagamoyo declined in importance and population, in dramatic
contrast to Mombasa.

For another dominating circumstance in the history of the
institutions of the Mombasa area was the town's position in a

[24] L. Swantz, 'The Zaramo of Dar es Salaam: A Study of Continuity and Change',
TNR 71 (1970), 157–64.
[25] J. Iliffe, *A Modern History of Tanganyika* (Cambridge, 1979), 128–9, 161; Sutton,
'Dar es Salaam', 7.
[26] W. T. Brown, 'A Pre-Colonial History of Bagamoyo: Aspects of the Growth of
an East African Coastal Town', Ph.D. thesis (Boston, Mass., 1971), 90: id., 'Bagamoyo:
An Historical Introduction', *TNR* 71 (1970), 69–83.
[27] Iliffe, *Modern History*, 44–5.
[28] J. Glassman, 'Social Rebellion and Swahili Culture: The Response to German
Conquest of the Northern Mrima, 1888–1890', Ph.D. thesis (Wisconsin, 1988),
183–6.

colonial economy, the future of which was perceived to lie in European enterprise. In the late nineteenth and early twentieth centuries the coast around Mombasa was partly given over to new, European-owned plantations, and the town itself became the harbour and railway terminus of the colony. In the early years of the British East Africa Protectorate, Mombasa's new economic role enhanced the power of patrons in the town—whose control over labour and trade put them in a position to benefit from increased demand. Their control was soon under threat, however, for the supply of labour both in the hinterland and in the town became a matter of considerable importance in the economy of the colony, and thus of great concern to the administration—particularly since local officials were acutely aware of the economic disruption occasioned by what some felt to be the overly rapid abolition of slavery. It was this issue which intensified the struggle for control of Mombasa, for the social institutions through which the town was constructed were inimical to the needs of the colonial economy, offering as they did alternative employment and means to evade the legislation through which the administration sought to control workers.

These institutions were equally offensive to the contemporary understanding of how African societies worked and to the machinery of administration developed within that understanding. The official perception that the problems of labour supply and administration on the coast were bound up with these institutions of clientship was expressed through the metaphor of disease, and the suggested response to these problems used similar imagery—isolation was to prevent the spread of contagion. This discourse became bound up with the issue of ethnicity on the coast, and particularly with the use of the term 'Swahili'.

Being Swahili, Becoming Mijikenda

Much has been written on Swahili identity, most of it implicitly or explicitly addressing two questions; are the Swahili African or not, and are they a tribe or not?[29] Some have argued

[29] C. Eastman, 'Who Are the Waswahili?', *Africa*, 41 (1971), 228–36; W. Arens, 'The Waswahili: The Social History of an Ethnic Group', *Africa*, 45 (1975), 426–38; A. I. Salim, 'The Elusive Mswahili: Some Reflections on his Culture and Identity', in J. Maw and D. Parkin (eds.), *Swahili Language and Society* (Vienna, 1985), 215–27.

that Swahili identity is constructed by a dominant ideology which the Swahili themselves are powerless to influence, which fixes their position in an ethnic hierarchy in which they are the hopelessly aspiring underdogs, their subordination ensured by their ambitions.[30] Others have sought to establish the Swahili, or some of them, as a tribe, in the sense of a group defined by descent, in reaction to a popular discourse which has, particularly since the 1920s, both denied that the Swahili are a tribe and given this ethnonym a pejorative implication.[31] In this context, the legal differentiation in colonial Kenya between Arab and native, and the incentive to claim Arab identity which this offered, has been stressed.[32] But the wider manipulation of ethnic identity as a means for evading the control of the colonial state *and* other kinds of authority has not been discussed. By showing here how the use of the term Swahili was manipulated by various players in the early twentieth century, I hope to place the debate on Swahili identity in the context of a more modern debate on the nature of identity, which suggests that ethnic identity is a dynamic thing, created and recreated constantly through negotiation. There is no single 'definition' of the Swahili. Different people, in different situations, may appropriate this ethnonym or apply it to others, according to their perception of their own advantage. The Swahili are not a discrete, enduring unit—but neither are the members of any other tribe.

There has recently been a considerable literature on the creation of ethnicity in the colonial period, and the apparent invention of the Mijikenda in the 1930s and 1940s may be seen as another example of this.[33] The reinvention of the Swahili as a discrete and bounded group may also be seen in these terms, and both these examples clearly exemplify an important point:

---

[30] F. Constantin, 'Condition swahili et identité politique', *Africa*, 57 (1987), 219–33; id., 'Social Stratification on the Swahili Coast: From Race to Class', *Africa*, 59 (1989), 145–61; D. Parkin, 'Swahili Mijikenda: Facing both Ways in Coastal Kenya', *Africa*, 59 (1989), 161–76.

[31] H. Kindy, *Life and Politics in Mombasa* (Nairobi, 1972), 46–52.

[32] A. I. Salim, *The Swahili-Speaking Peoples of the Kenya Coast, 1895–1963* (Nairobi, 1973), 182–9.

[33] L. Vail (ed.), *The Creation of Tribalism in Southern Africa* (London and Berkeley, Calif., 1989); C. Ambler, *Kenyan Communities in the Age of Imperialism: The Central Region in the Late Nineteenth Century* (New Haven, Conn., 1988), 31–49.

that while colonial officials and academics tried to control and define ethnic identity, they did not do so in a vacuum—the people of the coast were not helpless bystanders at their own definition. It is important to stress, as some of the literature on the creation of tribalism does not, that tribal identity in itself is not a product of colonialism. Although the idea acquired new implications, boundaries were redrawn, and new categories created, the idea of identity at this level was not a wholly alien one. There already existed institutions which—like the initiation-sets of the Giriama and Rabai—dealt in identity at a level which can be called that of a tribe. The distinctive contribution of the colonial state was to try and fix these categories, and to make them the dominant institutions through which social networks were created, whereas before they were but one of a number of alternative institutions. To a degree, the state was successful in this.

This emphasis on the central importance of the tribe was not a cunning colonial plan, it was a product of contemporary understandings of how African society worked. In a sense, it offered initial advantage to Africans; in the first decades of colonialism, the manipulation of identity at the level of tribe became, precisely because the state attached such importance to it, an important weapon of Africans in resisting the demands of the state. Nor was it only the power of the state which could be evaded through the manipulation of ethnicity and other levels of identity—this was a weapon deployed also in the struggles between patron and client, and patron and patron. In the continuing redefinition of being Swahili, and in the invention of the Mijikenda, the state was by no means the only player, nor was tribalism simply an ideology in the service of the state.

Making History

This idea, of ethnicity as an institution which people manipulate in attempts to define, or redefine, the relationships of obligation which they have to others, has evident implications for the study of culture, and therefore of oral history. Recent writing, critical of structuralist approaches to the analysis of

culture, has emphasized the conscious role of individuals, who
constantly create culture through discourse and who do so
in pursuit of their own interests.[34] Such discourse is carried
on in the context of both general and particular relations of
power, so that the discourse of some people will be of more
influence than that of others. Culture, in other words, is
dynamic, synchronically diverse, and subject to innovative
diachronic change in response to political and economic
circumstance.

The presentation of history must then be seen in the same
terms. This is a point of central importance for any researcher
seeking to use oral history as a source. It would seem that in
many human societies, historical precedent is believed to provide a firm basis for social construct: so that people present
history in ways which conform with the institutions of ethnicity
through which they themselves organize their relationships with
others. This is true for the coast, too; debates over ethnic identity
are implicitly involved with questions of economy and society.
Consciously aware of the need for history to accord with their
presentation of their own identity, and what identity means,
people adjust their presentation of history. As informants, they
too are historians, marshalling the facts in support of their
argument, and revealing only those details which they deem
pertinent.[35]

An awareness of this requires a cautious, but not negative,
approach to oral history. The accepted version of the history
of the Mijikenda is built on a straightforward understanding of oral history: that historical truth can be found in unity
and consistency.[36] It is, it might be argued, a very democratic
approach, in that what the majority of informants say is taken

[34] S. Feierman, *Peasant Intellectuals: History and Anthropology in North-Eastern Tanzania*
(Madison, Wis., 1990); J. Willis, 'The Makings of a Tribe: Bondei Identities and
Histories', *JAH* (forthcoming).

[35] A study of the same phenomenon elsewhere can be found in D. Cohen, *Womunafu's
Bunafu: A Study of Authority in a Nineteenth Century African Community* (Princeton, NJ, 1977),
13–15; and J. Willis, ' "And So they Called a *Kiva*": Histories of a War', *Azania*, 25
(1990), 79–85.

[36] The orthodox history is contained in T. T. Spear, *The Kaya Complex: A History
of the Mijikenda Peoples to 1900* (Nairobi, 1978); a view slightly modified in id., *Traditions
of Origin and their Interpretation: The Mijikenda of Kenya* (Athens, Oh., 1982). The consistency approach guided earlier generations; see A. Werner, 'The Bantu Coast Tribes
of the East African Protectorate', *JRAI* 45 (1915), 326–54.

for the truth. However, it tends to stifle historical debate, by assuming some kind of community of interest among inform-ants;[37] this approach isolates one view of history, ensures its dominance, and then invests it with the status of truth, just as colonial officials sought to resolve the ambiguities of power in some African societies by investing an individual as chief. In the case of the Mijikenda, this approach has ensured the dom-inance of a particular view of history which developed from the 1920s along with a new set of economic relationships be-tween the people of the hinterland and those of the town. The speed with which historical presentation can change and the manipulability of historical stories are striking; for the new Mijikenda history incorporated and modified the Shungwaya story, a presentation of history which had itself only become common among hinterland groups since the turn of the cen-tury, and which had been the historical background to a quite different set of relationships between coast and hinterland.

Most of the oral historical information on which this book is based is concerned with personal and family histories of the recent past. More subtle analyses of history than the consist-ency approach have suggested that this kind of material, called 'historical gossip', is the raw material of history, as yet un-structured by the inclusion of mnemonic devices or of themes and clichés expressing the identity of the group. It is the inclusion of these which turn this material into the more struc-tured and less simply historical 'oral tradition'.[38] The logic of the analysis of ethnicity and culture advanced above would deny this, and it would seem that, in the Mombasa area at least, the distinction between 'oral tradition' and 'historical gossip' does not hold. Informants' discussion of their own lives, like their discussion of original group migrations, may be structured by their perception of their own interests. One man gave me one account of his early life which fitted in with his general historical presentation; which was one of separation

---

[37] The assumption of unanimity of interest on the part of informants is implicit in T. T. Spear, 'Oral Tradition: Whose History?', *HIA* 8 (1981), 165–81.

[38] J. Vansina, *Oral Tradition as History* (Madison, Wis., 1985), 17. The validity of this distinction has also been challenged in D. Cohen and E. S. Atieno-Odhiambo, *Siaya: The Historical Anthropology of an African Landscape* (London and Nairobi, 1989), 30.

and hostility between the people of Mombasa and its hinter-land. In a later discussion, a quite different life history was given, in which it emerged that the man had for a long period lived in Mombasa as a client/family member of an Arab patron. It is quite clear that informants consciously edit and structure what they say about the past. Here too, the options are not limitless—but individuals, constrained as they are, make use of these options as best they can, to what advantage they can.

Other historians have focused on the abominable conditions in which some workers lived in colonial Mombasa.[39] This book does not seek to contradict that presentation, nor to deny the level of suffering and everyday oppression experienced by the African population of a colonial city. Nor is the emphasis on the role of individual decision intended to suggest that the choices available were limitless, or attractive in absolute terms. It is rather that, closely constrained by the colonial state, by employers, and by others, people exercised what choices were available, to make the best of what was often a decidedly bad lot. In doing so, they made the town a place of resistance and celebration, as well as one of oppression and poverty.

[39] A. Clayton and D. Savage, *Government and Labour in Kenya, 1895–1963* (London, 1974), 216–18.

PART I

'Singwaya was a very big city':
The Swahili and the Nyika to 1890

The population of Mombasa's hinterland was, in the nineteenth century, generally described as the Nyika. Today this is a term seen simply as a pejorative forerunner of the name Mijikenda, which is now used of a grouping of nine peoples who live in Mombasa's local hinterland, share some cultural features, speak related languages, and who now share a common story of their origins. Yet the meaning of the two words is not the same; both the boundaries and the very conception of identity have changed. Nyika referred to a wider grouping of people than does the term Mijikenda, and defined them in a rather different way.

The first chapter of this book discusses differing understandings of the history of the coast and its hinterland, and examines in particular the now standard version of Mijikenda history. It is suggested here that documentary evidence from the nineteenth century runs counter to this historical presentation; particularly to traditions of an original migration from Shungwaya, or Singwaya and subsequent residence of whole ethnic groups in the settlements known as *kaya*s.

Historical accounts of the concentration of population in the *kaya*s are seen here in the context of continuing generational conflicts within hinterland communities. A history of migration from Singwaya, it is suggested in later chapters, was an early twentieth-century innovation, and was the result of changing relationships between the population of the hinterland and that of Mombasa. The second chapter discusses these relationships in the nineteenth century. In that century, and perhaps before, disputes over authority and tensions within homesteads, often exacerbated by food shortages, led to considerable movements of population. Individuals or small groups crossed the boundaries of identity in search of new patrons or protectors, and such movements created a multiplicity of kin ties which linked the populations of the local hinterland and of the coastal towns.

The division of these populations into Swahili and Nyika cut across these kin ties, for these wider identities were of a different order to those of kin or clan membership. They expressed not origins or consanguinity but the orientation of an individual's interactions with others. Nyika were those whose ties of dependence and obligation were located outside the coastal towns, while Swahili were those, of whatever origins, whose personal networks of patronage or clientage were located within the towns, participating in a patronage system based ultimately on access to the credit networks of the Indian Ocean. To move from one of these groups to the other, as a subordinate at least, was not difficult, but to belong actively to both was impossible.

1

Histories of the Coast, and the Structure of Hinterland Communities

> There seems to be a general consensus that the 'Wanyika' come from Sungwaya
>
> (Werner, 1915)

A few miles inland from the coast on which lies the island of Mombasa the land climbs, forming a steep ridge on the seaward side. It is a relatively fertile and well-watered area, stretching from Kilifi in the north, and continued to the south of Mombasa by the Shimba hills. Further west, this ridge gives way to drier and increasingly infertile scrubland. The island of Mombasa itself, and much of the immediately surrounding mainland, is not distinguished by its fertility. Coral lies just below the topsoil, and the ground holds little water. Wells can be dug, but often give only brackish water. The sea that surrounds the island, is, however, rich in fish, and these, dried or fresh, are an important source of protein throughout the area.

Between the coast and the main ridge is an area of hillocks and small valleys, a narrow band of undulating land much richer than the coastal plain. Here, annual crops such as sorghum, maize, and rice flourish. In the past, the top of the ridge behind this was densely forested, but now much of this land (like the poorer land along the coast) is planted with fruit trees: mango, cashew, orange, and, most commonly of all, coconut palms. While maize and other annuals can be, and indeed usually are, planted among fruit trees, they do not flourish. The spreading roots of coconut palms, in particular, provide too much competition for them. There is considerable potential complementarity between the agriculture of ridge, foothills, and shoreline.

The rains come in two seasons; the short rains in October or November, and the long rains in April or May. In the nineteenth century, crops of sorghum were planted for both rains: now maize is similarly double-cropped. Should the short rains fail, as not infrequently happens, there is no harvest in January. The long wait from August, the main harvest, to the long rains of the following year can cause general shortages. A poor crop or failure in the following August can bring general famine. The history of the coast is cruelly punctuated by such famines, whose names (or at least, the popularly accepted etymologies of them) hint at their severity and the strains they placed on social relationships. The *kabushutsi*, 'face turned down' famine was so named in remembrance of how those with food would avoid meeting the glances of their hungry relatives,[1] while the *mwakisenge*, 'move along', records how, each time those fleeing hunger found refuge with a new patron or provider, they would be followed by other hopefuls, and eventually forced to seek another refuge.[2] The search by the hungry or weak for a better patron is a major theme of the area's history.

The rains, or lack of them, may affect the area very unevenly: while the people of Kinung'una have a good harvest, those of Kwale, thirty miles to the south, may at the same time face shortage.[3] As a result, migrations of people within this area are common, and the ability to transport food grains is of great importance.

Diseases rule out the use of pack animals, and the broken nature of the land behind the coast makes head porterage difficult. Water has, in the past, been the most important means of transport. At Mombasa, Kilifi, and Mtwapa, creeks navigable by small vessels reach several miles inland, as far as the foot of the main ridge. These creeks were in the past the focuses of transport and trade routes in the area.[4] Along these creeks, and over the sea to which they led, the peoples of Mombasa's immediate hinterland had access to the agricultural products of hundreds of miles of coast and islands: particularly

---

[1] Int. 2c.   [2] Int. 47a.
[3] See e.g. PC to CNC, 8 Aug. 1919, KNA PC Coast 1/2/105.
[4] C. Guillain, *Documents sur l'histoire, la géographie et le commerce de l'Afrique Orientale* (Paris, 1857), ii. 2, 229; Int. 40a, 21b.

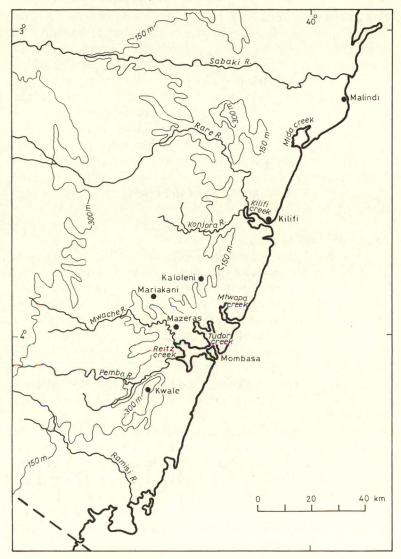

MAP I. *Mombasa: coast and local hinterland*

to the produce of the island of Pemba. It was a link which
proved invaluable in time of famine, and which gave considerable power to those who controlled it.

The sea structures the economy of the area in another way.

For centuries there have been trading contacts with the Middle East and India, bringing a demand for certain high value products—ivory, civet, rhino horn, orchilla weed, and others—which could not be met solely by the inhabitants of the towns which developed along the seashore. So the people of the hinterland also became involved in supplying this demand. While the two rains set the seasons for the farmers of the coast, the winds that carry them set the seasons for sea-borne traffic. From December to March, a wind from the north brought sailing boats from the Gulf, from Aden, and from India. From April to November another wind carried them north again, leaving the inhabitants of the coast free to collect their August harvest.[5]

Along the line of the East African coast itself lies a chain of towns and the ruins of towns. These are, and have long been, populated by Muslims, all speaking dialects of a language which is common to settlements along hundreds of miles of this coast. These people are generally known as the Swahili. Some of these towns were many acres in extent, with buildings of coral set in lime cement, as well as of clay and timber.[6] Mombasa is among these towns, and has existed for hundreds of years.[7] Yet while Arab and Portuguese geographers and colonists wrote of Mombasa, visited, and conquered it,[8] the ridge that lies only ten miles from the island remained a mystery to them, as did its inhabitants.

The population of Mombasa's local hinterland make brief appearances in the records of these visitors, usually as the armed allies of one Mombasan faction or another, mutely waving their bows in the background of Mombasa's dramatic performance. The Portuguese gave them a name: 'The fortress of Mombasa is situated on the east coast of Africa in Cafraria on an island of the Cafres who are called Mozungulos'.[9] But the identity,

[5] See M. Horton, 'Early Settlement on the Northern Kenya Coast', Ph.D. thesis (Cambridge, 1984), 55–60, for a discussion of winds and tides.
[6] Horton, 'Early Settlement', 1–12; J. S. Kirkman, *Men and Monuments on the East African Coast* (London, 1964), 18–29.
[7] H. Sassoon, 'Excavations on the Site of Early Mombasa', *Azania*, 15 (1980), 1–42.
[8] See J. Strandes, *The Portuguese Period in East Africa* (Nairobi, 1961); G. S. P. Freeman-Grenville, *Select Documents of the East African Coast* (Oxford, 1962); id., *Mombasa Martyrs of 1631* (London, 1980).
[9] J. M. Gray, 'Rezende's Description of Mombasa in 1634', *TNR* 23 (1947), 2–28, 7.

politics, and economy of the Mozungulos remain mysterious. Apparently fickle in the extreme, the Mozungulos appeared at one time fighting for the Mombasans against the Portuguese, at another supplying the beleaguered Portuguese garrison of Fort Jesus, and at yet another removing and selling to the Portuguese the head of a rebellious Sultan of Mombasa who had fled to them for protection.[10] That they remained unknown to the Portuguese clearly did not make them powerless or irrelevant. In 1610 the Sultan of Mombasa was bankrupted by his obligation to entertain Mozungulo visitors, who seem to have made a point of outstaying their welcome.[11] The Portuguese took over from the Sultan of Mombasa the burden of paying a yearly sum to pacify them, and maintained forts at the ford which leads to the island to discourage those not satisfied with this arrangement.[12]

For historians, this apparently hostile relationship has been taken as the most extreme manifestation of a curious feature of the urban Islamic culture of the coastal towns—its failure to expand, to move inland, indeed to have any apparent impact on the continent to the edge of which it clung. Books on the history of East Africa have tended to treat the coast and the interior in separate chapters, and those chapters discussing the coast deal with the coastal towns, and the overseas trade,[13] not with the 'half-savage' (as two historians have put it[14]) inhabitants of the narrow strip of populated hinterland that lies immediately behind the towns. The oral and written traditions of the towns seem to emphasize this detachment, with their accounts of the magical separation of islands from the mainland, the identification of even the local hinterland with outsideness and danger, and their concentration on the superiority of urban, Muslim, culture over the pagan culture of the world without the town walls.[15]

---

[10] Typescript trans. of extract from Botelho, *Memoria estatistica sobre os dominos porteguezes na Africa oriental*, in Fort Jesus Library, Mombasa; Strandes, *Portuguese Period*, 170, 127.

[11] Typescript trans. of extract from Bocarro, *Decada XIII da historia da India*, in Fort Jesus Library, Mombasa.   [12] Strandes, *Portuguese Period*, 16.

[13] See e.g. F. J. Berg, 'The Coast from the Portuguese Invasion', in B. Ogot (ed.), *Zamani: A Survey of East African History* (Nairobi, 1974), 119–41.

[14] C. R. Boxer and C. Azevedo, *Fort Jesus and the Portuguese in Mombasa, 1593– 1729* (London, 1960), 43.

[15] Freeman-Grenville, *Select Documents*, 37, 222. A generation of archaeologists emphasized that the coastal settlements were sited with fear of attack from the

Yet these are expressions of an idealized view of town culture, the view of the world held by the towns' élite. The hostility was ambiguous, the separation illusory. The mainland around Mombasa was not unknown or threatening to the townspeople in the seventeenth century, for the twelve 'Cafres' villages within it paid a yearly tribute of grain to the rulers of the town[16]—which puts the Sultan's payments of cloth in the light of exchange, rather than of a protection racket. While the Sultan's attempt to seek refuge in 1614 was less than successful, tales of Mombasa in the eighteenth century emphasize the role of the mainland as a refuge from the political struggles of the island,[17] reversing the common image of the islands as havens from the turmoil of the interior. While some of the literature of the coastal towns emphasizes the distinct and superior nature of urban culture,[18] other works, long extant in Mombasa and other coastal towns, are more ambiguous. Fumo Liongo, a legendary hero of Swahili history, has been presented by European writers as the epitome of urban culture, a genteel prince and poet of the towns who embodies the distinction (which many European observers have been anxious to emphasize) between the civilization of the Swahili coast and the savagery of the hinterland.[19] Yet Liongo was also, in other stories, a hunter, a man of the wilds beyond the town; the son, indeed, of a pagan mother.[20] At the centre of urban life, Liongo was also its antithesis.

Most ambiguous of all in this relationship of town and

mainland in mind; N. Chittick, *Kilwa: An Islamic Trading City on the East African Coast* (Nairobi, 1974), 6. For the emphasis on the Arabic element in coastal literary culture, see L. Harries, *Swahili Poetry* (Oxford, 1962), 1–2; for more of the debate on the importance of Arab influences on coastal culture, see J. de V. Allen, 'Swahili Culture Reconsidered: Some Historical Implications of the Material Culture of the Northern Kenya Coast in the Eighteenth and Nineteenth Centuries', *Azania*, 9 (1974), 105–38.

[16] Gray, 'Rezende's Description', 10.

[17] Harries, 'Swahili Traditions of Mombasa', *Afrika und Uebersee*, 43 (1959), 81–105; 'Mombasa Chronicle', in W. F. W. Owen, *Narrative of Voyages to Explore the Shores of Africa, Arabia and Madagascar, Performed in HM Ships Leven and Barracouta* (London, 1833), i. 418.

[18] See e.g. J. de V. Allen, 'Introduction', in id. (trans.), *Catechism of a Soul* (Nairobi, 1977).

[19] E. Steere, *Swahili Tales* (London, 1870), Intro.; W. Hichens, 'Liyongo the Spearlord', typescript in SOAS library, MS 20500.

[20] See 'The Bow Song' in Harries, *Swahili Poetry*, 182; Allen, 'Traditional History and African Literature: the Swahili Case', *JAH* 23 (1982), 227–36.

hinterland is the question of ethnicity, a subject of heated debate, intense conflict and negotiation that runs through the history of Mombasa and its local hinterland from the earliest references to the town to the present day. This debate still stirs intense emotion among the people of the coast and heated controversy amongst historians.[21] There were some people of Middle Eastern origin in the towns, for the sparse historical records and archaeological evidence show signs of the presence of traders and settlers from the Middle East in the coastal towns from an early date.[22] But these were probably a small minority. In the twentieth century, many of those who describe themselves as Swahili, or who are described by others as such, have claimed long genealogies that locate their origins in Arabia or Iran. Yet in 1847, a French visitor to Mombasa, Guillain, was told that the Kilindini, the largest subgroup of the Mombasa Swahili, came from the mainland, where the remains of their settlements could still be seen, and that they had originally come from a place called Shungwaya, to the north.[23] Shungwaya, or Singwaya, is a name and an idea that winds its way through the history of the area, and through developing ideas of ethnicity, its meaning metamorphosing dramatically over time.

There is no more recent historical cognate for the Portuguese term Mozungulos. In the eighteenth century, a new word for the people of Mombasa's local hinterland became current. An Arabic history of Mombasa records that in 1728 a Mombasan delegation to seek the help of the Sultan of Oman in expelling the Portuguese from Fort Jesus was accompanied by representatives of the 'towns of Vanikat'.[24] Through the nineteenth and much of the twentieth centuries, the hinterland population continued to be called Wanyika by others, and on

[21] See A. H. J. Prins, *The Swahili-Speaking People of Zanzibar and the East African Coast* (London, 1967), 11–12; C. Eastman, 'Who are the Waswahili?', *Africa*, 41 (1971), 228–36; W. Arens, 'The Waswahili', *Africa*, 45 (1975), 426–38; H. Kindy, *Life and Politics in Mombasa* (Nairobi, 1972), Intro. and Ch. 4; A. I. Salim, *The Swahili-Speaking Peoples of the Kenya Coast, 1895–1963* (Nairobi, 1973), 221–43; id., 'The Elusive Mswahili: Some Reflections on his Culture and Identity', in J. Maw and D. Parkin (eds.), *Swahili Language and Society* (Vienna, 1985).
[22] See nn. 4 and 6.   [23] Guillain, *Documents*, ii. 2, 240.
[24] 'Mombasa Chronicle', in Owen, *Narrative*, i. 418.

occasion by themselves. This term is itself laden with the implications of the distinction between town and hinterland already mentioned. *Nyika* is the scrubland beyond the ridge, connotes uncivilized life as against the life of the town, and is in a sense a definition of the peoples of the hinterland by what they are not rather than what they are. It is not a term expressing any perceived commonality between these people, and many of those consigned to this category by outsiders have rejected it.[25] Moreover, while twentieth-century ethnographers have restricted the meaning of this term to the nine tribes living near Mombasa, in the nineteenth century the term also embraced the population in the hinterland of towns on the Tanzanian coast.[26]

While there was in the seventeenth to nineteenth century no term expressing their overall identity, there does seem to be a degree of continuity in the names of the individual tribes or groups who were living around Mombasa in the seventeenth century and those there today. Portuguese records mention the Arabaja and the Chogni,[27] names clearly identifiable as those now written as Rabai and Chonyi. Since the 1940s, these groups around Mombasa have had a collective appellation. Now they are called the Mijikenda, the 'nine towns', and the nine constituent groups have been recorded and fixed by politicians, ethnographers, and historians. These are the Giriama, the Digo, the Rabai, the Chonyi, the Jibana, the Ribe, the Kambe, the Kauma, and the Duruma.

The historical traditions which are perceived as underlying this unity have been collected and analysed by Thomas Spear in two books.[28] Today the Mijikenda all share a common and in many ways remarkably consistent tradition of origin: that they came from Singwaya, a place in the north, whence they were driven by a war with the Galla, a pastoralist group who play the role of destructive villains in many

[25] W. W. A. Fitzgerald, *Travels in the Coastlands of British East Africa and the Islands of Zanzibar and Pemba: Their Agriculture and General Characteristics* (London, 1970 (first 1898)), 103; A. H. J. Prins. *Coastal Tribes of the North-Eastern Bantu* (London, 1951), 35.
[26] In J. Emery's Journal, from the British Protectorate of 1824–6, in PRO ADM 52. 3940. Also T. Boteler, *Narrative of a Voyage of Discovery to Africa and Arabia* (London, 1835), ii. 176–8.   [27] Strandes, *Portuguese Period*, 170, 217.
[28] T. T. Spear, *The Kaya Complex* (Nairobi, 1978); id., *Traditions of Origin and their Interpretation* (Athens, Oh., 1982).

historical traditions and written histories of the East African coast.[29] From Singwaya, the Mijikenda came south. Around Mombasa, they found refuge from the Galla in *kaya*s, settlements in clearings within dense stands of forest, only entered by narrow pathways. These are described as ridge-top settlements, and there was one for each group, hence the name of the nine towns.

Spear argues that these traditions are a fairly accurate rendering of actual historical events: that the Mijikenda do come from Singwaya and that this common origin is both a charter for and an explanation of a set of institutions based around the *kaya*s, a system of government which broke down in the nineteenth century as more and more people moved out from the *kaya*s. In this analysis, the durability of the stories is a mark both of their historical truth and of their role in maintaining the integrity of these institutions.[30] Spear dates the migration from Singwaya to the sixteenth or seventeenth century, a date obtained by comparing the names of age-sets among the Mijikenda and reducing them to a consistent core. The validity of this process and the reliability of the dates it produces have been challenged.[31]

Spear adduces some evidence from historical linguistics, and some names on Portuguese maps, as support for his argument. The cartographic evidence is flimsy and the linguistic evidence is contentious. Hinnebusch has suggested that Spear's timescale for linguistic change is inadequate, and that linguistic evidence indicates that the 'Sabaki' languages (Mijikenda, Swahili, and Pokomo) developed to the south rather than to the north of Mombasa. This group is most closely related to the ' Seuta' languages (Zigua, Bondei, Shambaa) of northeastern Tanzania.[32] It is interesting to note that groups speaking 'Seuta' languages share some of the cultural features which Spear associates with Singwaya; notably the use of *fingo*

[29] For an example of this, see S. Kiro, 'The History of the Zigua Tribe', *TNR* 34 (1953), 70–4.
[30] Spear, 'Traditional Myths and Historians' Myths: Variations on the Singwaya Theme of Mijikenda Origins', *HIA* 1 (1974), 67–84.
[31] M. Walsh, 'Mijikenda Origins: A Review of the Evidence', unpublished typescript in the library of the British Institute in Eastern Africa, Nairobi.
[32] T. Hinnebusch, 'The Shungwaya Hypothesis: A Linguistic Reappraisal', in J. T. Gallagher (ed.) *East African Culture History* (Syracuse, NY, 1976), 1–42.

charms to protect circular, palisaded settlements and a male initiation ceremony in which initiates are smeared with clay.[33]

Essentially, Spear's argument is based on the consistency of the traditions; that such a widely known and repeated story must be historical. Yet there stands against this one dramatic and overwhelming fact: the Singwaya story of Mijikenda origins was never recorded before the turn of this century.[34] No exhaustive collection of traditions was undertaken before this time, but other stories of Mijikenda origins, and other stories of Singwaya, were recorded by missionaries, travellers, and explorers, some of whom lived in the area for many years. It seems inconceivable that a story as widely told and known today as that of the Mijikenda migration from Singwaya could have escaped the notice of these observers.

Challenging Spear's thesis, Morton has argued that the existing Singwaya story, a Swahili myth of origin was transferred to the population of the hinterland by the Arabs and Swahili of the coastal towns. This was done in an attempt to seek historical justification for the coastal people's relationship with the Nyika, and particularly the practice of pawning children in return for food, which the British had effectively banned.[35] This version accounts admirably for the sudden emergence of Singwaya as an origin for the Nyika in coastal texts such as the *Kitab al-Zanuj*. Yet viewed in these terms, it is harder to see why the story should so swiftly have been adopted by the hinterland people themselves; and in following chapters, it is argued that the Singwaya story was adopted as a historical explanation for a much wider coincidence of interests between the people of Mombasa and its hinterland. This adoption must have been strikingly swift, though some of the stages of it can be glimpsed: Hollis, in 1897 or 1898, is the first to mention Singwaya as a place of origin for the Nyika,[36] but Johnstone's

[33] H. Cory, 'The Sambaa Initiation Rites for Boys', *TNR* 58–9 (1962), 2–7; G. Dale, 'An Account of the Principal Customs and Habits of the Natives Inhabiting the Bondei Country', *Journal of the Anthropological Institute*, 25 (1895), 181–239; O. Baumann, *Usambara und seine Nachbargebiete* (Berlin, 1891), 124–5, 132–3.

[34] R. F. Morton, 'The Shungwaya Myth of Mijikenda Origins: A Problem of Late Nineteenth-Century Kenya Coastal Historiography', *IJAHS* 5 (1972), 397–423; id., 'New Evidence Regarding the Shungwaya Myth of Mijikenda Origins', *IJAHS* 10 (1977), 628–43.

[35] Morton, 'The Shungwaya Myth'.   [36] Ibid. n. 399.

account of 1902 makes no reference to it, saying instead that the Kambe are from Taita, the Digo 'indigenous', and the Duruma descended from the slaves of the Portuguese.[37] By 1915, Werner noted that 'there seems to be a general consensus that the "Wanyika" come from Sungwaya'.[38] It is a consensus that has been maintained since then.

Seen in this light, of recent adaptation, consistency becomes questionable evidence of truth. It is, anyway, partly an illusory consistency, constructed by disregarding differences in the stories. They are consistent in the inclusion of Singwaya, but not in the dating or manner of the migration—nor in the reasons adduced.[39]

That Singwaya was first a story of the origins of some of the Swahili was crucial to its shifting meaning in the twentieth century. In 1847 Krapf was told of 'Shunguaya, a now ruined town on the coast of Malinde and the original seat of the Suahili, who being ejected by the Galla fled to Malinde; thence expelled again they retreated to the creek of Killefi and finally to Mombas.'[40] The story for the Swahili was not, however, a part of the construction of identity. In the nineteenth century some of the Swahili claimed quite different origins:[41] it was not necessary to come from Singwaya to be called a Swahili. Yet now, among the Mijikenda, the story is intimately connected with the reconstruction of identity: the Mijikenda are the Mijikenda because they come from Singwaya.[42] It has been

[37] H. B. Johnstone, 'Notes on the Customs of the Tribes Occupying Mombasa Subdistrict, British East Africa', *JRAI* 32 (1902), 263–72, 263. There are several other references to non-Singwaya origins for the Mijikenda: Fitzgerald, *Travels in the Coastlands*, 101, and J. L. Krapf, Journal, 11 Oct. 1847, CMS CA 5. 0. 16. 171–2. Both these men heard references to Singwaya, but as a Swahili, not Mijikenda, place of origin.

[38] A. Werner, 'The Bantu Coast Tribes of the East African Protectorate,' *JRAI* 45 (1915), 326–54.

[39] See Spear, *Traditions of Origin*, interviews (hereafter referred to as MHT) 1, 23, 38, 43, 65, 71, 72; Werner, 'The Bantu Coast Tribes', 328. Famine and disputes with other neighbours are given as causes for migration in MHT 43, 33, 45, 63, 66. See also this chapter, below.

[40] Krapf, Journal, 11 Oct. 1847. Krapf was at another time told of Swahili, Galla, and Segeju origins in 'Shungaya or Shiras', Krapf, 'Journal of Journey to Usambara', 19 July 1848, 25–6, CMS CA 5. 0. 16. 173.

[41] Werner, 'A Swahili History of Pate', in *JAS* 14 (1914–15), 148–61, 152; 278–97; 392–413.

[42] Spear, *Kenya's Past: An Introduction to Historical Method in Africa* (Nairobi, 1981), 54–7.

argued elsewhere that consistency in such origin stories marks not historical truth, but their function.[43]

Traditional and other evidence is at variance with the ideal picture of history presented by Spear on several points. The neat picture of the nine *kaya*s, all similar, and the nine groups dwelling within them, seems questionable. There are considerably more than nine *kaya*s, and by no means all of them are on the ridge.[44] Kaya Fungo, the main Giriama *kaya*, is considerably to the west of the ridge, and Guillain described the Duruma settlement of Mtswakara, often referred to as a *kaya*, as a dispersed collection of homesteads in a valley.[45] While the name Mijikenda has fixed the number of constituent tribes at nine, and the list of nine has been recorded and fixed, the historicity of this cannot be assumed. Nineteenth-century sources give a number of other Nyika names: Shimba and Lughuh;[46] Bombo, Malife, Mohane, Muzador, Mukuomame;[47] and Taoota, Wangoombe, Makhshingo, Mannamokee, Mackoolo, Amprengo.[48] Some of these are recognizable as clan names among the modern Mijikenda, but clearly at this time the number nine had no significance, nor was the distinct unity of each of the current nine in every case established.[49]

There still exists some confusion among the Mijikenda themselves as to who the nine tribes are. At the beginning of the century, officials often included the Taita and Segeju among the Nyika,[50] and informants today may number the Pokomo and Segeju, sometimes the Taita, sometimes the Kamba, among the Mijikenda. These groups may also be mentioned in traditions of migration from Singwaya.[51] Since there have to be nine members of the Mijikenda, these informants exclude some of the 'real' nine, the list made absolute by written ethnography and history. Historians may attempt to fix and limit the idea of the Mijikenda, but as an oral tradition it remains dynamic.

[43] A. D. Roberts, *A History of the Bemba* (London, 1973), 27.

[44] Werner, 'The Bantu Coast Tribes'; H. Mutoro, 'The Spatial Distribution of the Mijikenda Kaya Settlements on the Hinterland Kenya Coast', *Trans-African Journal of History*, 14 (1985), 78–100.   [45] Guillain, *Documents*, ii. 2, 277.

[46] Owen, *Narrative*, i, 418.   [47] Emery, Journal, 15 Oct. 1825.

[48] Krapf, 'Voyage from Aden to Zanzibar', CMS CA 5. 0. 16. 163.

[49] The Digo, e.g., seem not to have been perceived as one group in the 19th c.; see Krapf, *Travels and Missionary Labours during an Eighteen Years' Residence in Eastern Africa* (London, 1968 (first 1860)), 159.

[50] K. MacDougall, 'Notes on the History of the Wanyika' (1914), KNA DC KFI 3/3.

[51] MHT 8, 16, 44.

There are considerable variations in the details of traditions of the migration itself. The Digo, for example, have a
tradition of a northward migration,[52] as do the Rumba clan
of the Jibana.[53] To accommodate the Singwaya story, this is
presented as a remigration. This seems remarkably similar to
the apparent adaptation of the nineteenth-century stories of
Rabai origin in Rombo.[54] Spear himself now doubts, on these
grounds, that the Rabai (and the Duruma) come from
Singwaya.[55] The inclusion of Singwaya in the Digo stories may
be a similar emendation. The Digo, like the Rabai and the
Duruma, and unlike the other Mijikenda, were in the recent
past matrilineal.[56]

It is in the differences between versions that the extreme
negotiability of all the details of this tradition becomes apparent. It is clear from these differences that history is seen to
legitimate present claims and is therefore continually remade
in new situations. Through their presentation of details of the
tradition, story-tellers seek to establish a hierarchy between
the Mijikenda groups, to find precedents and claim rights. Some
groups claim seniority over others by virtue of the order in
which they left Singwaya,[57] or by the order of birth of their
ancestors.[58] Most vividly, disputes between the Ribe, the
Kambe, the Chonyi, and the Jibana find expression in stories
of splits and conflicts on the journey from Singwaya, or in
competing claims to be the first arrivals in an area.[59] The
simmering conflict over land between the Kambe and their
neighbours[60] comes out in the story that the Kambe were not
at Singwaya, and in their counter-claims that they were the
first to leave.[61] Through the Singwaya story, claims to brotherhood through common origin are intertwined with competing
claims to places in a hierarchy established by that common
origin. The story is consistent only where all the tellers are

---

[52] Int. 5*a*.   [53] MHT 8.

[54] Krapf, Journal, 11 Oct. 1847; L. Harries, 'The Founding of Rabai: A Swahili
Chronicle by Mwidani bin Mwidad', *Swahili*, 31 (1961), 141–9; cf. MHT 43.

[55] Spear, *Traditions of Origin*, 12.

[56] There were also considerable differences in the age-grade system between the
Digo and other groups; cf. Int. 57*a* with Prins, *Coastal Tribes*, 71–3.

[57] MHT 31, 38, 71, 72.

[58] MHT 23; Werner, 'The Bantu Coast Tribes', 328.   [59] MHT 12, 38, 45.

[60] For mention of these land disputes, see T. H. R. Cashmore, 'A Note on the
Chronology of the Wanyika of the Kenya Coast', *TNR* 57 (1961), 153–72, 161; and
Int. 44B.   [61] MHT 38, 45.

making a similar claim—and that is, today, that they share a collective identity as the Mijikenda.

In the context of the creation of identity, Singwaya has proved to be a most versatile story, and has even acquired an archaeology of its own; an archaeology which has proved as transferable as the story. The Bajun, whom some consider to be a Swahili group, once inhabited the coast and islands north of Lamu, but have in the last two centuries become established along much of the coast south of Lamu. In the 1890s a traveller was told that 'the ruins I saw near Burkau were built by a Bajoni named Shingwaia and were the remains of a wall intended to resist the Galla attacks'.[62] Since then, these ruins at Birgao, near the Somali border, have been pressed into service by others as the site of the Mijikenda Singwaya.[63]

The consistency of the migration stories, then, lies mainly in the mention of Singwaya: a consistent element recently attached to the traditions. The most frequently mentioned cause of migration from Singwaya, like the reference to Singwaya itself, links this provenance with Mijikenda identity. In this case, the war with the Galla is said to have been caused by the murder of a Galla boy during a Mijikenda initiation ritual: both the Mijikenda and their culture come from Singwaya.

Singwaya itself was a very big city. There the Mijikenda started the custom of *mung'aro*. They used to *ng'ara* when they marked the beginning of an age-grade. At the end of *mung'aro* they had to kill a man from a different tribe. One time they killed a Galla and cut off the parts they wanted. They buried the body in a cattle kraal and marked the spot with a stick . . . The Galla came to the kraal, dug up the place marked, and produced the bones. That is what started the war of the Galla against the Mijikenda. The Galla speared their victims and the rest quickly started to disperse.[64]

There are, however, other perspectives on history; other motives adduced for the migration.

These other perspectives connect the migration with a dispute over the nature and bounds of authority. The most common of these locates the war, usually with the Galla, in a dispute over access to the reproductive power of women:

---

[62] Fitzgerald, *Travels in the Coastlands*, 65.
[63] Freeman-Grenville, 'The Coast, 1498–1840', in R. Oliver and G. Mathews (ed.), *History of East Africa* (Oxford, 1963), i. 129–68, 130.   [64] MHT 10.

At Singwaya, when a Giriama married, a Galla had first to sleep
with his wife. One time a man married for the second time and this
wife was much more beautiful than his first. He decided that he
would not allow a Galla to sleep with her first. But because it was
the custom, a Galla youth forced his way into the house and slept
with the new bride. The husband took a knife and killed the Galla.[65]

A related theme is that of the ability of some men to make
demands on the labour of other men: 'When we were there
(Singwaya) we were the slaves of the Galla. For instance, if
one cultivated maize, and harvested it, a Galla would come
and eat first. Or before moving one's homestead, a Galla had
to sleep with one's wife.'[66]

These themes curiously reappear in one tradition of migration recorded earlier; a tradition of migration from the *kaya*,
rather than from Singwaya. According to an account given to
a District Commissioner in the 1920s, the Digo left *kaya* Kwale
because their leader 'commenced to force labour for work on
his own gardens and also to force fathers to give their daughters
to him in marriage'.[67] Unlike the *mung'aro* incident, these
stories form a discourse concerned not with Mijikenda identity
but with struggles over power: the power of men over other men;
men's power over women; and men's power over other men's
access to women. This discourse is central to the tensions within
Mijikenda groups in the nineteenth and twentieth centuries,
and it is continued in the historical presentation of the *kaya*s.

Before turning to this, however, there is another strand in the
Mijikenda migration traditions to consider. In the traditions
of several groups, notably the Digo, Ribe, Jibana, and Chonyi,
there are stories of residence on the island of Mombasa. The
theme of most of these is similar: a hunter tracked a wounded
elephant to the island of Mombasa, which was empty bush at
the time, to find that the elephant had died on the site of Fort
Jesus.[68] The hunter and his people settled on this site, which
was at that time a cave:[69]

---

[65] MHT 23.   [66] MHT 3.

[67] 'Further Notes on the Wadigo', Digo District Station Diary, Oct. 1925, 2, KNA
PC Coast 1/12/222. Cf. the story of Mzee Fungo, in S. Ushuru, 'How the Nyika Came
by their Names', in KNA DC KFI 3/3.

[68] Int. 21*b*, 46*a*; MHT 27, 65; 'Further Notes on the Wadigo', Digo District Station
Diary, Oct. 1925, 5.   [69] Int. 21*b*.

At that time there was no Mombasa, it was just bush . . . they were living in Mombasa, at the place called Fort Jesus, the elders tell us that that was the place where they hunted the elephant. So it was bush, they went and cleared it, they put skins there, at the Fort, they put the skins there to dry . . . Mwandadza was the hunter, in hunting those animals, he shot it with arrows, until it fell, where it fell there he skinned it.[70]

If the Singwaya traditions are taken as historical fact, these stories articulate rather poorly with them:[71] on Spear's dating, the Mijikenda would have arrived to find the Fort under construction, the passage to the island guarded by Portuguese soldiers, and a not inconsiderable town long established on the island. And these traditions conflict with those of Singwaya in more than chronology.

On one level, in the often tense political atmosphere of the twentieth century, these traditions act to claim political primacy for the Mijikenda at the coast: when they came, the island was empty, so their presence predates that of the Swahili or Arabs. The Fort, long the effective symbol of authority on the coast, is claimed for the Mijikenda, and is made both indigenous and a place of some good fortune by the tale of the elephant. At the same time, the story of the elephant wandering on the island emphasizes that the island was bush, a place of wild animals, uncultivated and therefore unclaimed by others. Yet the story has significance beyond this.

A number of anthropologists and historians have noticed the special relationships existing between certain inhabitants of Mombasa and some of the Mijikenda.[72] These have generally been seen as alliances, and debate on them has centred on the relative balance of power between the two sides, as though the relationship were one between two governments.[73] But, as we shall see, executive authority was rather limited among the Nyika and in Mombasa, and consisted of a set of balances and alliances between patrons on either side, a set of alliances fraught with tensions.

[70] Int. 30a, 7.   [71] See MHT 38.
[72] Krapf, 'Excursions to Dshombo', 25 Mar. 1845, CMS CA 5. 0. 16. 167; Guillain, Documents, ii. 2, 244.
[73] Prins, Coastal Tribes, 37–8; F. J. Berg, 'Mombasa under the Busaidi Sultanate', Ph.D. thesis (Wisconsin, 1971), ch. 2; Spear, The Kaya Complex, 71–3.

Mijikenda informants, moreover, have a completely different perception of these 'alliances'. The Ribe, for example, say
not that the Kilifi clan of the Swahili Twelve Tribes are their
allies, but that they are *themselves*: the Kilifi are Ribe, and the
Ribe are, or rather can be, Kilifi.[74] The Kilindini clan similarly are not, according to Mijikenda informants, allies or representatives of the Digo; they *are* Digo.[75] The relationship is one
of kin. The term *adzomba*, used by some Mijikenda of the
Swahili, similarly claims a relationship. Meaning both
'mother's brother' and 'sister's son', it locates this relationship
particularly in the movement of women from hinterland to
town: a frequent occurrence,[76] and a common cliché in the historical presentations of all groups.[77] It is a cliché that neatly
fits the ideal picture of patrilineally inherited identity which now
prevails: women from Mijikenda groups who married men in
the town bequeathed their relatives, but not their identity, to
their children. As a cliché, it obscures the fact that numbers of
men from Mijikenda groups have also made the transition to
being members of town groups, regardless of the theoretical
rules of patrilineality.[78]

The Mijikenda stories of Mombasa thus can serve to locate
these kin links in history: the Mijikenda and the Swahili are
the same people because the Mijikenda were the first inhabitants of Mombasa, and have remained there since.[79] However,
this cliché may be reworked into a different historiography, of
Mijikenda independence. Used thus, it becomes a story not
of enduring alliance, but of dispossession and hostility.[80] The
changing significance of the elephant at Fort Jesus, like that of
coming from Singwaya, has been intimately bound up with
changing economic and social relationships on the coast. In
the never-ending process of adaptation to new circumstance,
oral history can take up new stories, but it can also rework the
meaning of existing ones.

The idea of Mijikenda residence in Mombasa does not, of
course, cohere with the presentation of the Mijikenda as discrete

[74] Int. 20*a*. This presentation has not always been confined to the 'Nyika' side of
the pairings. In 1913, the elders of the Kilifi clan of the Twelve Tribes described
themselves as 'elders of Wakilifi from the Nine Tribes, elders of Ribe in the town of
Mombasa'; see Document, 15 Aug. 1913, KNA PC Coast 1/11/197.

[75] Int. 5*b*, 21*b*.   [76] Int. 47*a*.   [77] Int. 5*a*, 9*b*.
[78] Int. 5*b*.   [79] Int. 20*a*.   [80] Int. 3*a*.

groups living in *kaya*s until the later nineteenth century. The *kaya*s are none the less an essential component of much of the historical presentation of the Mijikenda, and though Spear has linked the two concepts of migration from Singwaya and residence in the *kaya*s,[81] they are separate: Singwaya was never mentioned in nineteenth-century sources, while the *kaya*s frequently were. Moreover, the Singwaya stories are now widely told, while the *kaya*s are, in Spear's analysis, greatly reduced in significance. An examination of the evidence suggests that the presentation of Mijikenda residence in the *kaya*s until a dispersion in the later nineteenth century is a problematic one.

No *kaya* was ever seen with the entire group population living within it. Indeed, eye-witness accounts almost always note that the population had been living in the *kaya* but had recently dispersed. There is a curious consistency in these accounts over time: whether they be of the Rabai in the 1840s,[82] the Kambe in the 1890s,[83] or the Giriama in the 1910s.[84] In 1845, the missionary Krapf noted that the Giriama were recently scattered from their *kaya*, while in 1913 Champion, a District Commissioner, recorded a similarly recent dispersion.[85] Some elderly informants today insist that their parents' generation lived within the *kaya*,[86] a suggestion which would place the dispersion rather later than Spear dates it, and which curiously echoes the accounts given to Champion in 1913—by the very generation which these modern informants say *did* live in the *kaya*. The presentation of the population as having recently dispersed seems fixed over time: they have always dispersed recently.

The presentation of the *kaya* should be seen rather in the context of the power of old men, with which it is clearly linked.

---

[81] Spear, 'Traditional Myths and Historians' Myths', 69.
[82] Krapf, 'Excursions to the Country of the Wanika Tribe of Rabbay', 1, CMS CA 5. o. 16. 166.
[83] C. New, *Life, Wanderings and Labours in Eastern Africa* (London, 1971 (first 1877)), 78.   [84] A. Champion, *The Agiryama of Kenya* (London, 1967), 4–5.
[85] Cf. the above with Krapf, 'Excursion to the Wanika Division of Keriama', 13 Feb. 1845, CMS CA 5. o. 16. 166.
[86] Int. 2*a*, 8*b*. The somewhat scanty archaeological evidence is also at variance with Spear's presentation—it has been claimed that some of the *kaya*s were occupied from the 10th c., and that there was some dispersion from them in the 16th c.—see H. Mutoro, 'An Archaeological Study of the Mijikenda *Kaya* Settlements on Hinterland Kenya Coast', Ph.D. thesis (UCLA, 1987), 178, 262.

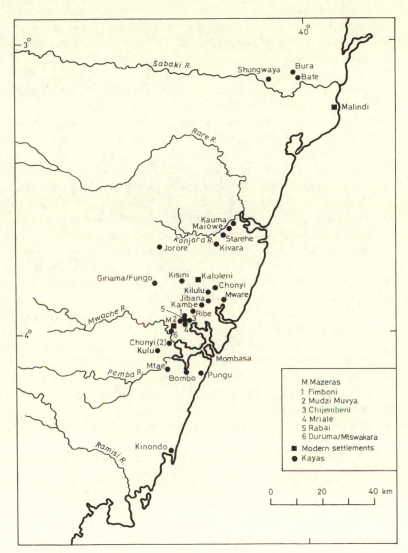

MAP 2. *The* kayas

One informant told me simply that when men reached a certain age they could move into the *kaya*.[87] Knowledge and care
of the *kaya*s is still in the hands of old men now, and one informant explicitly characterized the *kaya* as a source of power
for him, by describing how he had built a considerable reputation as a preacher within the Seventh-Day Adventist Church.
On being expelled from the church for polygamy he became
one of the elders of the *kaya* at Rabai: 'Now I've taken myself
in to being a *kaya* elder, and well, I get more knowledge, I get
more knowledge'.[88]

Thus playing a central role in the power of old men, the *kaya*
takes a central place in their historiography. The current ideal
residence pattern common to all the Mijikenda groups, which
is of a patrilocal homestead consisting of two or three generations of men and their wives, is portrayed as a recent development, marking a decline in the power of the male *kaya* elders.[89]
Yet the evidence is that this has been the pattern for some
time, and that the presence of the *kaya* in the traditions should
be seen in the context of a continuing dispute over the nature
and extent of old men's power, rather than as the historical
pattern of an institution.

There was, and still is, considerable conflict over power
within the patrilocal homestead. The eldest male allocated land
to the younger men for themselves and their wives to work on,
and demanded their labour on his own fields.[90] He was responsible for providing his sons (which group might in practice
include both brothers' sons and grandsons) with bridewealth
when they wished to marry, and he thus had control of the
timing of at least the first marriage of young men.[91] It was he
who received the bridewealth for daughters who were married
by others. Responsible for providing his sons with chickens or
goats to trade if they so desired, he could claim the ultimate
right of disposal of any resulting wealth. Constant redistributive
rituals, such as the system of double funerals, meant that such

---

[87] Int. 44*a*.   [88] Int. 56*a*, 11.

[89] Prins, *Coastal Tribes*, 59–61; Champion, *The Agiryama*, 17, 19; C. Brantley,
'Gerontocratic Government: Age-Sets in Pre-Colonial Giriama', *Africa*, 48 (1978),
248–64.

[90] Int. 17*a*; J. B. Griffith, 'Glimpses of a Nyika Tribe (Waduruma)', *JRAI* 65 (1935),
267–95, 280.   [91] Int. 1*a*, 17*a*, 47*a*, 20*a*; Prins, *Coastal Tribes*, 68–71.

wealth was often immediately used, rather than being saved to buy a bride for the man who had earned it.[92] The homestead was the productive unit, and the homestead head controlled both production and reproduction within the homestead. He was, at the same time, in competition with younger men for young wives.[93] There could be many years between the birth of a man's first child and that of his last, so that he himself could still be marrying new wives and bearing children when his children were doing so.

The homestead head was, however, generally anxious to maintain, even to expand, the number of men in the homestead, for they increased the homestead's productive potential, as farmers, herders, and petty traders, whose wives would similarly work. Men from outside the kin group might be welcomed in and given bridewealth and land, to build the homestead. Where there was little wider authority, a large homestead was the ultimate guarantee of the security for both its members and its head. As one informant put it to me, talking of his grandfather's large following of dependants, 'If you have nobody, you are nobody.'[94]

Even these basic outlines of the homestead structure are somewhat reified: I do not wish to replace one static picture of Mijikenda societies with another. The 'rules' governing the homestead were not fixed, but subject to intense negotiation. There was, for example, no definite point at which fission of the homestead always occurred. Direct testimony on the subject and life histories make clear that some men set up a new homestead on marrying, others when their children were born, and others only on the death of their father or uncle.[95] Essentially this was a matter of negotiation, of individuals sizing up their options. Similarly, the degree of control which a father could exercise over wealth earned by his sons, wives, and other subordinates was disputed. Yet this idealized picture has a function, in identifying the basic points of tension inherent in the structure.

Dominating the negotiation over these issues was the option

---

[92] For the double funeral system see Griffiths, 'Glimpses of a Nyika Tribe', 274; also Int, 69a. For the homestead head's control of earnings, see Int. 3a, 17a.
[93] Champion, *The Agiryama*, 15.   [94] Int. 53a.
[95] Int. 17a, 43a, 47a; Champion, *The Agiryama*, 10.

of flight, by men or women, to seek better terms elsewhere. That flight is explained in some traditions of migration as a way of avoiding authority and demands upon labour is symptomatic of the importance of this option. Men or women leaving their homesteads could move to other hinterland homesteads, but they could also move to the coast.[96] The coast offered a whole different set of patrons, different opportunities, and different constraints: in times of hardship or shortage in the hinterland, patrons on the coast had access to food and other goods from abroad. At all times the position of the coast, and particularly of Mombasa, in the oceanic trading system gave some of its inhabitants considerable wealth and considerable potential as patrons.

The homestead head's authority was not the only form of government among the Nyika in the nineteenth century. There was a wider system of authority, again one based on gender and age. This was expressed through the age-grade system, and it was here that the power of old men and the *kaya* were interlinked. The eldest tier of men in the age-grade system had privileged access to the *kaya*.[97] Through their knowledge of *kaya* ritual, older men controlled the rain. The magical objects of the *kaya*—the *fingo*, or charm, which protected it, and the *mwanza*, the friction drum used during ceremonies—could only be seen and used by elder males.[98] Rituals against ill-luck and sickness all involved intercessions to the spirits of ancestors by the elder males: which ceremonies again centred on the *kaya*. Such intercessions required the elders to exact from everyone else meat, grain, palm wine, and cloth, to be consumed and worn at the ceremony.[99] Arbitration of disputes allowed the elders to charge fees, which they kept.[100] They could also exact fines from those who saw the *mwanza*.[101] This system

[96] For migration to other homesteads, see Int. 49*a*, 41*a*: for migration to the town see Int. 5*b*, 49*a*. In the later 19th c., missions provided a new option for refugees, see Mackenzie to Euan-Smith, 15 Nov. 1888, IBEA File 1*a*; also R. F. Morton, 'Slaves, Freedmen and Fugitives on the Kenya Coast,1873–1907', Ph.D. thesis (Syracuse, NY, 1976).

[97] Brantley, 'Gerontocratic Government'; Prins, *Coastal Tribes*, 74–6; Champion, *The Agiryama*, 16–20; Werner, 'The Bantu Coast Tribes'.

[98] Krapf, Journal, 4 Feb. 1847.

[99] Ibid. 16 Apr. 1847; Fitzgerald, *Travels in the Coastlands*, 110.

[100] Krapf, Journal, 11 Nov. 1847.   [101] Ibid. 4 Feb 1847.

continually redistributed wealth, if not in a very equitable fashion, channelling it towards the elders: the *kaya* was thus of considerable importance in maintaining their ability to act as patrons, and thus their authority within the homestead.

There also existed a number of secret societies, each with its own oath, the membership of which was drawn from men able to pay the entry fees: which were normally of livestock, grain beer, or palm wine.[102] Members of these societies were able to cast and remove spells and to administer oaths to the parties in contested cases. The power and the membership of these societies overlapped with that of the age-grades, the members of the most powerful society, *vaya*, all being drawn from the *kambi*, the top three sections of the ruling age-grade.

There was, however, some ambiguity in the support which the *kaya* offered to homestead heads. It reinforced the authority of old men, and gave them control over the accumulation of wealth, and therefore the power of patronage, of others. But it also tended to enforce a kind of equality amongst elder males. It did not allow a great accumulation of wealth by the elders, for the goods exacted as fines or fees were often consumed immediately. Those elders who did accumulate wealth found themselves subject to exactions from other elders.[103] The old men who dominated Nyika society doubtless had some very enjoyable parties, but few became very wealthy. At the same time that the institutions of the *kaya* increased the power of old men within the homestead, these institutions also limited old men's ability to accumulate as individuals, and thus their own power to act as patrons.

Yet the system did generally support the authority of old men over young men, and of both over women. Those younger men who tried to set up homesteads on their own were excluded from this level of power, and were thus particularly vulnerable to the exactions of the elders. Such young men had had no opportunity to build up the degree of wealth, and the consequent following, that was the effective guarantee of property or personal security.

Thus, the source of hinterland elders' power lay in the *kaya*.

[102] Champion, *The Agiryama*, 22–5; Werner, 'The Bantu Coast Tribes', 345; Fitzgerald, *Travels in the Coastlands*, 103–11.   [103] Krapf, Journal, 25 Dec. 1848.

Constantly engaged in a struggle to maintain this power, they presented, and still present, a history which symbolizes the apogee of their power: all lived within the *kaya*, and so their power was complete. Hence the stress in accounts of dispersion from the *kaya* on the consequent decline in the authority of elders.[104] The two processes are synonymous, and possibly neither is historical fact. These accounts of what Mijikenda society was are equally statements of what informants feel that it should be; they are a part of a process of negotiation over the nature of power within society. Where the informant was talking to colonial officials anxious to strengthen a 'traditional' system in order to govern through it, such information was a particularly powerful weapon in this negotiation.[105] There was a circularity to this: the testimony of these men was valid because they hold a position within the *kaya*, and the legitimation which the *kaya* gives to history was underlined by their testimony.[106]

Brantley, assuming the historicity of the static picture of Mijikenda society as presented by the traditions, has characterized Mijikenda society in the nineteenth century as a gerontocracy.[107] Yet the gerontocrats constantly sought to reaffirm their position through the manipulation of history, for the gerontocracy was an insecure one. The young men of Rabai acknowledged the power of older men by singing 'We are yet young men, but we shall be elders'.[108] But not all were willing to wait; the power of elders could be challenged. In the nineteenth century, the challenge to the power of elders fell into two categories, one being flight in search of other patrons, and the other the construction of alternative sources of power not drawing on the *kaya*.

Those who remained could seek to appropriate the symbols of power. Krapf recorded the presence of a women's friction drum in Rabai in the 1840s, which was used to exact fees from outsiders who inadvertently saw it.[109] Krapf also mentioned the

[104] Champion, *The Agiryama*, 1.
[105] Seen e.g. in the debate over the institutions of the Duruma, in the Political Record Book, 67, KNA DC KWL 3/5, and Lambert, ADC Rabai to PC, 5 Oct. 1918, KNA PC Coast 1/9/52.
[106] Werner, 'The Bantu Coast Tribes', 320–32; Spear, *Traditions of Origin*, 36, 52.
[107] Brantley, 'Gerontocratic Government'.
[108] Krapf, 'Excursion to Rabbai Empia', 9 Apr. 1846, CMS CA 5. 0. 16. 170.
[109] Krapf, Journal, 11 July 1847; also ibid. 29 Dec. 1848.

delicate relationship between the *kaya* elders and the 'dreaming woman', who was periodically possessed and became a medium for messages from the ancestors.[110] Much has been written concerning spirit possession among Mijikenda women, and how it is and was used to extract material goods from ungenerous men.[111] Such possession is not dealt with by *kambi* elders, nor is knowledge of it derived from the mysteries of the *kaya*, although women possessed by spirits might, as did the 'dreaming woman', make a tactical alliance with the *kaya* elders.

That the power of elders was not complete or unchallenged can also be seen through the disputes over rain magic. In an area where the failure of rain threatened famine, control over the rain was a highly valued skill. It was a source of ritual power for *kaya* elders, as it was their duty to organize ceremonies should the rain fail.[112] But they also faced physical attack and accusations of witchcraft for 'stopping up' the rain. Such accusations could result in murder. There is one well-recorded example of this from the beginning of this century, where young men in Chonyi countered what they suspected to be rain witchcraft by older men with simple violence. One elder encouraged the young men, fired by personal animosity, but this does not disguise the active generational conflict that inspired the violence.[113] It is a basic conflict: between the physical power of young men and the ritual power of old men. A few years earlier a British official had noted a similar challenge to elders' power:

When rain fails, the Nyere (uninitiated men) maintain that the Kambi elders have stopped it . . . the Nyere go to a leading *muganga* (ritual specialist) who sniffs at some medicine and wanders about until he arrives at a place where he says that the 'pot with the mischief in it' is buried or hidden . . . At other times the Nyere make for several Wakambi, tie them up and roast them before a fire until they say where they have buried the 'pot'. When the Nyere are about

---

[110] Ibid. 11 May 1847; also 10 Jan. 1848.
[111] Krapf, 'Excursions to Dshombo', 26 Mar. 1845, 27–8; R. Gomm, 'Bargaining from Weakness: Spirit Possession in the South Kenya Coast' *Man*, NS 10 (1975), 530–43; also M. K. Mumba, *The Wrath of Koma* (Nairobi, 1987), 29–33.
[112] Krapf, Journal, 8 Dec. 1848.
[113] PC Coast to DC Malindi, 22 May 1915, KNA PC Coast 1/10/53.

this quest, the Wakambi bury pots, in case they may be seized and nothing saves them except showing where the 'pot' is.[114]

This vulnerability to physical coercion was not the mark of a recent decline in the power of elders. In 1848 Krapf had witnessed an almost identical confrontation.[115] Nyika government may have been a gerontocracy, but it was never an unchallenged one.

The nineteenth century, then, saw not the steady breakdown of an established order but the continuation of a dispute over what that order should be. The unity and common origins of the Mijikenda were not established, and their institutions were not uniform or fixed. The expansion of trade, the growth in the wealth and population of Mombasa, and the establishment of mission and runaway slave settlements during the century may have exacerbated disputes within society, but the idea that hinterland society was, in the early part of the century, in a sort of ideal state from which all later history was a decline cannot be accepted: Mijikenda history both displayed more continuity, and was more dynamic, than the vision of abrupt change suggests.

---

[114] Murray, 'Native Laws and Customs of the Takaungu Subdistrict; Wanyika, Wagiriama, and Smaller Tribes' (1898), 3, KNA PC Coast 1/1/138.
[115] Krapf, Journal, 27 Dec. 1848.

2

Clients and Slaves in the Nineteenth Century

The liwali had pity on them and provided them with
rations, and sent many Duruma families to Pemba.

(Al-Amin Mazrui, n.d.)

Through the differing and often conflicting perspectives on
nineteenth-century history provided by European observers of
the time, and by more recently recorded family histories and
traditions, a set of historical processes and changes can be
identified. It is these which reveal the themes—of migration,
and of co-operation and conflict between different sets of patrons—which dominated the relationship between the Nyika
and the people of Mombasa in the nineteenth century.

This was a period of considerable political change at the
top. At the beginning of the century Mombasa was ruled by
the Mazrui family, who had originally been installed as governors by the Sultan of Oman in the eighteenth century, but
who had effectively become independent from Oman when the
Yaarubi dynasty there was replaced by the Busaidi. Following
a long struggle, during which the Mazrui briefly (from 1824 to
1826) entrusted Mombasa to British protection, the Busaidi
finally took control of Mombasa in 1837. They continued to
govern Mombasa until 1887, when the Busaidi Sultan (who by
this time ruled from Zanzibar, not Oman) leased Mombasa as
a concession to the British East Africa Company, which in
1888 became the Imperial British East Africa Company. In
1895, the Company surrendered its claim and the coast became,
again, a British protectorate, under the nominal authority of
the Sultan of Zanzibar.[1] Despite these changes, there was a

---

[1] For a description of politics at this level, see C. S. Nicholls, *The Swahili Coast: Politics,
Diplomacy and Trade on the East African Littoral, 1798–1856* (London, 1971).

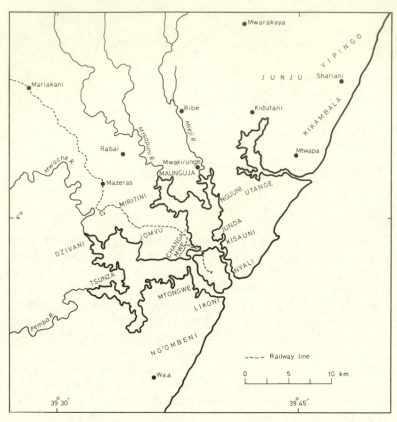

MAP 3. *The mainland around Mombasa Island*

considerable continuity through the nineteenth century in the relationships between the people of Mombasa and those of its hinterland.

The first of the written accounts of this period is that of Lieutenant Emery, who kept a daily log of events during his two-year posting as commander of the 1824–6 British Protectorate.[2] Emery's political and social dealings were almost exclusively with the Mazrui clan of Omani Arabs, who had an uneasy control of such government as there was. Information on the

---

[2] Contained in PRO ADM 52. 3940. See also J. Emery, 'A Short Account of Mombasa and the Neighbouring Coast of Africa', *JRGS* 3 (1833), 280–3.

mainland beyond Mombasa is drawn from them, for Emery showed a marked unwillingness to venture beyond the island.[3]

The Mombasa described by Emery was a small town, with the Mazrui settled near to the Fort and the 'Sohilli' a little distance away.[4] The island itself was not heavily cultivated, and neither was the mainland around Mtwapa creek[5] to the north, where there developed, in the second half of the nineteenth century, a large settlement and a considerable area of slave-cultivated fields. The people of Mombasa did cultivate on the mainland in Emery's time, though; Mombasa's population varied markedly with the seasons, there being at times very few people on the island.[6] There were slaves in Mombasa at this time, for a number were given to Emery as soldiers by the Mazrui. Emery wrote much of the difficulty of disciplining them, since, unhappy with the rather strict regimen of the Royal Navy, these soldiers frequently ran away.[7] These problems gave Emery his most intensive contacts with the 'Whaneka', as he called the people of the hinterland: it was they who captured and returned to Emery, and to other inhabitants of the island, the slaves who had fled from them. For this service they were paid in cloth, and sometimes in grain.[8]

The Whaneka made other appearances in Mombasa. Often Emery's log simply notes that there were Whaneka in town.[9] At times they came with ivory, which they themselves had received from the Kamba.[10] They also brought other goods for the maritime trade in luxuries: gum copal and calumba root.[11] These visits with trade goods were markedly seasonal, occurring in October to May, when maritime traffic was at its peak. But in August and September, when the harbour was almost empty, the Whaneka came to town without ivory or gum. In September 1824, Emery wrote, 'The Whaneka are

[3] The death of his predecessor on an exploratory mission may have underlain Emery's reluctance to venture into Mombasa's hinterland; J. M. Gray, *The British in Mombasa, 1824–6* (London, 1857), 64–5.

[4] See Emery, 'Short Account'; also W. F. W. Owen, *Narrative of Voyages to Explore the Shores of Africa, Arabia and Madagascar* (London, 1833), i. 423.

[5] Emery, Journal, 15 Oct. 1824, PRO ADM 52. 3940.

[6] Ibid. 21 May 1826, 6 June 1826, 22 Sept. 1825.   [7] Ibid. 12 Feb. 1825.

[8] Ibid. 3 Nov. 1824, 17 Dec. 1824, 8 Mar. 1825.

[9] Ibid. 2, 8 Sept. 1824, 13 Oct. 1824.   [10] Ibid. 6 July 1826.

[11] Ibid. 21 Nov. 1825, 4, 10 Dec. 1825.

daily coming into town. I suppose they come for grain as it is near harvest.'[12] Captain Owen, who established the Protectorate, thought that the Whaneka's main interest in trade was to secure palm wine and hence oblivion, an opinion formed by hearsay rather than observation and one which accorded well with his view of the Arabs as wily and exploitative traders.[13] Emery's comment on grain may be closer to the truth.

Mombasa's role as an entrepôt port in the Indian Ocean trade has attracted a good deal of historical attention—perhaps a natural corollary of the perceived separation of coast and hinterland. Yet the importance of this role might be questioned. Emery records that ships did call at Mombasa from India and the Gulf, with salt, dried fish, cloth, earthenware, iron, and brass,[14] taking away ivory and foodstuffs. But this transoceanic trade was not flourishing. Some ships called and then sailed off, finding no market for their goods,[15] and for many of these vessels Mombasa was but one of many stops.[16] Emery, seeking to convert cloth into ivory, organized expeditions to other ports along the coast, so bad was the market in Mombasa.[17]

This was not a new situation. In the Portuguese period, two hundred years before, the takings from customs at Mombasa were considerably less than the costs of maintaining the garrison.[18] As Rezende noted, 'owing to the trade and population of Mombasa there will be a deficit'.[19] Guillain's description of coastal commerce in the 1840s suggests that most trade goods were scarcer and more expensive in Mombasa than elsewhere on the coast, with the exception of food grains.[20] Mombasa's major trading role was not in the intercontinental exchange of luxuries, but rather, as Rezende recorded in 1634: 'There are large supplies of corn, rice and cows. This is one of the reasons why this port is of vital importance to the rulers of the coast.'[21]

Mombasa's own resources were minimal, but the island was

---

[12] Ibid. 3 Sept. 1824.
[13] Owen, *Narrative*, ii. 187; for Owen's view of Arab business practices, see ibid. 150.
[14] Emery, Journal, 6, 21 Dec. 1825.   [15] Ibid. 20 Oct. 1824.
[16] Ibid. 7 Nov. 1824, 26 Feb. 1826.   [17] Ibid. 28 Feb. 1825.
[18] C. R. Boxer and C. Azevedo, *Fort Jesus and the Portuguese, in Mombasa, 1593–1729* (London, 1960), App. F.
[19] J. M. Gray, 'Rezende's Description of Mombasa in 1634', *TNR* 23 (1947), 2–28, 11.
[20] C. Guillain, *Documents sur l'histoire, la géographie et le commerce de l'Afrique Orientale* (Paris, 1857), ii. 2, 300–37.   [21] Gray, 'Rezende's Description', 15–16.

a clearing-house in the trade up and down the coast and between the islands off the coast and the hinterland. It was a
complex trade. In the same month that Emery reported
Whaneka coming to town to buy grain, Mombasan merchants
were receiving boatloads of grain from the north mainland,[22]
and exporting grain by sea to ports as distant as Sayhut in
Arabia and Bombay.[23] Shortly thereafter, grain was arriving
in Mombasa by sea from Pemba.[24] The Nyika were not always
importers of food; it is unclear whether the grain grown on the
north mainland was produced by Nyika farmers, but Emery
did at times specifically note that Whaneka were bringing
foodstuffs into town.[25] In the 1840s, Mombasa certainly was
exporting grain grown by hinterland farmers.[26] Whether or not
any particular area on the coast was, over the year, a net im-
porter of grain, it seems likely that some people from that area
at some time would need to bring food in from outside. If there
were a general failure of rains throughout the local hinterland,
as happened in 1837, 1884–5, and 1898–9, food could be brought
in through Mombasa from Pemba or further afield. In Emery's
time, most of the boats that entered and left Mombasa were
bound to and from the local coast, Pemba, the Tanzanian coast,
or the Lamu Archipelago; and they were loaded with grain,
coconuts, and occasionally livestock.[27]

Mombasa's role as a famine reserve for the hinterland led to
a particular kind of population movement. In the 1840s Krapf,
a missionary of the Church Missionary Society who had established himself at Rabai, noted that the Nyika had turned
to Mombasa for food during a major famine in 1837: 'The
Mombassians who had food in store provided them with such,
but required them to give up their children who were forth-
with sold to Arabia'.[28]

Krapf lamented this process as slavery, and there were other
references to it as such during the nineteenth century.[29] There
is little actual evidence of children being sent to Arabia,
however, and the history of the Mazrui clan refers to the practice

[22] Emery, Journal, 28, 30 Sept. 1824, 2, 5 Oct. 1824, 6 Nov. 1824.
[23] Ibid. 6, 9 Oct. 1824.   [24] Ibid. 17, 26 Nov. 1824.   [25] Ibid. 3 Nov. 1824.
[26] Guillain, Documents, ii. 2, 265.   [27] Emery, Journal, various entries.
[28] J. L. Krapf, 'Excursions to Dshombo', 24 Mar. 1845, 14, CMS CA 5. 0. 16. 167.
[29] C. New, Life, Wanderings and Labours in Eastern Africa (London, 1971 (first 1877)), 128.

in rather more favourable terms, describing events some time around 1820: 'In the liwaliship (governorship) of this Abdallah bin Hemed [*c.*1814–23] a very bad famine hit Duruma country . . . crowds of them left their country for Mombasa seeking food . . . the liwali had pity on them and provided them with rations and sent many Duruma families to Pemba.'[30] This history was written in the twentieth century by a Mazrui anxious to demonstrate the benign dominance of Arab rule in the nineteenth century, and our appreciation of Abdullah's philanthropy may be a little diminished by the knowledge that the Mazrui maintained numbers of slave cultivators on the island of Pemba. Clearly, though, Krapf's dislike of the 'senseless Muhammedan master'[31] shaped his perception of this practice.

Krapf suggested that the process of lending food in time of famine was transformed by the Busaidi, who took control of Mombasa from the Mazrui in 1837: a previous practice, whereby children were given as temporary security for a loan of food, was thus distorted into slavery.[32] Yet the exchange and movement of people was more complex than that. The Busaidi could not simply have changed the arrangement, for it was not one between governments—indeed, it was not one arrangement at all, but a series of little agreements between hinterland homesteads and wealthy men (and women) in Mombasa.[33] The importance of people as a resource in Nyika groups has already been noted, and while dependants might move between homesteads of their own volition, they could also be transferred from one homestead to another by the head of the homestead. Hinterland people not only belonged in, but belonged to, the homestead:[34] the homestead head had rights over the persons of his juniors, rights that extended to transfer or sale. In 1898 an official noted that dependants could be transferred as compensation for crimes, as a form of blood-money: 'The persons handed over appear to occupy a somewhat

[30] Al-Amin Mazrui, 'History of the Mazrui Clan', 3, typescript in Fort Jesus Library, Mombasa.   [31] Krapf, 'Excursions to Dshombo', 24 Mar. 1845, 14.
[32] Krapf, Journal, 3 May 1848, CMS CA 5. 0. 16. 171–2; this analysis is followed by T. T. Spear, *The Kaya Complex* (Nairobi, 1978), 100.
[33] Krapf, Journal, 3 Sept. 1848.
[34] A distinction in meaning noted in S. Miers and I. Kopytoff (eds.), *Slavery in Africa: Historical and Anthropological Perspectives* (Madison, Wis., 1977), 10.

menial position, but being essentially strengtheners of the family are not regarded as slaves . . . Boys handed over in the above manner among the Wa-Digo are on coming of age permitted to return home, but not so the girls.'[35] In the same way, dependants could be transferred to the households of Mombasans: 'During the great famine she [a Swahili woman] had provided an Mnika mother and her child with 20 pishis or measures of Turkish corn, then to the value of 4 or 5 dollars . . . in consequence of this act she considered the persons she had maintained to be her slaves.'[36]

While Krapf saw this as slavery, one informant used the term *kore*, 'blood-money', of children given to Mombasans in this way, underlining the similarity of this type of movement to that in compensation between hinterland homesteads.[37] Where such movements were arranged through the relationships that existed between Nyika groups and the Swahili Twelve Tribes, the similarity of this movement to the transfer of 'rights in persons' between homesteads was even more clear. Such 'pawning' was not a relationship unique to the Mombasa area. Around Dar es Salaam 'Zaramo were sold or sold themselves into slavery' in time of famine.[38] The Kerebe, on Lake Victoria's coast, received pawns in exchange for foodstuffs,[39] and it seems that this was a transaction in which there was always the possibility that the pawns could be sold, should the original loan not be repaid. The status and ultimate fate—return, incorporation, or sale as slaves—of Maasai who were pawned or pawned themselves to Kikuyu during famines similarly depended very much on individual circumstances: and particularly on the existence of previous ties between the lineages involved.[40] In Mombasa, what Krapf saw as a transformation wrought by the Busaidi was a possibility always present in this

---

[35] 'Laws of Kenya' (1898), i. 98, KNA DC KFI 3/3.
[36] Krapf, Journal, 8 Feb. 1847.   [37] Int. 60a.
[38] J. E. G. Sutton, 'Dar es Salaam: A Sketch of a Hundred Years', *TNR* 71 (1970), 1–19, 6.
[39] G. Hartwig, 'Changing Forms of Servitude among the Kerebe of Tanzania', in Miers and Kopytoff (eds.), *Slavery in Africa*, 261–85, 269–72; see also R. A. Austen, 'Slavery among Coastal Middlemen: The Duala of Cameroon', ibid. 305–33, 316; for the Maasai, see R. Waller, 'Emutai: Crisis and Response in Maasailand, 1883–1902', in D. A. Johnson and D. M. Anderson (eds.), *The Ecology of Survival: Case Studies from North-East African History* (London and Boulder, Col., 1988), 73–112.
[40] Miers and Kopytoff (eds.), *Slavery in Africa*, 10.

type of relationship, the terms of which may well have varied from one individual to the next. The creditor might demand not just a period of labour by the dependants, but also repayment of the food advanced before they were returned.[41] Some were not returned. Others, after going to Mombasa, converted to Islam there, under the tutelage of their patron, becoming a part of the household.

The relocation of dependence and obligations that such a move could involve was a complete one, as a Digo informant explained of a nineteenth-century ancestor:

So a relative on my father's side went and lived in Mombasa and he owned a piece of land there, which is still existing, but during these days before he died he announced to his people, 'Whatever I own in the island should not be inherited by those on the mainland'. . . . He was a pure Digo . . . the parents here thought he was taken away by some Arabs or Swahilis as a slave and sent away, and so it was until they had to go to the island to sell some firewood or charcoal, and they saw him somewhere . . . and his parents went there . . . to his place, when they went there they asked for him in his native name, but he was already Muslimised, they said, 'We do not have these Nyikas here,' but he heard them and he came out to see them, and they asked him if he was a slave, and he said, 'No, I'm here by choice, I have already married.'[42]

Having exchanged one set of claims and obligations for another, this migrant himself became a potential patron for migrant Digo kin—the informant's father and aunts were brought up in Mombasa, as townspeople, among this man's family.

Converting in this way, these people shifted their identity as well as their physical location, from Nyika to Swahili. Glassman has suggested that in Pangani this constant process, of becoming Swahili, was a form of resistance on the part of lower-status outsiders: identifying themselves as Swahili they implicitly demanded equality of treatment.[43] Yet equality of treatment is an ambiguous idea in a society where everyone

---

[41] Krapf, Journal, 3 Sept. 1848.

[42] Int. 5b, 3 (this interview was conducted in English). Even in death, such incorporated Nyika had their new identity reaffirmed, by interment in the burial grounds of their adoptive clan; see Int. 61b, 21b.

[43] J. Glassman, 'Social Rebellion and Swahili Culture: The Response to German Conquest of the Northern Mrima, 1888–1890', Ph.D. thesis (Wisconsin, 1988), 99–100, 180–1.

belongs, is subordinate in some way. Becoming Swahili in it-self involved the acceptance of dependent status. It was resist-ance to the elders of the homesteads whence the immigrants came, rather than to the patrons of the coastal towns: resist-ance through renegotiation of the terms of subordination, not through escape from subordination.

Since young men and young women were the least power-ful people in the homestead, it was they who bore the brunt of any shortage of food. Similarly, members of small or weak homesteads could be expected to suffer more from the effects of shortage than could the dependants of wealthier patrons. The wealthy could call in their debts in time of famine, and rely on the support of those networks which their wealth had allowed them to construct.[44] The dependants of lesser patrons, denied this support, sought to place themselves in new net-works by leaving the homestead of their paternal kin in search of new patrons, anticipating any attempt by their seniors to sell them or pawn them for food.

Such migration was not always in response to the social strains imposed by famine : 'there was a great-uncle, my grand-father's elder brother, he left here because he was mad, he even cut my grandfather with a knife, then he ran to Mombasa and studied Islam, and he got better'.[45] The competition over dependants, and over the right to dispose of them, could force others to flee to Mombasa: 'there was one of my great-uncles, a Muslim, he ran away, he married a wife there [Mombasa], he stayed there, until he died there . . . he ran away because he sold his nephew, he sold him to the Arabs, and he was going to be killed by his father.'[46]

Perceptions of these processes have been affected by the im-plications of the term slavery. Spear has argued that essentially the Nyika held no slaves, for servile labour was incorporated into the household. The implied difference between this and the servile labour of Mombasa is made explicit by Morton in his discussion of incorporability. Slaves in Mombasa society, even when manumitted, could never attain the status of the free-born, and neither could their children. Thus, while the

---

[44] A general point made in Johnson and Anderson (eds.), *The Ecology of Survival*, 9.
[45] Int. 27*a*, 1.   [46] Int. CHONYI/2, 2.

Nyika did buy, sell, and kidnap people for their labour power, they were not slaves, and movement as a servile labourer to Mombasa was of a different order to movement from one hinterland homestead to another.[47] This argument, based though it is on the expressed tenets of Mombasan culture, yet ignores the extent to which Nyika (if not slaves from elsewhere), were able to establish themselves within Mombasa as members of high-status groups, notably within the Twelve Tribes of the Swahili.[48] It is difficult to generalize about the position of slaves in a society where the continuum of 'rights in persons' stretches from children, through adopted kin and debtors, to servile labourers bought and sold in the market, and Glassman has shown for Pangani that the lines between slave and client-kinsman are not clearly drawn.[49] The ancestry of such migrants was gossiped over and hinted at, but it did not always hamper them and, whatever the 'rules', there was a degree of incorporability in Mombasa, as well as among the Nyika, which makes questionable the distinction drawn between slavery on the coast and incorporation in the hinterland.

The transfer of 'rights in persons' could take many forms: war, kidnap, sale, debt, or even sale of oneself. The forms of bondage resulting were similarly diverse. Imports of bought slaves by sea seem to have been small until the mid-1840s, when ironically, the Hamerton Treaty and other anti-slave trade measures led to an increase in the use of bought slaves in East African coastal agriculture.[50] In 1824 Emery banned the slave trade in Mombasa, but though he frequently mentions the presence of slaves around Mombasa he seems to have found little actual maritime trade in slaves to suppress. The Mazrui Sultan objected rather more strongly to the tax on the grain trade from the north coast than he did to the banning of the import of slaves by sea.[51]

---

[47] T. T. Spear, *The Kaya Complex* (Nairobi, 1978), 98–9; R. F. Morton, 'Slaves, Freedmen' and Fugitives on the Kenya Coast, 1873–1907', Ph.D. thesis (Syracuse, NY, 1976), 90.   [48] Int. 5d, 9d.

[49] Miers and Kopytoff (eds.), *Slavery in Africa*, 6; Glassman, 'Social Rebellion and Swahili Culture', 183; cf. F. Cooper, *Plantation Slavery on the East African Coast* (New Haven, Conn., 1980), 219, where Cooper takes the distinction to be both clear and fundamental.

[50] Sheriff, *Slaves, Spices and Ivory in Zanzibar* (London, Nairobi, Dar, Athens, Ohio, 1987), ch. 1.

[51] Re Emery's anti-slave-trade activities, see Emery, Journal, 29 Aug., 8 Nov. 1824;

In 1847, Guillain was told that 4,500 of the 6,000 inhabitants of Mombasa's mainland areas were slaves.[52] This is a large figure: it would make Mombasa's slave labour force at this time as large as that of Malindi in the 1870s—a force which needed the import of 600 slaves each year to maintain its numbers.[53] There is no sign of such a volume of slave imports at this time, and it seems more likely that many of these slaves were dependants, debtors, and clients rather than slaves bought and sold in the market.

The assumption that people from the local hinterland played little part in Mombasa's servile labour force—because they could so easily have run away—needs to be re-examined in the light of the evidence on pawning. Flight from Mombasa was not always easy: Nyika elders sometimes returned those who, having been given to Mombasans, fled to the mainland.[54] Patrons on either side could collude in the control of subordinates, rather than compete in their acquisition.

In the context of this discussion on the varying nature of bondage, the contrast which Cooper has noted for the later nineteenth century between the control of slave cultivators in Mombasa and in Malindi, forty miles to the north, seems significant.[55] Malindi was resettled by Arabs and Swahili only from the 1840s onwards, and here there were large plantations, cultivated by slaves who worked under supervisors. The slaves were set an amount of work on their owner's plantation each day, and were given subsistence rations. In Mombasa, it was more usual for slaves to live in their own villages, and organize their own time, paying a part of the crop which they grew to their owners in recognition of their obligations. It seems likely that this arrangement incorporated relationships between Mombasan creditors and Nyika debtors and dependants.

Non-agricultural slaves in Mombasa could also enjoy a considerable amount of freedom. Some controlled their own time, working not for their master but for others, and paying a proportion of the wages earned to their masters. Others worked as

and for the Sultan's attitude to the ban on slaves and the tax on grain, see ibid. 29 Sept., 5 Dec. 1824.

[52] Guillain, *Documents*, ii. 2, 239.   [53] Cooper, *Plantation Slavery*, 86–8.
[54] Krapf, Journal, 8 Feb. 1847.
[55] Cooper, *Plantation Slavery*, 17; Morton, 'Slaves, Freedmen', 75.

crew or fishermen on boats owned by their masters, and earned a share of the takings.[56]

In these circumstances, where slavery involved, in day-to-day terms, no more than the recognition of a continuing obligation, it was a status which overlapped with that of the client or debtor, never actually bought or sold, but none the less similarly obligated. This is not to say that slavery on the coast was 'benign':[57] it is rather that 'slavery' comprised a number of institutions, whose intricate but flexible hierarchy was marked by different terms for different statuses.[58] In this hierarchy of slaves and dependants, similarity of language and family connections in the town put the Nyika immigrant, whether bought, pawned, or personally indebted, above the slave marched or shipped from Malawi or Mozambique. Miers and Kopytoff have suggested that the essential mark of the slave is that of being an outsider, without kin:[59] yet the historic movement of people from hinterland to island meant that Nyika who moved to Mombasa would have been surrounded by potential, if not necessarily acknowledged kin, although they were transplanted to a new identity and status. Moreover, the presence of kin, as well as the general demand for dependants, made it much easier for people from the local hinterland to move to Mombasa by themselves, outside the control of the homestead head.

The 'pawning' arrangement, then, was not simply a sale into slavery. Nor was it as entirely one-sided as Krapf believed. To homestead heads it offered an alternative to the unplanned, independent flight of their subordinates in search of better options. In return for the loan or outright surrender of the labour power of some of their dependants, they would receive food which confirmed their position as providers to their homesteads. To the wealthy men (and some women) of Mombasa and Swahili and Arab clan heads and traders, the arrangement was similarly important. There were many uses for the 'pawned': the economy of Mombasa, and its local

[56] Cooper, *Plantation Slavery*, 187–9; 'Questions on Slavery', Tritton, 30 Jan. 1903, KNA PC Coast 1/1/93; Administrator to IBEA Sec., 22 Mar. 1893, IBEA File 12 (3).

[57] An assumption warned against in Miers and Kopytoff (eds.), *Slavery in Africa*, 20.

[58] Cooper, *Plantation Slavery*, 219; cf. the similarly detailed Duala terminology of servitude, in R. A. Austen, 'Slavery among Coastal Middlemen: The Duala of Cameroon', in Miers and Kopytoff, *Slavery in Africa*, 308.

[59] Miers and Kopytoff, *Slavery in Africa*, 15.

hinterland was largely agricultural, and given the abundance of land and the prevailing level of technology, the production of wealth was largely dependent on the availability of labour to the men who controlled the land. The acquisition and control of subordinates within the household of the Arab or Swahili landowner was as important as it was within the Nyika homestead, economically and as a display of status.

The practice of pawning shows clearly that in controlling their subordinates, patrons in Mombasa and among the Nyike could co-operate, curtailing but not eliminating the evident potential for conflict between these sets of patrons. The lack of any strong central authority on either side meant that this co-operation took the form of a number of small alliances and accommodations, between particular individuals or between particular families or clans.

The absence of central authority in hinterland society has already been explored. While the coastal towns have more often been seen as states by historians,[60] a study of the evidence of both Emery and Krapf suggests that authority and law in nineteenth-century Mombasa were diffuse.

Emery was most concerned, indeed obsessed, with the nature of power: acutely aware of the small size of the British Establishment, but equally aware that he was His Majesty's representative and should therefore be the ultimate authority on the island, he struggled to assert himself. In this, he received little support from the Mazrui governor who was, theoretically, the ruler of Mombasa. Emery, suspicious and isolated, was inclined to view the governor's attitude as deliberate obstructionism,[61] but it seems rather to have reflected a very real lack of power. When one governor displeased several different factions in Mombasa, he was quickly replaced by a more congenial member of the family.[62] The governor's power was circumscribed, and he governed indirectly, through the heads of the clans and great families of Mombasa, whose consent and co-operation he constantly sought.[63] Mombasa was

[60] J. de V. Allen, 'Witu, Swahili History and the Historians', in A. I. Salim (ed.), *State Formation in Eastern Africa* (London and Nairobi, 1986), 216–49.

[61] Emery, Journal, 2 Aug. 1825; see also Gray, *The British in Mombasa*, 119–43, for Emery's problems of authority.   [62] Emery, Journal, 5 Oct. 1825.

[63] Ibid. 3 July, 2 Aug. 1825; Owen, *Narrative*, i. 408–9.

an agglomeration of self-governing groups, held together by the diplomacy and arbitration of the governor, and Emery even referred to the governor simply as 'Head of the Arabs' at one stage.[64]

The Swahili and Arab clans were not the only parties to this accommodation of interests. Emery referred to Whaneka 'chiefs', as did Krapf twenty years later.[65] While there was no individual with executive power over any hinterland group, there were some men who benefited from a relationship with powerful figures in Mombasa, whose power and influence as homestead heads and *kaya* elders might be increased as a result of the wealth which this relationship brought them. The importance to these 'chiefs' of their relationship with Mombasa, and the jealousies that this could arouse amongst them, were described by Krapf (although he interpreted this as a sign of a lack of authority, rather than a dispute over access to the sources of authority): 'A great number of Wanika were in town today for the purpose of making our chief pay a bullock, for he had allowed the slaves of Sheikh Jabiri of Mombas to cut down a tree without the permission of the other chiefs. The powerless chief was fined by his own people.'[66] These 'chiefs' were called to Mombasa for events such as the installation of the new governor,[67] and while in Mombasa they were entertained by, and received gifts from, the governor and other prominent men.[68] The Mazrui governor, like the Portuguese 200 years before, was paying an annual sum to some of the Nyika chiefs.[69]

While the Mazrui sometimes acted as arbiters to settle disputes between hinterland groups in the 1820s,[70] they lacked the physical force to rule directly, having very little in the way of a standing army. In time of trouble, they relied on the numerous slaves and clients of the individual members of the Mazrui

[64] Emery, Journal, 5 Oct. 1825.
[65] Ibid. 5 Aug. 1825; Krapf, *Travels and Missionary Labours during an Eighteen Years' Residence in Eastern Africa* (London, 1968 (first 1860)), 171.
[66] Krapf, Journal, 25 Dec. 1848. Krapf had a preference for clear and unambiguous central authority, and regarded all else as rather obstructive chaos; see his comments on Usambara and Shoa as against the Mombasa area, *Travels and Missionary Labours*, 274–5, 370–2.   [67] Emery, Journal, 14 Oct. 1825.
[68] Krapf, 'Excursions to Dshombo', 25 Mar. 1845, 25; Emery, Journal, 14 Oct. 1825.   [69] Emery, Journal, 25 Feb. 1825.
[70] Ibid. 3–6 Aug. 1825.

family, and on the family itself, which was fairly large. In a
serious military confrontation, as when they went to war with
the Busaidi in Pemba, they called on the Nyika as allies.[71]
Even mediation was not the preserve of Mombasans: in the
1840s the Swahili of Jomvu turned to the elders of Rabai for
help in settling a dispute.[72]

These arrangements brought other benefits beyond co-
operation in the control of subordinates: Krapf noted that
Mombasan merchants had specific trading partners among
the Nyika, with whom they could exchange cloth and other
goods for ivory, gum copal, foodstuffs, and the right to cut
timber. These arrangements offered the merchants a degree of
protection; safety for themselves and for their goods in the
hinterland.[73] These hinterland partners, in turn, controlled the
channels of trade and thus the distribution of wealth from that
trade: a homestead head, could, through such an arrangement,
ensure that his dependants could not independently amass
wealth through this trade and threaten the head's position as
the controller of wealth and production in the homestead. The
support which these arrangements lent to the gerontocracy is
expressed most directly in various stories concerning the gates
of the *kaya*, which recount how these gates were given by the
Mazrui or by Swahili.[74] In a Duruma version of this story, the
connection with the movement of labour is made explicit;
the gates of the *kaya* were said to have been paid for with
children.[75] Other parts of the ritual regalia of the elders were
also said to come from Mombasa.[76] The elders sought to incorporate some elements of Islam into their rituals, having
Muslims slaughter the animals which they exacted from the
populace as offerings, thus seeking to counterbalance the ritual
power lent to some of the alternative institutions, such as spirit
possession, by itinerant Muslim religious specialists.[77]

Where disputes did occur between the Nyika and the people
of Mombasa, they centred on the flight of dependants: the

[71] Ibid. 9 Oct. 1824.   [72] Krapf, Journal, 6 Oct. 1847.
[73] Krapf, 'Excursions to Dshombo', 25 Mar. 1845, 2–25.
[74] MHT 31; Harries, 'The Founding of Rabai: A Swahili Chronicle by Mwidani
bin Mwidad', *Swahili*, 31 (1961), 141–9.
[75] ADC Rabai to Land Officer, 28 Mar. 1914, KNA PC Coast 1/11/218.
[76] Krapf, Journal, 25 Apr. 1848.
[77] Ibid. 13 Mar. 1848. id., 'Excursions to Dshombo', 28.

most tense point in the relationship, and that which made it so necessary.[78] A constant movement of individuals from the hinterland to Mombasa, and from Mombasa to the hinterland, outside this framework of alliances, allowed patrons on one side to build their followings at the expense of those on the other. This was a problem that intensified in the later nineteenth century. The Nyika perceptions of Mombasa recorded by Krapf should be seen in the light of this struggle to control the movement of dependants.

Krapf was frequently told by Rabai and other informants that they dared not visit the island, for fear of being made slaves and sold abroad:[79] for them the island was a strange and dangerous place. It is an attitude which mirrors the perception, evident in some coastal texts, of the mainland as a wild and hostile place. Like this perception, it was ambiguous. Krapf in fact met and saw numbers of Nyika in Mombasa, as Emery and Owen had done before him.[80] This ambivalence, the perceived division of two groups between which there was constant contact and a considerable, if asymmetrical, movement of population, was a product of the systems of patronage which located people within one group or the other. Membership of the group was not a matter of kin, nor even of residence, for the mainland settlements of some Swahili clearly intermingled with those of some Nyika. Rather it was that a population sharing space and sharing kin ties was divided into two groups by the orientation of patron–client links. The impression of danger implicit in the ambivalent presentation of each group by the other was intended to limit contacts between the two groups to the channels established by the elders and wealthy men: thus hinterland elders hoped to prevent the independent movement of individuals to Mombasa. It is perhaps significant that most of the Nyika that Krapf met in Mombasa seem to have been 'chiefs'.[81]

During the nineteenth century there was an intensification of the tensions in these relationships, but their nature was

[78] Emery, Journal, 28–30 Nov. 1824.
[79] See e.g. Krapf, 'Excursions to Dshombo', 24 Mar. 1845, 14.
[80] See e.g. Krapf, 'Journey to Pemba, Tanga and Mombas', 13 Mar. 1845, 15, CMS CA 5. 0. 16. 165.
[81] Krapf to Revd. Venn, 26 Sept. 1855, 3, CMS CA 5. 0. 16. 114.

unchanged, and a degree of co-operation between powerful men in the hinterland and in Mombasa continued. Busaidi rule has been seen as a turning point,[82] but the introduction of a new set of governors did not immediately transform Mombasa as a state. Like the Mazrui, the Busaidi governors ruled essentially by compromise, leaving the Arab and Swahili clans and families to govern themselves, and mediating in disputes between them.[83] Unlike the Mazrui, the Busaidi possessed a moderately effective armed force of their own, and so did not rely on Nyika allies in time of war. But the assumption that the Busaidi had less to do with the population of the hinterland than did the Mazrui seems incorrect. Indeed, the increased wealth which the new governors drew from their share of Mombasa's growing customs revenues allowed them to play a considerable role as patrons to migrants.[84] A series of economic shifts, partly the result of innovation by some hinterland people, were more directly significant in nineteenth-century change.

In the 1840s, when Krapf and Guillain arrived there, Mombasa was still not a great entrepôt, although the first Kamba caravans bearing ivory and other trade goods had made their way to the coast,[85] and the Indian traders of Mombasa and Zanzibar were beginning to finance caravans into the interior.[86] These developments deprived the population of the hinterland, particularly the Giriama, of their role as middlemen in the trade in high-value goods. But in other ways it drew them more firmly into the Mombasan commercial economy. The growing demand for caravan labour, as the number and size of these up-country expeditions increased, led some Nyika to enlist as porters.[87]

There was another, equally significant change in the second half of the nineteenth century, which slightly post-dated the

---

[82] Spear, *The Kaya Complex*, 136–7; F. J. Berg, 'Mombasa under the Busaidi Sultanate', Ph.D. thesis (Wisconsin, 1971), ch. 2.

[83] Berg, ibid., 98.   [84] Int. 60a., Int. 53a.

[85] Guillain, *Documents*, ii. 2, 213.   [86] Ibid. 238.

[87] There is some dispute over how many porters were from the local hinterland and how many were actual or runaway slaves of other origins; cf. Morton, 'Slaves, Freedmen', ch. 2, with D. C. Sperling, 'The Growth of Islam among the Mijikenda of the Kenya Coast', Ph.D. thesis (London, 1988), 50.

inception of the caravan trade. This was the planting of the island of Pemba with clove trees, and the concomitant decline in grain cultivation on that island, long the bread-basket of the area. This gave a new importance to grain cultivation on the Kenya coast. The new demand for grain was met largely from Malindi, but production in the Mombasa area also increased.[88] Mombasan landholders expanded their cultivation, and hinterland farmers became more involved with, and indebted to, an expanding class of planters-cum-traders from Mombasa. The dispersal of many members of the Mazrui family from Mombasa and their establishment at Gasi and Takaungu provided new focuses for these relationships,[89] at Takaungu in particular.[90]

Agricultural expansion and the demands of the caravan trade combined to make the later nineteenth century a period of high demand for labour. In the earlier nineteenth century there had been a bearable complementarity between the demands of maritime trade and those of the harvest, the peak season in each coming at a slightly different time. The caravan trade was not so seasonally restricted, and could involve journeys of many months, so that demands for labour conflicted. Heads of households in Mombasa and in the hinterland faced increasing difficulties in controlling the time and product of their dependants and slaves, for subordinates could easily find other work and new patrons. In 1888, one of the conditions set by the 'people of Mombasa' for the acceptance of Imperial British East Africa Company rule was that 'should any domestic slave wish to engage themselves for work they are only to be employed with the consent of their masters. NB The idea is to prevent their slaves being sent into the interior on Caravan duty which causes their own shambas and other affairs being neglected for want of labour.'[91]

In 1845, when Krapf established his mission station in Rabai, he was perturbed by what he regarded as a new development—the presence in the hinterland of coastal Muslims: 'These people

[88] Cooper, *Plantation Slavery*, 100.
[89] P. Koffsky, 'The History of Takaungu, East Africa, 1830–1895', Ph.D. thesis (Wisconsin, 1977).   [90] Int. 53*a*.
[91] Attached, Mackenzie to Euan-Smith, 25 Oct. 1888, IBEA File 1*a*.

craftily possess themselves by degrees of the lowlands of the Wanika, and constructing villages, here and there, along the mountain range, people them with their slaves, gain over the Wanika by trifling presents, and purchase their produce very cheaply.'[92] Krapf perceived the Nyika as simple heathens, apt to be bamboozled by the more civilized people of the coast. It was a view of the dynamics of coastal society that persisted into the period of British rule, when historically minded officials were wont to quote Krapf's comments.[93] Krapf's views were also shaped by his personal experiences. He had initially relied on Muslim acquaintances to establish himself among the Rabai, but turned against these Muslims when he discovered that they were, not altogether surprisingly, trying to limit his activities.[94] Indeed, his changing attitudes were a striking precursor of the changing attitudes of officials in the colonial period.

Krapf's initial ally and eventual opponent, the archetype of the land-grabbing Muslim, was Abdullah bin Pisila.

Abdalla (son of a Hindoo named Pisila) is a native of Cutch in India. He came hither in merchant business like all the other Hindoos who are here, chiefly natives of Cutch. He turned Musulman (as many of his countrymen do) some 20 years ago. At first he lived in the village Rabbay amongst the pagan Wanika, whose favour he had won by prudent conduct and by accommodation to their superstitious practices. A dying Wanika made him the heir of a considerable piece of ground situated near the creek . . . on the foot of the hill of Rabbay. There he erected a cottage and cultivated a plantation which provides him with coco-nuts, rice, maize and other eatables. A pagan family associated with him assists him in digging the ground etc.[95]

Abdullah also traded in Nyika-produced foodstuffs.[96] He had achieved this position partly through marriage to the daughter of Bwana Hamadi, whom Krapf called the Swahili 'chief' of the Rabai and of the Chonyi.[97] Abdullah's life story makes clear the fluidity of ethnic boundaries, the ease with which the

[92] Krapf, *Travels and Missionary Labours*, 139.
[93] See e.g. Hollis, 'Report No. 4, on Mile 7.2–9.5', 23 Dec. 1906, KNA AG/4/2055.
[94] Krapf, *Travels and Missionary Labours*, 181; id., Journal, 3 Sept. 1848; ibid. 30 Sept. 1847.   [95] Krapf 'Excursions to Dshombo', 23 Mar. 1845.
[96] Krapf, Journal, 10 Feb. 1847.   [97] Ibid. 8 Feb., 11 Oct. 1847.

normative rules of class and marriage could be broken in Mombasa's community, and the ease with which a Muslim could live amongst the people of the local hinterland—despite the assertion, common in the colonial period, that even Nyika who converted to Islam were driven out, lest they alienate their clans' land under Muslim law.[98]

Abdullah had a family 'associated with him', who farmed for him: the ease with which such figures could obtain dependants, through their own superior access to credit and trade goods, is striking. Krapf was several times asked to provide money to help those unable to get money from their fathers for a bride-price, or who were short of food. Some offered a gift, called *heshima*, 'respect', to acknowledge the obligation thus placed upon them.[99] Others sought to obtain help through a religious expression of their obligation to Krapf: 'I was approached by Marunga, who said that the people would embrace my doctrines, if I would lay out a sum of 100 dollars to buy corn for the time of famine which would most likely come upon them in consequence of there being no rain.'[100]

Krapf failed to establish such relationships, indeed, he campaigned against them and once noted with satisfaction that 'they commence to perceive that they cannot expect from me what the Mohammedan leaders are obliged to give them'.[101] The mission gained no following. It is perhaps illustrative of the increased wiliness (and wealth) of missionaries, that from the 1870s a number of missions—the Anglicans at Rabai and Freretown (in Nyali) and then the Methodists at Jimba—built and occasionally lost followings through the same processes which Krapf refused to participate in: the shifting movements of individuals seeking better terms from new patrons.[102]

Abdullah, for his part, is the first recorded example of a type of whom we hear much more in the early colonial period—a trader and planter, with indebted clients acquired through

---

[98] R. W. Hamilton, 'Land Tenure among the Bantu Wanyika of East Africa', *JAS* 20 (1920), 13–18. For further discussion of this, see Ch. 5.

[99] Krapf, Journal, 1 May 1848.   [100] Ibid. 31 Dec. 1848.

[101] Krapf, 'Excursions to Dshombo', 29 January 1845, 2.

[102] Morton, 'Slaves, Freedmen'; T. Herlehy and R. F. Morton, 'A Coastal Ex-Slave Community in the Regional and Colonial Economy of Kenya: The Wamisheni of Rabai, 1880–1963', in S. Miers and R. Roberts (eds.), *The End of Slavery in Africa* (Madison, Wis., 1988), 254–81, 263–4.

trade, and with land in the hinterland worked for him by local people growing grain or fruit for the Mombasan market. Many of these individuals prefigured by Abdullah were, like him, members of the Swahili Twelve Tribes by birth or marriage.[103] Some were born of parents in the hinterland,[104] or had Nyika mothers or other kin. Bwana Heri, the great trader and patron of the Pangani area, had a similarly ambiguous ethnicity, variously claiming Zigua, Swahili, and Arab identity.[105] It has been suggested that blood brotherhoods and hypergamous marriages (the giving of women from a less to a more prestigious group, without reciprocity) forge 'pacts of general responsibility' which are necessary to a coast–hinterland trading system where the coastal people's greater access to credit makes them dominant: the relationship of kin thus established allows a trust system and the use of credit which is essential to the trade.[106] This is to an extent true of the Mombasa area, and conforms to the expressed rules of identity and culture in Mombasa. The relationship went further, however: Nyika men also joined Twelve Tribes groups, so that while the kin ties between the people of the coast and the hinterland were, nominally, fictive or matrilineal, they could in actuality be patrilineal. In Pangani, by marrying 'marginal' women from clans of Arab origin male outsiders could gain full status in those clans for their children if not for themselves.[107] It is possible that this happened in Mombasa, but it was in a sense unnecessary: male outsiders seem to have gained status in the Twelve Tribes anyway. Such newcomers might be vulnerable, as the twentieth century was to show, but if no strain or hardship occurred their marginality remained hidden within the considerable negotiability of norms and history in a largely oral society.

Krapf treated Abdullah's presence in the hinterland as a new phenomenon. Seventy years later, British officials similarly refused to accept that such people could have been established for any length of time in areas that had by then been designated

---

[103] Such as Said bin Sheikh in Kilifi, and Ali bin Salim al-Mandhri in Kidutani.
[104] Int. 50*a*, 5*c*, 68*a*.
[105] Glassman, 'Social Rebellion and Swahili Culture', 107.
[106] Austen, 'The Metamorphoses of Middlemen: The Duala, Europeans and the Cameroon Hinterland, *c*.1800–*c*.1960', *IJAHS* 16 (1983), 1–25, 4.
[107] Glassman, 'Social Rebellion and Swahili Culture', 251–7.

as 'native reserves'.[108] The officials were clearly wrong, and
Krapf may have been. Abdullah had been trading for twenty
years, since Emery's time, before the caravan trade brought
Mombasa an expanded role in Indian ocean trade, before
Pemba was planted with clove trees. None of the conventional
arguments suggest any changes in economic patterns in the
1820s that would help us to understand Abdullah as an in-
novator, and see his role as a novel one . Such figures as he
may long have been intermediaries in the local trade. However,
the nineteenth century did see an increase in their numbers,
their influence, and their wealth, as the grain trade grew.

The ties of debt woven around such traders were complex.
Almost all creditors were also debtors, in a chain of indebtedness which led to Mombasa and ultimately to the Indian Ocean
networks of merchant capital. The trader Tshakka, to whom
the Rabai 'chief' was indebted, and who held the chief's
daughter as security for this debt, was himself indebted to
traders in Mombasa and avoided going there.[109] When the
missionaries hired Bwana Heri (not the same as Bwana Heri
of Pangani), a Mombasan caravan leader, to guide an expedi-
tion to Chagga, he was promptly kidnapped by his Mombasan
creditors, and Krapf and his colleague Rebmann had to bail
him out.[110] Some of the porters hired for this same trip would
only come to Rabai at night, to avoid their creditors. Despite
this precaution, one of them was apprehended, and lost most
of his wages before he had earned them.[111]

These events reveal a little of the complexity of the obligations imposed by debt. Some debts were incurred by homestead heads, seeking bridewealth to buy wives for themselves
or for their sons. Other debts were taken on by young men,
perhaps in an attempt to circumvent the control of elders over
their earnings. Such debts could take the form of an advance
given for a future delivery of grain, timber, fruit, or sometimes
other goods.[112] Increasingly, the spread of coconut palm and

---

[108] See the Judgment in Civil Case No. 60 of 1913, KNA PC Coast 1/10/209; see also
Ag. DC Kilifi to SC, 10 Aug 1822, KNA PC Coast 1/1/177.
[109] Krapf, Journal, 3 Sept. 1848.   [110] Ibid. 13 Nov. 1848.
[111] Ibid. 12, 14 Nov. 1848.
[112] Krapf, 'Excursion to the Wanika division of Keriama', Feb. 1845, 21, CMS CA
5. 0. 16. 166; H. K. Binns, 'Recollections in 1898 of Experiences in 1878', MS in KNA
H. K. Binns Collection, 28; see also PC Coast to ADC Rabai, 12 Dec. 1913, KNA PC
Coast 1/10/188.

other fruit tree cultivation in the hinterland provided another form of security for loans.[113] In this case, the product of the fruit trees so mortgaged would go to the creditor, in lieu of interest, which was forbidden by Islamic law.[114] Deprived of their earnings from the mortgaged trees, debtors found repayment difficult, and some handed over their junior kin to repay advances.[115] The growing trade in grain and fruit from hinterland producers, and advances within this trade, became involved in the movement of people from hinterland to coast: and movement from one patron to another.

Some of these debts were never repaid, and quite possibly no one expected them to be. As in the case of Bwana Heri and the porters, a debt could simply be a claim on the potential earning power of the debtor, a claim which could be called in when that potential was realized. Debts were another aspect of transactions in 'rights in persons', though unlike the movement of individuals from one homestead to another, they did not immediately redefine the identity of the debtor: the transaction was not necessarily a total transfer, but it could result in such a transfer, of the debtor or one of his dependants.

The expansion of debt was closely connected with inflation of bridewealth during the second half of the nineteenth century. Informants' suggestions that until the mid-nineteenth century bridewealth was a fixed, non-negotiable amount are perhaps an idealization of the past,[116] but it is clear that there has been intense inflation of bridewealth over the last 150 years:

It was money, a *shami*, a *shami* was bridewealth. A *shami* is a dollar [Maria Theresa dollar = 2 rupees = 4 shillings] . . . my wife got one hundred and ninety dollars, my father-in-law was given it, and I got a wife. Now it's gone up, five thousand, six thousand shillings for one wife. . . . my mother was married for forty dollars, just forty dollars for my mother. My grandmother got twenty-two dollars, and my great-grandmother was given for just three dollars, just like giving her away, a whole wife![117]

Mijikenda informants now blame this inflation of bridewealth, as they blame much else, on the Arabs, who began to

[113] Krapf, Journal, 1 May 1848; also George David to CMS, 2 Apr. 1879, CMS CA 5. o. 6. 5. [114] Chancellor to Wright, 4 Feb. 1874, CMS CA 5. o. 5. 2. [115] Binns, 'Recollections', 25. [116] Int. 20*a*. [117] Int. 25*a*, 3.

offer money to buy women from the hinterland as brides.[118] Krapf too blamed the practice on the Arabs when he reported it in Rabai in the 1840s, at which time the price of a bride was three or four dollars.[119] Yet the inflation was almost certainly more to do with the nature of accumulation within hinterland homesteads, and with elders' attempts to keep control of the increasing amount of money circulating.

The growth in the market for grain, ivory, and other goods offered new opportunities, but to take advantage of these required an ability to call on the labour of others, as farmers and porters, on a regular basis, and to call on this labour at a time when others might have their own work to do, at harvest time. Some forms of casual labour existed, usually involving the clearing of ground for cultivation in return for a payment of grain or palm wine.[120] But this offered no permanent and reliable labour force for the weeding and harvesting of crops, for protecting the ripening grain against birds and wild pigs, or for the lengthy process of turning the harvested grain into flour and carrying it to the creeks for shipment. There were no contracts, nor means of enforcing them, and the only institution for controlling labour was the homestead. To acquire more labourers, the homestead head could either marry more wives or he could provide wives for his sons and dependants, in the hope that these dependants would not leave the homestead. The increasing amounts of wealth, and particularly of cash, circulating in the later nineteenth century produced something of a dilemma for homestead heads.

By pushing up the price of the resource which they controlled, their marriageable daughters, elders sought to control the increasing amount of money that the growth of the grain trade and of caravan portering had introduced into the economy; bridewealth payments became essentially a transfer of money from young men to old. Thus old men continued to be able to compete with younger men for brides, although young men now had access to cash from wages or the credit trade. This very inflation, however, made the position of homestead heads as providers of brides to their sons more difficult, for prices

[118] Int. 20a.   [119] Krapf, Journal, 90–1, 1 Dec. 1847.
[120] Int. 66a, 17a.

were higher. An intensification of competition within the homestead was inevitable. Among the Duruma and Digo matrilineality had moved such tensions outside the homestead, as the maternal uncle was responsible for bridewealth.[121] But the practice developed of buying slave, or at least non-Duruma, wives, whose offspring would belong to the patrilineage since they had no matrilineage. For such wives, the maternal uncle would not pay bridewealth, so that the tension over the use of resources within the homestead, over who should get the wife, emerged here too.[122] Disputes frequently arose, with young men leaving to seek better treatment elsewhere, in another homestead or in Mombasa.[123] If the head of the homestead had taken on a debt, mortgaging trees or future crops, junior males in the homestead would have greater incentives to flee, or rather fewer reasons to stay: their prospects for inheritance would be dim, and the head of the homestead would have little chance of raising bridewealth for them.

For many women, flight, and particularly flight to Mombasa, was an increasingly attractive option. Women had even less control of the product of their labour than did young men; demands on their labour within the homestead were considerable, and newly married women in particular were very much at the mercy of their in-laws.[124] Women did most of the work in cultivation, in fetching water, and in collecting firewood. Migration to Mombasa offered (and still does offer) alternatives to this, usually relieving a woman at least of her duties as a cultivator: a Muslim woman should not labour in public, in the fields or elsewhere. Moreover, under Islamic law women may inherit property and enjoy the product of it for themselves, rights which were generally denied to women in hinterland homesteads. Islam is often accused of imposing restrictions on women, yet it could offer women a degree of protection, and a level of autonomy, not available elsewhere.

To describe these conflicts within hinterland homesteads is not to suggest that life in Mombasa was, in contrast always

---

[121] Thanks to Jeanne Bergman for much useful discussion on this point.
[122] Annual Report, Rabai Subdistrict (1912), KNA PC Coast 1/1/15.
[123] Int. 1a.
[124] Int. 6a; also H. M. T. Kayamba, 'Notes on the Wadigo', TNR 23 (1947), 80–96, 87.

easy for slaves and clients, the men and women who generally did the least pleasant work for little or no remuneration. Many voted with their feet against life in Mombasa, fleeing from there either to the mission stations or to found their own run-away slave communities in the hinterland.[125] It is rather to suggest that the movements of people around Mombasa have to be assessed in their entirety, for the complexity of these movements clearly shows that people were constantly evaluating the options open to them; and Mombasa was by no means always the worst option for them. While the flow of runaway slaves from Mombasa to the missions has received considerable attention from historians,[126] it was in fact runaways from hinterland homesteads who first sought refuge at Rabai mission:

About the end of the year 1876 there commenced a movement which in later years assumed very extensive and alarming proportions and caused no little trouble and anxiety to the missionaries. I refer to the migration of the runaway slaves towards the mission stations. I remember quite well the first man and his wife who came . . . they were the slaves of a Giriama man . . . it was not until some time after this that slaves from the coast began to come to us.[127]

Some individuals ran from Mombasa to the missions or to the runaway slave settlements, some ran from their homesteads to the missions, some ran from their homesteads to other homesteads, some ran from homesteads to Mombasa. From the 1870s, some of those of Malawian and other origins, 'freed' by the British anti-slavery naval patrols and settled in the mission station at Freretown, escaped from there to the more easy-going mission establishment at Rabai,[128] or joined hinterland homesteads. Some Nyika men, such as Mwavuo among the Giriama[129] and Mkoka wa Mbeu among the Kauma,[130] built followings of hundreds of dependants, far larger than any

[125] Morton, 'Slaves, Freedmen', 183–229; Herlehy and Morton, 'A Coastal Ex-Slave Community', 257.
[126] See e.g. A. I. Salim, *Swahili-Speaking Peoples of the Kenya Coast, 1895–1963* (Nairobi, 1973), 48–50.
[127] Binns, 'Recollections', 9–10; Herlehy and Morton, 'A Coastal Ex-Slave Community', 263.
[128] Morton, 'Slaves, Freedmen'; Herlehy and Morton, 'A Coastal Ex-Slave Community', 261.
[129] Champion, *The Agiryama*, 15.   [130] Int. 53a.

homestead, yet similarly structured, drawing in clients from other hinterland groups in the process. Such confused activity might seem bizarre, but it was rooted in the considerable variations in the treatment of subordinates that seem to have existed between one Nyika homestead and another, and between one Mombasan household and another.

Kin ties and the intermingling of mainland settlements facilitated such movements. On the shores of Port Reitz, the southern arm of the creek around Mombasa, stood in the 1840s both Nyika homesteads and Mombasan plantations, and the village of Dshombo on the mainland was divided into Muslim and pagan halves.[131] Guillain, from the information of his town informants, listed a number of villages of the Swahili Twelve Tribes on the mainland.[132] Among these were some—Kidutani, Kinung'una, and Mwakirunge—where today the inhabitants insist that they are Ribe or Jibana, and always have been, and that the villages are on their land: and that, of course, the Swahili tribes to whom Guillain attributes these villages are they themselves by another name.[133]

The movement of some Nyika to dependence on Mombasan patrons increased this intermingling. Some settled on the mainland immediately around the island of Mombasa, in Likoni, Mtongwe, or Kisauni, where they became small farmers, having their own plots of a few coconut palms and other trees.[134] Krapf noted such a settlement of Digo at Mtopanga, north of Mombasa, in 1845.[135] Their transition to the following of a new patron was signalled by their conversion to Islam, and they might be given land by the Mombasan who converted them. Active proselytism had never been a feature of coastal Islam, but the establishment of these client communities gradually increased the number of Muslims on the coast, as the clientage relationships expressed by conversion to Islam expanded. For the migrants, Islam marked not only their attachment to a new patron, but their freedom from the demands of the elders, from a gerontocracy which drew its strength from non-Islamic ritual and belief.

---

[131] Krapf, 'Excursions to Dshombo', 13 Mar. 1845.
[132] Guillain, *Documents*, ii. 2, 239.   [133] Int. 20*a*, 40*a*.   [134] Int. 5*c*.
[135] Krapf, 'Forty Miles Journey to Takaongo', 5 July 1845, 34–5, CMS CA 5. 0. 16. 168.

The new patron could assume the role of father even more completely, supplying the migrant with bridewealth,[136] or with a bride from among his own following. Some Digo converts to Islam were settled by their Muslim patrons around the head of Mtwapa creek, towards Junju, as trading agents.[137] Those settled in Mtongwe and Kisauni helped harvest the nuts from their patron's palms, or cleared his ground for cultivation. Such migrants could assume membership of one of the Swahili Twelve Tribes.[138]

All these movements took place in a context of increasing insecurity. Increasing competition for dependants did not only bring a wider range of options for clients: there was an intensification of attempts to secure dependants by force, which attempts might take the form of kidnapping small children by stealth, or of minor battles to secure captives. Krapf had noted the kidnapping of children in the 1840s,[139] but kidnapping and raiding seem to have worsened later in the century.[140] The insecurity this generated increased the importance of belonging to a large homestead, of being *mtu wa watu*, 'a person belonging to people': the parallel of the importance to the wealthy of having followers.[141] Again, such insecurity could motivate flight from one patron in search of another.

The Mombasa to which many of these migrants moved was, at the end of the nineteenth century, still a society in which personal security depended on the individual's relationships to other individuals, rather than to the state. Members of the population usually defined themselves in terms of the clan or family to which and in which they belonged.[142] Patterns of residence on the island still generally reflected group membership and allegiance, not personal wealth or status. Some quarters of the town were named after the family or clan which occupied them: such as the Mandhry quarter, populated by the members of this family and by their slaves and clients.[143]

---

[136] Int. 61*b*.   [137] Int. 9*a*, 9*d*.   [138] Int. 61*b*.
[139] Krapf, Journal, Nov. 1847, 87–8.
[140] Int. 53*a*; see also Proclamation of 1 May 1890, contained in 'Ordinances and Regulations of the IBEA Company', 7 June 1894, PRO FO 2. 74.   [141] Int. 53*a*.
[142] See the Transactions Register in Mombasa Lands Register Office, the A books, nos. 1–20, for examples of identification.
[143] See Entry 56A of 1895, Register A3.

The town still showed the divisions which Guillain had described in the 1840s: the stone-built quarter of the Arab clans
and their followers lying near to the Fort, and the clay-built
quarters of Kilifi, Bondeni, and Mji wa Kale, occupied by the
Swahili, lying towards Ras Kiberamuni.[144] However, to the
north and west of these areas a new area was developing.
Sometimes known as Miembeni,[145] this area contained the
quarters of Hailendi, Mwembe Tayari, Mwembe Kuku, and
Shehe Jundani. Most of the land here was owned by the Busaidi
governor, Salim bin Khalfan, and his son Ali bin Salim, and
on this land slaves, freed slaves, and clients built houses and
let portions of them to similar people.[146] Many, but not all, of
these people were the slaves or clients of Ali bin Salim.[147] Others
were connected by debt or religious conversion to other
Mombasans, and some were themselves constructing their own
little followings of clients. In the early colonial period it was
these people who came to provide the bulk of Mombasa's casual
labour force, until their communities were uprooted by the town
plans of the 1920s.

Like the other people of Mombasa, these newer arrivals did
not define themselves as members of a single group: they had
no general or agreed label for themselves. A few of those from
hinterland groups identified themselves as such, as Mdigo or
Mduruma. Some identified themselves as recent converts by
adopting *el-Muslim* as a clan name, one calling himself 'Mmake
el-Muslim of the Nine Clans', and so simultaneously claiming
recent arrival in the town and membership of the Mombasan
Nine Tribes. Others too associated their identity with that of
the patron who had converted them to Islam, one as 'Abdullah
el-Muslim, or convert to Muhammedanism through the in-
strumentality of Mbarak bin Muhammed el-Shikeli'. Some
simply identified themselves as 'slave of' or 'follower of'.[148] To
identify oneself as belonging to a clan, a town group, was more
important than to claim membership of some larger ethnic

---

[144] Guillain, *Documents*, ii. 2, 258.   [145] Int. 61a.
[146] Ibid.   [147] Int. 60a.
[148] See Entry 331A of 1900, Transactions Register A9; Entry 184A of 1895, Register
A4; Entry 423A of 1903, Register A14; Entry 648A of 1903, Register A14; Entries
193A and 275A of 1899, Register A8; also 185A, 205A, 352A, 361A of 1900, Register
A9.

group, though the status of the newcomer in their adopted group might be low.

Yet, by virtue of their position as clients in networks of dependence located in the town, all these people could be described, and could describe themselves, as Swahili. This was, as such, a potentially vast and highly permeable category, which served to obscure rather than to define the origins of the heterogeneous population which could lay claim to it. In the next few years, the 'Swahili' population of the coast grew apace. In the context of the chronic labour problems that afflicted the colonial economy on the coast, British officials came to find the negotiable nature of ethnicity, and the economic relationships associated with this negotiability, particularly trying.

PART II

'Why the natives will not work':
Labour, Trade, and the Story of Singwaya,
1890–1919

The blurring of ethnic boundaries on the coast challenged the colonial state in two ways. It was an affront to colonial notions of how African societies worked; to the image of clearly defined groups, each with its own political structure, that was essential to the system of administration through tribal authorities. It was also, partly because of the difficulty of control in such circumstances, a constant hindrance to efforts to obtain and control labour. The economic relationships bound up with this ambiguity of ethnic identity on the coast produced a serious and enduring shortage of labour for the administration and for European business enterprises.

In colonial Kenya, African involvement in wage labour, or refusal to become involved in it, has been analysed as a rational decision based on computations of the returns to be gained from homestead production as against those from wage labour.[1] But, for the people of Mombasa's local hinterland at least, the decision was not simply an economic one. The desire to keep, or gain, control over their own time was an important factor: the Nyika determinedly resisted the tyranny of the clock and the contract. The calculation of relative returns was, anyway, not a straightforward one based on producer prices for agriculture as against wage rates: for a member of a homestead, decisions on the relative attractiveness of wage labour and production in the homestead were governed by their position in the homestead. Labour migration was not solely a product of tensions within the homestead, but the impacts of taxes, prices and colonial legislation were all mediated through the structure of the homestead.[2]

In making these decisions, Nyika found that the proximity of Mombasa, and existing ties with the population there, offered attractive alternatives to wage labour on contracts: but at the same time, these links to the coast imposed constraints.

The two chapters in Part II explore the alternatives which the people of Mombasa's local hinterland exploited. These were of two types, fundamentally different yet intimately linked. The first was involved with networks of credit, trade, and agricultural labour on the mainland, and these alternatives involved

---

[1] S. Stichter, *Migrant Labour in Kenya: Capitalism and African Response* (London, 1982), 78–80.   [2] Id., *Migrant Labourers* (Cambridge, 1985), 6.

no shift of identity or abandonment of the homestead. The second set of alternatives was essentially tied up with the process of becoming Swahili, and with Mombasa's expanding casual labour force.

It is in the context of the expansion of these options that the spread of the Singwaya story must be understood. The shifting meanings of the term Swahili in the discourse of officials and of the Nyika themselves are similarly best understood in the context of the conflict over the control of labour between the state, hinterland elders, and Mombasan employers and patrons.

3

Squatting and Trade in the Hinterland

The shortage of labour on the coast was a constant complaint of private and government employers from the time of the Imperial British East Africa Company onwards.[1] Under the Protectorate, early enthusiasm for the potential of tropical plantation crops brought a number of European planters, and planting companies, to the coast,[2] and they complained bitterly of both the shortage of labour and the unreliability of such labour as was obtainable.[3] Government building projects were similarly hampered: when private contractors were unable to find labour in 1906, the Public Works Department took over construction of a new rail spur in Mombasa: but it had to import indentured Indian labour for the purpose.[4] Wages in Mombasa became, and remained, the highest in the Protectorate, so desperate were employers to attract labour.[5]

It was, initially, the freed slaves who bore the brunt of official displeasure for their failure to turn out to work,[6] but attention soon turned to the Nyika. In 1908 the Mombasa District Commissioner (whose district at that time stretched a

---

[1] W. W. A. Fitzgerald's book, *Travels in the Coastlands of British East Africa and the Islands of Zarzibar and Pemba* (London, 1970), 239–41, 259, paints an optimistic picture of the future prospects of the labour supply but is essentially propagandistic, and Fitzgerald's own labour difficulties (see pp. 52–3) and his suggestion that Tamil labourers be settled on the coast, reveal that there was a problem (pp. 207–9). The Company's internal correspondence refers more explicitly to a shortage of labour; see e.g. Letter 3 (524), précis of mail from Mombasa, 12 Aug. 1891, IBEA File 52 (3).
[2] J. F. Munro, 'British Rubber Companies in East Africa before the First World War', *JAH* 24 (1983), 369–79.
[3] Evidence of W. MacGregor Ross, Director of Public Works, in *Native Labour Commission, 1912–1913: Evidence and Report* (Nairobi, 1913), 43; *EAS* (D), 4 Mar., 20 Apr., 14 May 1912. 　　　　　　　　　　　　　[4] *EAS* (W), 4, 25 Aug. 1906.
[5] A. Clayton and D. Savage, *Government and Labour in Kenya 1895–1963* (London, 1974), 58.
[6] Tritton, Sub-Commissioner for Seyyidieh Province, 'Questions on Slavery', 30 Jan. 1903, KNA PC Coast 1/1/93, 18.

considerable distance north and west, inland of the island it-self) sourly noted that 'the local natives, Wagiriama and other Wanyika, supply practically no labour'.[7] The people of Mombasa's local hinterland were seen as potential labourers, not as independent producers, as the Provincial Commissioner, Hobley, succinctly explained in 1916: . . . 'a native can gener-ally contribute more to the wealth of the country by producing something under European supervision than by scratching the soil with a tiny hoe or digging stick'.[8] Only for a very brief period during the First World War, at a time of chronic food short-age, was encouragement given to local food production for the market.[9] Even then Hobley, Provincial Commissioner at the coast from 1909 to 1919, felt that, in Mombasa's local hin-terland, production of food for the market was important prin-cipally to provide for the plantation labour force, not as a general alternative to involvement in wage labour.[10] So the Giriama were, in 1913–14, expelled from the fertile lands north of the Sabaki, where their success as cultivators was unwelcome to those who saw Giriama agricultural wealth as the root of their reluctance to work elsewhere.[11] The crops of the new Euro-pean plantations were not food crops that were also grown by hinterland farmers, so that independent production could not augment the output of these plantations, as it had that of the pre-colonial grain plantations. Officials felt that it was their responsibility to ensure that the people of the hinterland in-stead went out to work, as the Provincial Commissioner in-formed a subordinate in 1907:

I have the honour to inform you that His Excellency wishes you to undertake a trip through the Nyika country and explain to the Chiefs and Elders that every endeavour must be made to induce

[7] Pearson, DC Mombasa to Ag. SNA, 17 July 1908, KNA PC Coast 1/1/138; see also e.g. 'Agricultural Returns', Rabai and Malindi Districts, Jan.–July 1905, KNA PC Coast 1/1/99; also Gilkison, Ag. PC to Governor, 27 June 1907, KNA PC Coast 1/1/141.

[8] Hobley, PC to DC Nyika, 17 Jan. 1916, KNA PC Coast 1/1/196; Hobley, PC to Ainsworth-Dickson, 4 Mar. 1918, KNA PC Coast 1/2/10; also Hemsted, DC Mombasa to PC, 12 Mar. 1917, ibid.

[9] 'Report of the Food Production Mission', Mar. 1918, Ali bin Salim and T. Ainsworth-Dickson, KNA PC Coast 1/2/1.

[10] Hobley, PC to Ag. Chief Sec., 15 Nov. 1917, KNA DC KFI 3/3.

[11] C. Brantley, *The Giriama and Colonial Resistance in Kenya, 1800–1920* (Los Angeles, 1981), 82, 93: Clayton and Savage, *Government and Labour*, 66.

their people to go to Mombasa and Malindi to work for the Government Departments and private individuals. . . . There appears to be no reason why the populous Nyika country, and especially Giriama, should not furnish its share of labour.[12]

Later in 1907, following the failure of this effort, the Secretary of Native Affairs himself undertook a mission to make enquiries in Mombasa's hinterland 'as to why the natives will not work and as to what steps could be taken to prevail upon them to do so'.[13] This mission met with no more success than did the previous one, and the complaints continued: 'It is estimated that the Wadigo tribes include some 8,000 able-bodied men of whom about 700 work, the remainder being content to loaf around and live on [sic] their women.'[14] These complaints reached their height in the evidence to the Native Labour Commission of 1912.[15]

It is in the context of this labour shortage that the reluctance of local officials to abolish slavery may be understood. While the historical recollection of many Mijikenda now associates British rule with the abolition of slavery and the end of what is presented as an oppressive Arab domination,[16] local British officials of the IBEA Company and the Protectorate were staunch opponents of the abolition of slavery until legal abolition was forced on them in 1907.[17] In a series of minutes and reports on coastal slavery, these officials portrayed it as a benign institution which would eventually fade away; but the immediate abolition of which would cause economic chaos.[18] The local newspaper, owned by a European entrepreneur with

[12] PC to MacDougall, 16 June 1907, KNA PC Coast 1/1/141.
[13] Hollis, SNA to Chief Sec., 28 Sept. 1907, KNA PC Coast 1/1/130.
[14] EAS (D), 29 May 1912.
[15] See the evidence of Mr Hollis, and other coastal witnesses, in Native Labour Commission, 1912–1913.   [16] Int. 40a.
[17] For the legal details of the abolition, see 'Abolition of the Legal Status of Slavery Ordinance' (1907), in KNA AG/4/429; for more discussion of this see Salim, Swahili-Speaking Peoples, 108–111; F. Cooper, From Slaves to Squatters: Plantation Labour and Agriculture in Zanzibar and Coastal Kenya, 1890–1925 (New Haven, Conn., 1980), 176–91.
[18] W. Hamilton, Principal Judge, 'Minute on Slavery', 15 May 1905, PRO CO 533 2; Tritton, 'Questions on Slavery'; Monson, Chief Sec., 'Report on Slavery and Free Labour in the East African Protectorate', 14 Apr. 1903, KNA AG/4/432; for a comment on the general tendency of European administrators of newly acquired territories to portray slavery in their colonies as essentially mild, see S. Miers and I. Kopytoff (eds.), Slavery in Africa (Madison, Wis., 1977), 6.

plantation interests, joined in this chorus.[19] The problem was, essentially, that freed slaves had generally refused to engage in wage labour for Europeans: large-scale manumissions at the end of the nineteenth century, organized by the missionary societies and the IBEA Company[20] had produced no flood of eager 'free' labourers.[21] Officials warned darkly that on abolition 'the whole country would be overrun by loafers, thieves and prostitutes'.[22]

On one level, this attitude to slavery was a defence of the economic base of the Arab landowning class who were, in the early years of the Protectorate, important political allies of the administration.[23] For many years after the abolition of slavery, local officials continued to attribute the coast's perceived economic backwardness to the abolition of slavery.[24] But at another level, officials were uncomfortably aware that Arab and Swahili landowners and merchants, if deprived of their slaves, were able to mobilize workers through ties of clientship and debt, thus obtaining labour much more easily than could European employers.[25] The IBEA Company had itself employed slaves,[26] and condoned the employment of slaves by other British subjects,[27] for similar reasons: no labour was 'free' in a society where everyone belonged, and it was easier to come to an arrangement with the patrons and owners of

---

[19] *EAS* (W), 31 Mar. 1906.

[20] F. J. Berg, 'Mombasa under the Busaidi Sultanate', Ph.D. thesis (Wisconsin, 1971), 303; P. L. McDermott, *British East Africa or IBEA: A History of the Formation and Work of the Imperial British East Africa Company* (London, 1895), 352–8.

[21] Tritton, 'Questions on Slavery'.   [22] Ibid. 21.

[23] A. I. Salim, *The Swahili-Speaking Peoples of the Kenya Coast, 1895–1963* (Nairobi, 1973), 75–89.

[24] 'Report on Coastal Production and Trade', Part I, 2, KNA PC Coast 1/1/65.

[25] Evidence of K. MacDougall, *Native Labour Commission, 1912–1913*, 95; Cooper, *From Slaves to Squatters*, 178–82. The continuing ties between ex-slaves and their former masters, so often criticized by Europeans (and occasionally the cause of court actions by ex-slaves who felt that the demands on them were too great) may reflect not so much a sentimental attachment on either part as the continuing need for a source of patronage in order to survive. For comments on ex-slaves and masters, see Criminal Appeal No. 7 of 1922, Mombasa Supreme Court, KNA DC MSA 8/3; and the discussion in KNA AG/4/430.

[26] Administrator to IBEA Sec., 22 Mar. 1893, IBEA File 52 (21); Letter 3 (512), précis of mail to Mombasa, 12 Aug. 1891, IBEA File 52 (3); Letter 5/46, précis of mail to Mombasa, 27 Jan. 1893, IBEA File 52 (23).

[27] Mackenzie to IBEA Sec., 12 Dec. 1888, and to Euan-Smith, 4 Dec. 1888, IBEA File 1*a*.

clients and slaves than it was to compete with these patrons for workers.

The relative ease with which Arab and Swahili landowners could find labour grew partly from the casuality of the arrangements which they made: the amount of labour which they demanded from those who lived on their land was often slight.[28] These sorts of arrangement were not all new developments resulting from the freeing of slaves: some landowners benefited from the relationships which they had built up as patrons to particular groups and families.[29] Nyika and other occupants of the coast used this and other aspects of the nineteenth-century patterns of patron–client relationships to evade attempts by the administration to force them into certain types of labour, finding in and around Mombasa preferable alternatives to the economic roles which the administration wished them to play.

Responses to the famines of 1898–9, 1912, reveal the ways in which the people of the hinterland exploited these alternatives in time of crisis, and the kinds of work which they *were* willing to do. In each of these famines, the government distributed food aid, and attempted to use food shortage to push Nyika men into employment on public works or European plantations: relief food was only to be given, or even sold, to young men so employed.[30] These attempts were not particularly successful: in 1912 the DC Malindi reported that the people of his district 'informed me frankly that they preferred to sell all their possessions before they would consider going out to work'.[31] Similar efforts in 1918–19 proved similarly unsuccessful.[32]

[28] Cooper, *From Slaves to Squatters*, 190, 227.
[29] The movement of Jibana from the area of *kaya* Kilulu to the area of Mtwapa creek seems to demonstrate such continuity, and to show the importance of the historical presentation of these arrangements; see Int. 30*a*, 29*a*, and some of 21*b*.
[30] 'Memo of Points Calling for Mention in Question of Famine Relief', Crauford (1898), KNA DC MSA 8/2; DC Malindi to Ag. PC, 24 July 1912, and DC Mombasa to Ag. PC, 22 Jan. 1912, KNA PC Coast 1/2/58; Circular No. 20, Monson, Chief Sec., 2 Mar. 1918; PC to Chairman, Famine Committee, 4 Mar. 1918; and Sec., Mombasa Chamber of Commerce to PC, 8 Mar. 1918; and Maize Distribution Record, Mar. 1918; all in KNA PC Coast 1/2/6.
[31] DC Malindi to Ag. PC, 24 July 1912, KNA PC Coast 1/2/58.
[32] Rodwell, Manager of Nyali Sisal Estate to DC Mombasa, 21 June 1920, KNA PC Coast 1/9/43.

Those affected by these famines did not, in fact, have to sell all their possessions. Their alternatives took two basic forms. The first was that of temporary migration, usually to squat on coastal land but occasionally to live on the island of Mombasa or its suburbs and work as casual labourers. Hobley noted in 1919 that 'A considerable number of Wanyika are working for daily wage [*sic*] on the Arab shambas at Changamwe and Kisauni',[33] and Binns had noted a similar movement in 1912.[34] Such migrations were built on existing contacts, some established by debt, but also by the previous migration of family members who had become 'Swahili':

We went to my father's sister, who had married in Mombasa. She became a Muslim, and was married, and we went and stayed with her. . . . [her husband] was a Giriama, a convert, like her. He was a convert, a Swahili, but a Giriama, of the Mwandui clan . . . I only met him as an *mjomba*, I just saw him as an *mjomba*, and my father's sister was taken by him and converted.[35]

Such temporary migrations had several advantages: they involved no contract, no regular discipline, no complete surrender of one's time. Labour on the land, or in the town (which, for these migrants, was usually building labour[36]) was casual, and usually paid daily. Whereas European employers generally insisted on contracts and regular attendance, and had at their disposal an array of coercive legislation to enforce their demands upon those who entered contracts,[37] no such constraints were placed on these migrants. They assumed an obligation, but it was ill-defined and negotiable. Moreover, the conditions, as well as the terms, of European employ could be atrocious: the major public works project of 1911–17, the Shimba Hills water scheme, became notorious for the high death-rate amongst labourers (almost all of whom were from up-country);[38] sisal plantation work was hard and uncomfort-

---

[33] PC to CNC, 5 Feb. 1919, KNA PC Coast 1/2/105; see also DC Rabai to Ag. PC, 11 Oct. 1919, ibid.; also DC Malindi to PC, 9 Jan. 1918, KNA PC Coast 1/2/86; Circular No. 5 (1918), PC, 28 Feb. 1918, KNA PC Coast 1/2/6. Famine could also result in a degree of migration within the hinterland, to join other Nyika groups living nearer to the coast; Int. 20a.   [34] Binns, CMS to PC, 7 Oct. 1912, KNA PC Coast 1/2/58.
[35] Int. 54a, 2–3; see also Int. 26c.   [36] Int. 41a, 54a.
[37] Clayton and Savage, *Government and Labour*, 30, 43–44, 98.
[38] Director, PWD to Principal Medical Officer, 20 June 1912, KNA MOH/1/912; Pritchard, 'Report on Labour Camp at Shimba, 28 Feb. 1913, KNA MOH 1/1186.

able;[39] and some European employers had an unfortunate propensity to cheat their employees of their wages or to extend their contracts by various tricks.[40]

Casual labour and squatting arrangements were not always a response to an immediate crisis. All along the coastal plain, from Mombasa to Malindi, Nyika squatters took up long-term residence on the land of Arab, Swahili, or Indian landowners, squatting and growing their own annual crops. Some planted trees, too, but the insecurity of their position as squatters tended to discourage arboriculture. In return for the use of the land, these squatters took on an obligation to work for the landowner: but for many, particularly those on the lands of ex-slave-owners who had no other way of using their lands, this work involved little more than a desultory harvesting of coconuts or a commitment to keep the landowners' trees free from weeds.[41] Living on these lands, the squatters could earn cash by casual harvesting of nuts, or by growing food for the Mombasa market.[42]

In some places the continuity of these arrangements from nineteenth-century ones was particularly marked, as specific relationships of patronage carried on: in the Kanamai–Mtwapa area, some landowners kept rather more control of their land by coming to share-cropping arrangements with gangs of Giriama labourers who were resident only temporarily, and who had established relationships with particular landowners.[43] Such arrangements, more lucrative for the landowners than the presence of more permanent squatters doing very occasional labour, were also noticed in the Malindi area. In 1919, the one European planter on the coast who employed a considerable number of local workers had established himself as a patron in order to obtain workers, lending out money for bridewealth.[44]

---

[39] Clayton and Savage, *Government and Labour*, 150; Int. 39a, 44a.

[40] See e.g. 'Report on BEA Cotton and Rubber Estates', 22 Feb. 1916, Ag. DC Malindi, KNA PC Coast 1/9/34; also Int. 44a for the 'ticket' system of reckoning days worked, which made months rather longer than usual.

[41] Int. 72a, 61a, 49a, 47a; Cooper, *From Slaves to Squatters*, 225–6.

[42] Int. 72a.   [43] Int. 70a.

[44] The European planter involved was Mr Lillywhite of Sekoke plantation; see DC Malindi to PC, 18 July 1919, KNA PC Coast 1/9/52. The arrangement was later pronounced illegal by the CNC. For the relationships between landowners and Mijikenda homestead heads in Malindi, see DC Malindi to PC, 9 Jan. 1918, KNA PC Coast 1/2/86.

Nyika farmers also produced for the Mombasa market on land further from the coast, on the foothills and the ridge behind the coastal plain. But by no means all of Mombasa's food was drawn from here. Food was brought in by train from elsewhere in British East Africa,[45] and some vegetables came by sea.[46] That Mombasa relied so heavily on these imports reflects the way in which local hinterland production for the market was structured and constrained by debt.

The abolition of slavery had not brought an end to the activities of those planter-traders who dealt largely in crops grown by their clients or debtors. This group was particularly active around Mtongwe, Mwakirunge, Kidutani, and Junju, and they dealt largely in items which were grown for subsistence as well as for trade; maize, sorghum, coconuts, rice, and bananas.[47] The traders gave advances for crops to be delivered, on terms very advantageous to themselves.[48] Farmers often sold too much of their crop immediately after the harvest, and later in the season had to borrow to buy grain back for the next planting.[49] These traders also gave advances on other trade items, such as timber, gum copal, and copra. Through the hold which these advances gave them over producers, they secured for a while a virtual monopoly of the trade in some items.[50] Defaulting Nyika debtors were charged in the Muslim courts (run under the authority of the British administration) in Mombasa or Malindi, and they rarely appeared to defend themselves. Punitive fines were thus added to the debts of these defaulters, giving their creditor an enormous potential claim on their future product.[51]

---

[45] 'Inspection of Mombasa Water Supply Works', Radford, 14 June 1912, KNA MOH/1/912; according to some observers, this reliance on grain from up-country became even greater as time went on, Par. 4402, 'Minutes of Evidence to the Joint Select Committee on Closer Union', 1 May 1931, PRO CO 533 411/6.
[46] e.g., see the discussion of Mombasa's onion supply, in PC to DC Voi, 21 Nov. 1917, KNA PC Coast 1/2/4.   [47] Int. 38a, 44a.
[48] See the evidence in Civil Case No. 60 of 1913, Mombasa High Court, in KNA PC Coast 1/10/269; also Ag. DC Kilifi to SC, 10 Aug. 1922, KNA PC Coast 1/14/127.
[49] 'Report on Food Production', Mar. 1918, KNA PC Coast 1/2/1; and DC Kilifi to Ag. PC, 17 June 1920, KNA PC Coast 1/19/1.
[50] 'Report on the Local Prices of Gum Copal', ADC Rabai, 6 Dec. 1913, KNA PC Coast 1/2/61; Tritton to HM Commissioner, 20 Jan. 1903, KNA PC Coast 1/1/93; Rabai Subdistrict Annual Report, 1911–12, KNA PC Coast 1/1/185.
[51] DC Malindi to PC, 22 Sept. 1919, KNA PC Coast 1/19/1.

Some of these traders also acted directly as money-lenders, lending money to Nyika who wished to marry, or who needed to pay the taxes imposed by the administration in the hope that they would force Africans out to work.[52] Such loans were secured on the fruit trees or standing crops of the debtor, and the mortgagee might even install a supervisor to oversee this property: usually a client converted to Islam.[53] In areas nearer to the coast, where grain agriculture using bought slaves had been more common, other Arab and Swahili traders also turned successfully to trade in foodstuffs produced by Nyika farmers.[54]

Such patrons, acquired through networks of credit and trade, were known as *tajiris*: literally, 'wealthy persons'. It was a role that bestowed both claims and obligations: the *tajiri* had a claim on the produce and time of his client, but the client could call on the *tajiri* for continued financial help, in the shape of extra loans, or for housing and assistance in Mombasa.[55] Many of the Mombasa-based traders were themselves in debt to others,[56] and their investment in loans to dependants was one which they could not afford to endanger by too strict an attitude towards debt repayment. Traders could not force their debtors to produce for the market, and their ability to profit from mortgaged trees or crops depended to a degree on the goodwill of the mortgager—who might after all, simply steal the crops or allow others to do so.[57] Some creditors tried to cash in their investment by selling to others the trees mortgaged to them, and the land on which they stood, but the ensuing legal complications discouraged buyers.[58]

[52] See District Book notes written in 1913, 137, KNA DC MSA 1/2; for lending and labour in the Mtwapa area, see Int. 51a; for lending in Changamwe and Miritini see Int. 19a; for mortgages of trees in Tiwi and Vanga, see the case of Magwayi, DC Mombasa to PC, 2 Oct. 1917, KNA PC Coast 1/11/267; and also Diary of Tour, Ag. DC Vanga, 9 Aug. 1918, KNA PC Coast 1/2/1.

[53] Int. 20c.   [54] Int. 53a.   [55] Int. 26c, 44a.

[56] K. Janmohamed, 'A History of Mombasa, c.1895–1939: Some Aspects of Economic and Social Life in an East African Port Town under Colonial Rule', Ph.D. thesis (Northwestern, 1977), 169 and elsewhere, comments on the vulnerability and indebtedness of many Mombasan traders.

[57] The administration tried several times to deal with the problem of coconut theft on the coast, but never did so successfully; see Coconut Trade Ordinance of 1915; Hobley, Memo, June 1915, KNA AG/4/2380.

[58] An example of such a sale is Entry 443A of 1905, in Transactions Register A19; and the Allidina Visram case offers the best example of the resulting problems. See Civil Case No. 60 of 1913, Mombasa High Court, KNA PC Coast 1/10/269.

Yet the relationship was an unequal one, and it did limit the returns which producers could expect from trade, by forcing them into reliance on a single buyer—their creditor. One engineer in charge of the Shimba Hills water scheme complained that all foodstuffs had to be brought in from Nairobi because 'the Wadigo natives of the district do not want to trade, and they are too lazy to bring comestibles up to the camps for sale', and his successor remarked on the same problem and resentfully suggested that the water scheme was being boycotted. But as the ADC Rabai pointed out, the reluctance of the Digo to trade was a result not of indolence but of their involvement in other arrangements: 'the whole of that part of the district is overrun with Shehiri and Swahili traders'.[59] The engineers were almost certainly witnessing the results of indebtedness, not of indolence.

Some hinterland farmers bypassed these hinterland networks of trade and credit, taking their own goods directly to Mombasa for sale. In this way too, they could obtain cash without labouring for a wage. Yet they too became involved in relationships with *tajiris*, people with more money or knowledge of the town upon whom they relied to sell their goods. Those who transported their produce to Mombasa along the creeks relied on the boat-owners of Kidutani or Mwakirunge to store their produce prior to transportation, or even to take it to Mombasa and sell it for them.[60] More usually, sellers went with their produce to Mombasa, unloading and selling it at the old port, on the north side of the island. Here, some relied on particular buyers to purchase their goods—counting on this special relationship as insurance against a glut of produce that could reduce prices or make their crops almost unsaleable.[61] The contacts which such relationships gave could be used to move permanently to the town, through adoption as family by their *tajiri*—a move from being Nyika to being Swahili.[62]

Through these relationships, just as through the opportunities which access to land as squatters gave them, homestead heads in the hinterland were able to meet tax demands and

[59] Linnell, Ag. Resident Engineer, Shimba Hills Waterworks to Ag. Director of Public Works, 1 July 1913, KNA MOH/1/1186: PC to all DCs, 10 May 1913, and ADC Rabai to PC, 13 May 1913, KNA PC Coast 1/14/11.
[60] Int. 21*b*.   [61] Int. 21*b*, 40*b*.   [62] Int. 21*b*.

maintain their position as providers to the homestead, without themselves having to go out to work and without having to send their juniors out as contracted labourers.

The trade in palm wine was also, in part, tied in to the relationships between Arab and Swahili employers and Nyika groups: 'a few of the Arabs of Malindi and Roka and the Swahilis of Changamwe refuse to sell palm wine to the Giriama until they have performed a certain amount of work in their shambas, or pay them in palm wine for work done'.[63] For official observers, this trade neatly associated the immorality of drunkenness with an involvement with Swahili and Arabs and a refusal to work for Europeans. The palm-wine trade within the hinterland was also an important earner for some— many Rabai, in particular, effectively specialized in palm-wine production from the later nineteenth century onwards,[64] exchanging it for grain, volume for volume, with the Duruma and Giriama, or selling it for cash.[65] The Rabai earned sufficient money from this trade to avoid contract wage labour— as officials were uncomfortably aware.[66] The Rabai were also much less involved in other forms of labour and trade than were other hinterland groups.[67]

The exploitation of these alternatives to the colonial labour market, though they offered a kind of freedom, paradoxically put homestead heads in an increasingly difficult position. The networks of debt and credit in which they were involved offered the means of evading some colonial pressures, but they also tended to limit the productive potential of the homestead. Indebtedness dimmed the prospects of juniors within the homestead, encouraging them to seek alternatives elsewhere, and the closeness of the relationship between many homesteads and traders from Mombasa provided juniors with contacts which made these alternatives more accessible.[68]

[63] Hollis, SNA to Sec. for the Admin., 28 Sept. 1907, KNA PC Coast 1/1/130.

[64] ADC Rabai to Ag. PC, 16 Oct. 1907, KNA PC Coast 1/12/47; 'District Economics', Political Record Book, 97–8, KNA DC KFI 3/2; for 19th-c. Rabai specialization in this trade, see T. Herlehy, 'Ties that Bind: Palm Wine and Blood Brotherhood on the Kenya Coast during the Nineteenth Century', *IJAHS* 17 (1984), 285–308.

[65] Int. 32a.

[66] Evidence of Mr Hollis, in *Native Labour Commission, 1912–13*, 2; ADC Rabai to PC, 16 Oct. 1907, KNA PC Coast 1/1/130.   [67] Int. 32a, 42a, 43a.

[68] See the case of Sudi bin Ali, in *EAS* (W), 21 July 1911.

The possibility of flight by their juniors was a major re-straining factor on homestead heads. Unwilling themselves to engage in contract labour, for reasons already mentioned, they were equally unwilling to push their juniors into this work. To force, or even to allow, their dependants to take up contract labour, as the administration wished, was to invite the 'loss' of these juniors: desertion from such contracts was common, and deserters fled to Mombasa and the anonymity of a new identity as Swahili,[69] rather than return to the homestead where they could be caught and punished.[70]

The very success of these strategies for avoiding contract labour made the position of homestead heads more difficult. Many officials felt that it was a decline in the authority of Nyika elders which limited the supply of labour—for the ad-ministration relied on indigenous authorities to enforce their wishes.[71] In analysing the results of this perception on Nyika groups, a problem concerning the definition of 'elders' must be noted. In a situation in which the age-grade initiations on which their power was claimed to have rested had not taken place for some time, the category of 'elder' had become a blurred one; a blurring that was worsened by the introduction of government-appointed headmen, and later chiefs.[72] The status of chief was claimed and contested by numbers of older men,[73] and to discuss the power of elders is to talk of two different but related tensions: the power of homestead heads over their own juniors, and the power of some homestead heads over others. In granting to some men the backing of the state, the admin-istration added an intra-generational conflict between home-steads to the inter-generational conflict within homesteads. Not all homestead heads were elders, but almost all elders were homestead heads.

A number of measures were adopted by the administra-tion to bolster the power of elders and to enlist this power in

---

[69] For more details on this movement, see Ch. 4.

[70] EAS (D), 20 Apr. 1912, and (W), 27 Oct. 1912.

[71] Rabai Subdistrict Annual Report, 1911–12, KNA PC Coast 1/1/185; ADC Kakoneni to PC, 5 Feb. 1917, KNA PC Coast 1/9/56; Evidence of Mr Hobley, Native Labour Commission, 1912–13, 86.

[72] ADC Rabai to PC, 28 July 1913, KNA PC Coast 1/11/144.

[73] ADC Rabai to PC, 27 Jan. 1913, KNA PC Coast 1/10/54.

support of the state: elders were gazetted, and in Rabai these 'official' elders were given a monopoly of palm wine sales.[74] The decisions of these elders were given the approval and, if necessary, the physical support of the state. In 1912, the Native Authority Ordinance gave these elders the right to demand labour from those in their location, and the power to fine those who refused these demands. Some headmen were fired for not using their new power to co-operate in labour recruiting.[75] During the First World War the Native Followers Recruitment Ordinance gave headmen even greater powers of coercion,[76] and in 1915 it was reported that the elders, with the 'assistance' of the District Commissioner, were providing labourers for sisal plantations near Kilifi.[77] Yet these levels of coercion were not sustainable and, despite government support, headmen commanded little respect and no popularity.[78] Given the risk of desertion to Mombasa, other homestead heads were unwilling to risk sending their own juniors out to work simply to help these 'elders' keep their jobs.

In trying to reinforce elders' power, officials only emphasized the weakest point in the authority of homestead heads: the ability of young women and men to flee from their control. Forcing elders to send out their own and others' dependants to work simply increased the motives for flight from the homestead; and forced labour under the Native Authority Ordinance and the conscription laws effectively encouraged migration to Mombasa, where refuge was sought from the demands of elders and the state; and from the demands of elders as the state.[79] In 1917, 125 out of 261 conscripted Giriama

---

[74] Ibid.

[75] Traill, ADC Kilifi, Handing-Over Report, 12 Nov. 1915, KNA PC Coast 1/1/196.

[76] Homestead heads were threatened with having their juniors conscripted for military service if they did not send them out for plantation labour: 'Minutes of Baraza', 21 Dec. 1916, KNA PC Coast 1/12/282. For more on conscription and forced labour in the First World War, see Hemsted, APC to PC, 18 July 1917, KNA PC Coast 1/3/114; G. Hodges, *The Carrier Corps: Military Labour in the East African Campaign, 1914–1918* (London and New York, 1986), 93; Int. 19a, 40a.

[77] 'Inspection of the Labour Camps of Sekoke Estate', 20 Mar. 1915, and 'Inspection of the Labour Camps of Powysland Estates', 19 Mar. 1915, KNA PC Coast 1/9/35.

[78] Int. 64a; Rabai Safari Diary, 12 Jan. 1918, KNA PC Coast 1/1/182.

[79] Int. 40a; Ag. DC Kilifi to Ag. PC, 7 Feb. 1920, KNA PC Coast 1/9/52; Hodges, *The Carrier Corps*, 102.

labourers deserted within a month, and disappeared without trace into Mombasa.[80] By the 1920s, elders were evidently too nervous to demand forced labour from young men, and were instead sending out women to do road work, despite the active disapproval of the District Commissioner:[81] the effect that this had on women's motives for flight can be imagined.

Homestead heads thus faced a dilemma: the already ambiguous relationships of conflict and co-operation with town patrons allowed them to evade some of the demands of the colonial state; but these relationships also threatened their control of the members of their homesteads. The alternative sources of patronage offered by other town figures discouraged homestead heads from sending young men out to work on contract: many homestead heads thus relied for cash on involvement in debt-bound trade, which in the long run further weakened their position, and in working arrangements with coastal landowners. Attempts by the colonial state to use homestead heads as co-opted agents to obtain labour undermined their position even further.

[80] DC Rabai to PC, 4 May 1916, and Executive Engineer, PWD to PC, 26 July, 20, 25 Sept. 1917, KNA PC Coast 1/9/51.
[81] T. R. Cashmore, 'Kaloleni Diary', 8 Sept. 1921, KNA MSS 225/2.

4

Casual Labour and the Swahili in Mombasa

> . . . they will work for a day or two and then knock off,
> and they do not wish for permanent employment.
>
> (Mombasa District Annual Report, 1906)

An understanding of why movement to Mombasa was such an attractive option for some people in the early colonial period demands an analysis of the Mombasa labour market of the time, as well as of the domestic economy of the hinterland homestead. The development of the debate over Swahili identity in this period can similarly be understood only in the context of the development of this labour market.

The arrival of European planters, civil servants, the railway, and the Conservancy and Public Works Departments had created in Mombasa a demand for contracted labour: that is, for workers who had signed legally binding contracts for periods of three, six, or nine months. But this was not the only kind of labour that was increasingly in demand. The dock experienced the peaks and troughs in demand for labour common to docks everywhere. Unlike other European employers, the shipping and shorehandling companies employed their labour on a casual basis, paying them at the end of each day.[1] The demand for portering and building labour within the town similarly fluctuated from day to day, and the many small employers involved here, mostly Indians, Arabs, and Swahili, also employed their workers daily.[2]

---

[1] Int. 71b, 26c, 67a; F. Cooper, *On the African Waterfront* (New Haven, Conn., 1987), 26–9; K. Janmohamed, 'A History of Mombasa c.1895–1939', Ph.D. thesis (Northwestern, 1977), 334–6; G. Wilson, 'Labour Conditions in the Port of Mombasa', in G. Wilson (ed.), 'The Social Survey of Mombasa' (1957), typescript in KNA library, 261–89.   [2] Int. 54a, 71b.

After 1910, the daily hiring of labour had even more attraction for the shipping and shorehandling companies, for the Masters and Servants Ordinance was amended in that year so as to require that employers housed and fed their contracted labour.[3] Much of the land on Mombasa Island was privately owned, and land speculation had forced up the price of land in the first few years of colonial rule, so that buying land and building workers' housing was an expensive undertaking. Since prices, as well as wages, were higher in Mombasa than anywhere else in British East Africa,[4] feeding workers was a similarly unwelcome responsibility. Other European enterprises with permanent labour, including some government departments, consistently failed to meet these requirements of the Ordinance: which violations were treated with rather more understanding than were those committed by employees.[5]

The feeding, housing, and care of much of the waged workforce was thus left to Mombasa's informal economy, which grew and thrived, creating new opportunities for migrants. Workers bought cooked food from Hadhrami Arab men or African women;[6] they bought firewood from men and women who cut wood on the mainland and hawked it on the island;[7] and they bought water from hawkers who drew the water from public wells.[8] Some women lived as prostitutes,[9] and others in a sort of concubinage, cooking for, sleeping with, and otherwise caring for a man for a period of time.[10] They might combine this work with water-hawking or food-selling.[11]

Many relied on systems of patronage for accommodation, eating and sleeping at houses in return for occasional household labour.[12] Those more established in the town could themselves rent a room and acquire their own hangers-on.[13] Even where cash payment for room and board was involved in such arrangements, it was not a fixed and regular amount.[14] And so

[3] Sect. 26, Masters and Servants Ordinance of 1910, KNA AG/4/1612; A. Clayton and D. Savage, *Government and Labour in Kenya, 1895–1963* (London, 1974) 43–4.

[4] Janmohamed, 'A History of Mombasa', 443–4.

[5] Clayton and Savage, *Government and Labour*, 149.

[6] Int. 24a.   [7] Int. 25a.

[8] Int. 51a; DC Mombasa to PC, 20 Jan. 1917, KNA PC Coast 1/9/56.

[9] Int. 34a.   [10] Int. 59a, 24a.

[11] Int. 24a. Women also worked as casual labourers. See *EAS* (W), 25 Aug. 1906.

[12] Int. 61a. CHONYI/1, CHONYI/2.   [13] Int. 40a.   [14] Int. 26b.

this informal economy fed and sheltered casual workers, and itself provided manifold opportunities for the avoidance of contract labour. This economy allowed the extreme irregularity which characterized casual labour in Mombasa; workers could skip waged work for a while, and they would not starve or be homeless; for others would support them, and they could always work cutting wood or hawking water on their own account. The Mombasa DC wrote despairingly in 1906 that: 'There are plenty of men but they won't work continuously— they will work for a day or two and then knock off, and they do not wish for permanent employment . . . The labour question is a difficult one. The people are too prosperous at present. There is no need for them to work, and they don't'.[15] For this casual work-force, there was no daily discipline, no legal contract backed by flogging or prison, no set time of work. On the docks at least, this casual labour also paid far better than any other kind of work.[16]

Access to all these opportunities was not entirely free, however: 'informal' though this economy was it lacked neither organization nor hierarchy. It was built of innumerable little hierarchical networks, which were based on unequal access to resources: some had a house; more money or better access to credit; some simply knew a particular employer. Others seeking these things relied on these patrons, and became obligated to and partly dependent upon their providers. For migrants from the local hinterland, initial introduction to these patrons often came through kin; family members who had migrated to the town and become Swahili.[17]

Obligation to these providers was expressed most completely when migrants were, like many of their nineteenth-century predecessors, taken into the house and family of a patron, incorporated as kin. Such incorporation was marked by conversion to Islam and the removal of social barriers that had initially marked the migrant as an outsider: 'We were at work, I worked for him, then he said, let me convert you to Islam. Because the *wajomba* then, at first, the *mjomba* ate at his house

---

[15] Mombasa District Annual Report, Draft version, 8 May 1906, KNA PC Coast 1/1/113.
[16] Cooper, *On the African Waterfront*, 27.   [17] Int. 20c.

and I ate apart, but when we were converted, we were together. When I was converted, I ate together with him.'[18]

Membership of these networks, and incorporation to the
town, was not always expressed through the structure of family, however: particularly as the population of Mombasa grew
and there was an increase in the number of petty patrons, who
were not themselves able to incorporate large numbers of
followers into their family. Other institutions developed as
structures for hierarchical networks of credit and obligation:
particularly dance societies and spirit possession groups.[19] The
nature of the bond formed through these institutions is illustrated through the contrasting terms *ndugu* and *jamaa*. A *ndugu*
is a relative, and in their first move to town migrants usually
relied on a *ndugu*,[20] someone originally from their home area.
Through this relationship they came into contact with others
in the town who became the *jamaa* of the migrant. *Jamaa* is a
vaguer term than *ndugu*, indicating common membership of a
community rather than a kin relationship:[21] these were people
joined by common participation in the institutions of town life:
work-gangs, dance societies, and the like.[22] While some immigrants from the local hinterland, in moving to Mombasa,
constructed new networks of kin there, others constructed networks through other institutions.

The importance of participation in these networks, and the
way in which they operated, can clearly be seen in the hiring
of casual labour. On the docks and elsewhere, casual labourers
in Mombasa were hired in gangs, not as individuals.[23] The
employer's relationship was not with the individual worker,
of whom he knew nothing, but with a gang-head whose responsibility was to find workers. It was the gang-head who
decided, on the basis of personal knowledge, which workers
were reliable and worked well. The gang-head picked out, from
the crowd of hopefuls who gathered each morning for work,
those who would get work.[24] The very term for casual labour,
kibarua, had its roots in such an indirect system of hiring: the

[18] Int. 54*a*, 6.   [19] Int. 59*a*, 67*a*.   [20] Int. 43*a*.   [21] Int. 51*a*.
[22] For a discussion of these terms as used elsewhere on the coast, see W. F. McKay
'A Pre-Colonial History of the Southern Kenya Coast', Ph.D. thesis (Boston, Mass.,
1975), 124.
[23] Cooper, *On the African Waterfront*, 37; Janmohamed, 'A History of Mombasa',
338.   [24] Int. 34*a*, 67*a*.

employment of one person's slaves or clients by another in the nineteenth century.[25] The *kibarua* was the note given to the slave indicating what his earnings had been, so that his master could be sure to receive his half-share. In nineteenth-century Pangani, migrants were similarly found work by patrons who claimed a share of their earnings.[26] In Mombasa, a worker had to maintain some relationship with a gang-head, and the gang-head in turn had to maintain his hold over the individuals in his gang. This was done both through his position as an intermediary who could find and allocate work and through advances to individuals, who would then be reliant on their creditor to find them work to repay their debt.

Many men come into Mombasa from up-country seeking work, they are at once got together by certain Headmen, who in olden days were recognised Caravan Leaders or engaged to recruit porters, now find their services are not required, yet still wish to live comfortably so deliberately rob these unfortunate men by taking a tax of a rupee or two from each individual when work is obtained.[27]

It was not only casuals trying to find work who fell into debt. The author of the same letter noted that regular labourers for the Public Works Department were borrowing money to survive until their wages were paid: 'None of these poor people have any money, they must live somehow, and the result is that nearly every one is in debt either to traders or these so-called headmen.'[28]

The patrons/creditors of these workers were clearly confident of their ability to share in the earnings of their dependants. In 1902, one was willing to pay for the privilege of supplying workers to the administration:

Having come to know that there is no arrangement from the Government at the Government wood store near the Fish Market to supply coolies for carrying wood from there to the town and that

---

[25] M. Beech, 'Slavery on the East Coast of Africa', JAS 15 (1915–16), 145–9; a description of the hiring of portering labour in Mombasa at the end of the 19th c. also suggests the importance of this sort of 'segmentary' hiring. See C. W. Hobley *Kenya: From Chartered Company to Crown Colony: Thirty Years of Exploration and Administration in British East Africa* (London, 1929), 197–8.

[26] J. Glassman, 'Social Rebellion and Swahili Culture', Ph.D. thesis (Wisconsin, 1988), 94–5.

[27] Director of Government Transport to SNA, 16 Aug. 1907, KNA PC Coast 1/1/130.

[28] Ibid.

this work is done by common Negroes wandering in the streets I must respectfully beg to submit my tender for supplying coolies . . . I shall pay monthly or yearly in advance the fee for the contract the Government will order me.[29]

The system of hiring casual labour through gang-heads survived on the docks until the 1940s.[30] This accommodation with systems of patronage and debt allowed the stevedoring and shorehandling firms to compete successfully for labour, in dramatic contrast to other European employers. In 1912 Smith-Mackenzie, the shipping line, was the only European concern in Mombasa to be content with the labour situation, reporting that its workers were 'recruited in Mombasa by their own headmen'.[31] Yet the arrangement was never entirely satisfactory for the companies: the power of the gang-heads allowed them steadily to push up wages by refusing to let their followers work. Their bargaining-power was particularly strong during the First World War, and in 1917 the Provincial Commissioner angrily wrote of the dock labour situation that:

a considerable proportion of the labour was not free to engage itself in the open market, as Asiatic agents still hold large numbers of men in gangs and withhold them from the labour market until some firm makes it worth their while to release them for work. This grip over gangs is obtained by a system of advances and illicit rewards; by keeping the *hamals* in debt they cease to be free agents and have to obey the behests of the labour agents.[32]

Elsewhere in the world, casual dock labour has been seen as an iniquitous result of a chronic oversupply of labour, and a similar system of hiring by foremen has been characterized as a tyranny.[33] But in Mombasa, while there was a general surplus of labour, there were daily shortages[34] that kept wages high. Workers turned out very irregularly, not because they could not get regular work, but because high wages and the lack of discipline allowed them to live on a few days' work a month.

---

[29] Mohamed bin Nahman to Ag. Sub-Commissioner, 6 Oct. 1902, KNA PC Coast 1/1/94.　　　　　　　　　　　　　　　　　　　　[30] Int. 71*b*.

[31] Evidence of Mr Denne, *Native Labour Commission of 1912–13*, 95.

[32] PC to Chief Sec. 9 Feb. 1917, KNA PC Coast 1/9/42.

[33] G. Stedman Jones, *Outcast London: A Study in the Relationship between Classes in Victorian Society* (Oxford, 1971), 67, 81–2.

[34] PC to Chief Sec. 1 Aug. 1917, KNA PC Coast 1/9/42.

At Dar es Salaam a similar system of recruitment through headmen was also associated with very irregular working.[35] Casual labour was a sought-after alternative to other kinds of work—better the tyranny of the gang-head than that of the Masters and Servants Ordinance.

As the demand for casual labour at the docks grew from scores to hundreds each day, it reached a scale at which personal relationships between a few gang-heads and each individual labourer became difficult to maintain. A chain of such relationships developed, with the head of the smaller network in a personal relationship to the overall head, and those within the smaller network dependent upon its head as a secondary intermediary in obtaining work. The gang leaders were known as *serang*s or *serahangi*s (a word which similarly had its origins in nineteenth-century patterns of employment[36]), and the leaders of the smaller networks were called *tindals*.[37]

The *beni*, or *gwaride* dance societies played an important role in this large-scale organization of labour. Until the 1930s these societies had a combined following that ran into thousands.[38] Writing on *beni* in East Africa has not generally focused on this aspect,[39] but Cooper has briefly noted the role of *beni* in the organization of dock labour,[40] and Glassman's work on Pangani suggests the importance of dance societies there in social organization and in the mobilization of caravan labour in the nineteenth century.[41] The *beni* were segmentary organizations, divided into regiments and companies, each with officers who both acted as patrons and could demand subscriptions from their followers.[42] As such they were admirably suited to the organization of a hierarchical series of patron–client links: 'Now the *beni*, that dance, then it was like work. The *tindals* had to be in it. They were in it, the *beni*, you see that's how the *beni*

[35] J. Iliffe, 'A History of the Dockworkers of Dar es Salaam', *TNR* 71 (1970), 119–48.
[36] J. L. Krapf, *A Dictionary of the Suahili Language, Compiled by the Reverend Dr. J. L. Krapf* (London, 1882), 326.   [37] Int. 71*b*.
[38] *EAS* (W), 14 Apr. 1906; H. Norden, *Black and White in East Africa* (London, 1924), 47.
[39] T. O. Ranger, *Dance and Society in Eastern Africa, 1890–1970: the Beni Ngoma* (London, 1975), 18–19 and elsewhere.   [40] Cooper, *On the African Waterfront*, 39–40, 40–5.
[41] Glassman, 'Social Rebellion and Swahili Culture', 136–7, 354.
[42] Ranger, *Dance and Society*, Intro.; Int. 9*b*, 12*b*, 44*a*, 53*a*, 55*a*.

became strong, because people wanted to obey the *serangi*, then they'd get a job.'[43]

Reliant as they were on the *serangis*, workers tended to stay in the following of one *serangi*, even if this meant that on occasion they failed to find work.[44] Disputes did arise between *serangis* over workers,[45] but the relationship between *serangis* and their followers seems to have been remarkably free of open conflict, if inequitable, and the *serangi*'s exactions from his followers might be fairly haphazard:

It was up to you. You see, if you do him right, he'll see you right. He doesn't ask, but you feel yourself, this one, I must give him a cigarette. . . . some days the *serangi* has no money, he'll come to you, he'll tell you 'Give me two or three shillings, I'll get it back to you.'[46]

Though the dock employers were willing to accept this arrangement, other European employers on the coast were less than happy with the alternatives which the casual labour market of the town offered. The local newspaper, sympathetic to planters, railed against the 'rascally Swahili crimps',[47] who tempted away labourers signed up to plantation owners, able to do so because of the 'ridiculous ease with which money can be earned doing odd jobs in Mombasa'.[48] The association of casual labour with the 'Swahili', an important stage in the debate over this ambiguous identity, will be explored further below.

The dock labour force was the focus of the largest of these casual labour networks, but there were other, smaller networks in which a real or adoptive family relationship played more of a role. The public boats which carried passengers to and from steamers anchored in the harbour were crewed not by their owners, but by the younger relatives of their owners, or by migrants converted and adopted by the owners.[49] The *beni* societies could play an organizational role in these arrangements too.[50] These networks were no more equitable than those among the dock labour force:

---

[43] Int. 71*b*, 3; see also Int. 53*a*.   [44] Int. 26*a*.   [45] Int. 25*a*.
[46] Int. 20*c*, 8.   [47] *EAS* (D), 29 May 1912.
[48] *EAS* (W), 27 Oct. 1906; also *EAS* (D), 20 Apr. 1912.
[49] Int. 44*a*.   [50] Int. 44*a*, 44*b*.

In the boat, in that rowing boat, I used to get *pesa nane* [one-eighth of a rupee] for a day. Or some days our bosses would come visiting, [then] they would leave us to finish off, well, we'd steal a shilling each, half a rupee. Steal it. If we were asked we'd just say we took *pesa nane* . . . they were bastards.[51]

This informant was discussing events around 1918, when a day's work at the docks would have brought in two and a half rupees. Clearly, while these networks allowed employment outside the legal constraints of the contract, they controlled and restricted workers in other ways, keeping them in one occupation and excluding them from others. It was an exploitation based on a different sort of power: the power of those longer established in the town or with more access to capital, rather than the power of Europeans with greater access to the legal machinery of the state.

These networks were not closed: migrants could and did gain access to them through adoption as kin or participation in other institutions of Mombasa: like Swahili identity, these other institutions were highly permeable. For people from the local hinterland, such incorporation was easier than for other migrants. The history of migration from the local hinterland to Mombasa had given many of them kin in the town who could shelter them and introduce them to the networks of the town.[52] Thus they had privileged access to the casual occupations which many observers reported to be the particular preserve of the 'Swahili'.[53] As officials noted at the time, and as informants now recall, the worst jobs in Mombasa, such as sweeping and cleaning for the Conservancy Department, were done by upcountry workers, who were known derisively as *machura*, the 'frogs'.[54] Yet the networks of the town did not include or exclude according to origins. Up-country workers too could be adopted,[55] or find their way into other institutions of the town, such as the dance societies.[56] People from the local hinterland had easier access, but it was by no means exclusive. Among

---

[51] Int. 49*a*, 4.   [52] Int. 5*c*, 55*a*, 40*a*.

[53] See e.g. in the Political Record Book (1913) 66, KNA DC MSA 8/2; also C. Eliot, *The East African Protectorate* (London, 1905), 113.

[54] Evidence of Mr MacGregor Ross, *Native Labour Commission, 1912–13*, 43; Int. 40*b*.

[55] See Int. 72*a* for the account of a Luo taken as a convert into an Arab family early in this century.   [56] Int. 61*a*.

the Nyika, some groups evidently had easier access to the networks of the town than did others: the Digo more so than the Giriama, for example; while it was the Giriama who took most advantage of the opportunities for squatting on coastal land north of Mombasa.

The extent to which the institutions of the casual labour force were considered to be 'Swahili' shows the importance of incorporation to those seeking casual work. Ranger has described beni membership as being composed of the 'young Swahili men of the town',[57] and contemporary reports always characterized the dancers as Swahili.[58] Informants today clearly associate participation in *beni* with membership of a town community.[59] In form the *beni* were completely different—in dress, songs, and instruments—to Nyika dances,[60] and involvement marked movement to and immersion in a new world, as one informant explained: 'When I went, I lived in the town, I plunged into the town, Mombasa. In Mombasa we danced those dances; here, the dances are different.'[61]

Those who danced *beni* were considered to be 'real townspeople',[62] and one Ribe man, anxious to emphasize that he had always maintained his obligations to his homestead and stayed out of the Swahili networks of the town (he was a Christian and, unusually, worked as a domestic for a European family) said: 'I never danced . . . if I got civilised there, well, I'd discard my parents, I'd just discard them . . . if you dance, then no question, they'll draw you into that gang.'[63] Others too used 'becoming civilized' as a synonym for 'becoming Swahili'.[64]

Thus, the networks of the town offered opportunities only to those who became incorporated. Hobley, noting an apparently paradoxical shortage of dock labour at a time of considerable temporary immigration from the hinterland during the 1918 famine, wrote that 'raw Nyika labour which may drift into the town owing to a lack of food is of no value for this work'.[65]

---

[57] Ranger, *Dance and Society*, 32–3.
[58] Mombasa Collector's Intelligence Diary, 13 June 1906, KNA PC Coast 1/17/33; *EAS* (W), 14 Apr. 1906.   [59] Int. 9b, 12b, 55a.
[60] Int. 44a; Ranger, *Dance and Society*, 21; Int. 12b.   [61] Int. 9b, 1–2.
[62] Int. 26a, 2.   [63] Int. 40a, 9.   [64] Int. 9b.
[65] PC to Chairman, Famine Committee, 14 Feb. 1918, KNA PC Coast 1/2/6. The shortage of labour caused considerable delays in the unloading of relief food for the famine; see also PC to Chairman, Famine Committee, 28 June 1918, ibid.

Effectively, he was recognizing and acquiescing in the exclusion of such unincorporated migrants from the most lucrative form of casual labour.

The importance of the continuities from nineteenth-century history in the development of this pattern may be demonstrated by the contrast between casual labour networks in Mombasa and Dar es Salaam. Casuality and the hiring of labour by headmen dominated the dock casual labour force in Dar too, but access here was not reserved to the Swahili alone: people who identified themselves as Zaramo played a major role in this work-force from an early date.[66] It is a difference that may reflect both the much smaller economy and the lower level of incorporation in the nineteeth century, and the relatively small number of established patrons in Dar es Salaam.

Because migrants to Mombasa needed to become incorporated to survive for any period there, such migration continued to be a major threat to the domestic economy of the hinterland homestead. Like the nineteenth-century migrants, in becoming Swahili these people abandoned their homesteads. Male migrants might be given wives by their patrons, or find concubines for themselves, so that they did not need the support of their homestead head in paying a bride price—while the cost of maintaining a wife or concubine in Mombasa, or the exactions of the *serang*, made financial expressions of obligation to the rural homestead impossible.

This process of becoming Swahili and so renouncing obligations to the rural homestead, was necessary for those seeking the least restrictive kinds of employ: and it was also attractive for other reasons. It has already been suggested that migration in the nineteenth century could be a result of personal dissatisfaction as much as of ecological crisis. Informants discussing migration to Mombasa in the twentieth century give a variety of motives: bridewealth, a desire to buy clothes, most simply a desire for more or better food.[67] There is a common theme: the desire to free their time, and the product of their

---

[66] Iliffe, *Modern History*, 161. In the later 20th c. at least, the Zaramo of Dar made a considerable effort to maintain their identity and their links with rural Zaramo communities; see L. Swantz, 'The Zaramo of Dar es Salaam: A Study of continuity and Change', *TNR* 71 (1970), 157–64. [67] Int. 25a, 26a, 21a.

labour, from the control of the homestead head. In evading the authority of the homestead, migrants to Mombasa were also, increasingly, evading the coercion and control of the colonial state.

Incorporation, conversion to Islam, and the assumption of a new, Swahili identity made migrants to Mombasa effectively untraceable by the authorities or by the aggrieved former employers from whom many had deserted.[68] Officials elsewhere on the coast suggested that some were using the anonymity of the town to pursue a modest career in desertion: 'Mombasa affords a ready asylum for the professional contract breaker, who at Mombasa gets an advance on his engagement to work here, and returns without fulfilling it.'[69]

Mombasa provided a refuge for tax-evaders, too. Collection of poll tax on the island was so inefficiently pursued that in 1912 it was suspended completely.[70] Attempts to carry out a census and begin taxing again in 1913 failed, owing to the complexity of housing arrangements in Mombasa; even where house-owners could be identified and taxed, it was easy for the dependants, relatives, and others who lodged with them to evade registration. Hobley wrote that 'there are in most houses adult lodgers who are legally liable for poll tax but who pay nothing'.[71] Beech, the Mombasa District Commissioner, suggested in 1914 that the only way to collect the tax was to post clerks at all the ferries to the mainland and refuse passage to those without a tax receipt.[72] The Provincial Commissioner rejected the suggestion, unwilling to countenance the disruption and the confrontation that it would entail,[73] and the collection of poll tax on the island remained extremely haphazard.[74] The Swahili population of Mombasa grew apace, as more and more took refuge in this identity. In 1914 population estimates for Mombasa District included the category 'Swahilis including residents of almost every tribe in Africa'. They were the

---

[68] *EAS* (W), 4 Aug. 1906.
[69] Sect. VIII, 'Labour', Takaungu Subdistrict Annual Report (1909), KNA DC MSA 1/1.   [70] PC to Chief Sec., 6 Dec. 1912, KNA PC Coast 1/12/71.
[71] PC to Chief Sec. 17 May 1913, ibid.
[72] DC Mombasa to PC, 17 Dec. 1914, ibid.
[73] Hemsted, for PC, to DC Mombasa, 24 Dec. 1914, ibid.
[74] It was reported in 1930 that tax collection was still very ineffective: 'Report on Native Affairs in Mombasa' (1930), 3, KNA DC MSA 3/3.

vast majority of the population.[75] The existence of such a category was a tacit admission of the inability of the administration to differentiate, classify, and regulate the population of
Mombasa.

By becoming Swahili, migrants could confound the systems
of control on which the administration relied: however superior the power of the state, its ability to enforce labour and tax
laws relied, as a minimum, on the ability to identify and locate
the individual. The colonial view of African society, as composed of discrete tribes, each with its own separate system of
authority, led officials to seek to identify and control individuals through their membership of a tribe. Yet on the coast,
ethnicity was negotiable, and there was no single and effective system of authority among the rapidly growing 'Swahili'
population of Mombasa. The state resolutely continued to
define Swahili as 'natives', resisting pressure from some members of the Twelve Tribes to be classified as 'non-natives':[76] the
Swahili population was theoretically subject to the full battery
of colonial tax and labour laws. But effectively, to become
Swahili in Mombasa was to step outside the colonial framework of control, just as it was to evade the control of the homestead head.

Homestead heads in the hinterland resented this evasion as
much as did European employers. Women and men who moved
to Mombasa are now referred to as those who became 'lost'.[77]
It is a term used not only by elders in the rural areas but by
some younger men in the town, who insist that they have retained their identity, have not become lost. To become lost was
not to deny one's origins completely—for the lost often helped
members of their family who came to Mombasa.[78] Rather, it
was to be lost to the redistributive networks of the homestead,
to renounce obligations to and claims on these networks.

---

[75] Population estimates contained in KNA PC Coast 1/1/328.

[76] H. Kindy, *Life and Politics in Mombasa* (Nairobi, 1972), 4; A. I. Salim, *Swahili-Speaking Peoples of the Kenya Coast, 1895–1963* (Nairobi, 1973), ch. 5; for the continuing legal attempts to define the term 'Swahili', see e.g. Sect. 2, Ordinance No. 15 of 1910, KNA AG/4/798.

[77] Int. 40a, 4c. Brantley has also recorded that Giriama elders felt that those who moved to the coast were 'lost', and that this was one reason why they were reluctant to encourage their young men out to work; C. Brantley, *The Giriama and Colonial Resistance in Kenya, 1800–1920* (Los Angeles, 1921), 67.   [78] Int. 5c, 26b, 40a.

It was a loss against which homestead heads struggled. The movement of women to Mombasa was a constant problem for them.[79] If an unmarried woman moved to town, her homestead head would be unable to gain the bridewealth from her marriage. If a married woman fled, the head of the homestead would face demands from the abandoned husband for return of the bridewealth already paid. Many women moved to the protection of a man in the town, sometimes a man who had had some relationship to the woman's husband or father, as a trading partner or host in Mombasa.[80] Reclaiming compensation from such men was difficult, since they were not subject to the operations of 'native' courts, nor were Nyika marriages recognized in the magistrates' courts.[81] Women, like men, were hard to trace in their new identity in the town:

If you look for her, you'll get tired, she's being hidden, oh, perhaps she's in that house, watching you, and you're wandering about looking for her . . . She's already had her clothes changed, she's wearing that *buibui* [Muslim women's covering], the black thing, right down to her feet. She could come right up to you and you wouldn't know her, she's already lost, that's it.'[82]

Muslim patrons could claim the bridewealth for migrant women who married in Mombasa.[83] Where such women lived as concubines, they often rented a room from someone else and shared it with their succession of subtenants/lovers.[84] In a phrase illustrative of the shifting meaning of the term, 'Swahili', these were called Swahili marriages,[85] and European observers were quick to identify as Swahili any women whose lives they saw as immoral.[86]

Neither were homestead heads willing to see their young

---

[79] Sect. (iv), 'Social Condition of the People', Malindi District Annual Report (1919–20), KNA PC Coast 1/1/412; also ADC Kilifi to SC, 7 Aug. 1924, KNA PC Coast 1/3/130; Int. 43a.

[80] See the case of Sudi bin Ali's murder, in *EAS* (W), 29 July 1911; similar practice is implied in DC Nyika Reserve to PC, 12 Mar. 1920, KNA PC Coast 1/1/130.

[81] Crown Counsel to SCC, 4 Sept. 1924, KNA PC Coast 1/1/130; ADC Mombasa to Res. Magistrate, 31 May 1922, KNA AG/4/2789; Mombasa Res. Magistrate, note, n.d., ibid.   [82] Int. 46a, 5.

[83] Payment of a bride-price in this way is implied in the evidence concerning the murder of Stephen Madema, reported in *EAS* (D), 15 Mar. 1912.

[84] Int. 44a.   [85] Int. 24a.

[86] See the comments on women and fertility in 'Population', Mombasa District Annual Report (1905–6), draft version, 8 May 1906, KNA PC Coast 1/1/113.

men 'lost'. In part, they needed the labour of these young men. Regular agricultural work was largely the work of women,[87] but young men played an important role in the local trading economy. In Rabai they tapped the palm trees of their homestead heads for wine, and transported the palm wine for sale.[88] Throughout the hinterland, young men and boys (and many of the migrants to Mombasa were young, some only 10 or 11) were needed to herd livestock or guard crops.[89] Males also worked for homestead heads as porters in the foodstuffs trade with Mombasa.[90] The long-term loss of male labour was a problem, but worse than this, young men lost to the homestead would not send money to buy wives for themselves or the homestead head: and so the homestead would be weakened by the absence of the women workers whom these young men would have added to it.

The conflicts engendered by this loss are reflected in the ambiguity of the term 'Swahili': just as the conflict between European employers, the state, and Africans on the coast was played out in the changing meaning and implications of this term.

For the people who now call themselves Mijikenda, the term 'Swahili' has many meanings, several of which may be operative for the same informant in different contexts. 'Swahili' is used by some to describe any Muslim,[91] by others to describe a town-dweller.[92] For some, the Swahili are their relatives who have decided to live in the town and forget or deny their Mijikenda identity,[93] while others living in Mombasa now describe themselves as Swahili and Mijikenda.[94] There are many kinds of Swahili, but essentially the Mijikenda identify the Swahili as of the town. Moreover, while some Mijikenda claim Swahili identity in certain circumstances, the term usually carries a sense of disapproval: 'A Swahili is someone who doesn't go home, someone who has got a bit lost.'[95] A Swahili, for many, is someone sly and deceptive.[96]

The reappraisal by Europeans of the significance of Swahili identity was similarly rooted in the conflicts of this period.

---

[87] Int. 40a.   [88] ADC Rabai to Ag. PC, 16 Oct. 1907, KNA PC Coast 1/12/47.
[89] Int. 17b, 21a.   [90] Int. 21b, 66a, 34a.   [91] Int. 21b.   [92] Int. 5c.
[93] Int. 40b.   [94] Int. 18a.   [95] Int. 4c, 2.   [96] Int. 18a.

Underlying the whole debate was the appreciation that becoming Swahili gave Africans new options, challenging the
ability of the state to record and control the population.

During the Company period, and in the first years of the
Protectorate, Swahili had not been a term of opprobrium. The
Company decided that 'Swahilis' would make the best police-
men;[97] missionary scholars hobnobbed with the literati of the
Twelve Tribes, impressed by the existence of a Swahili literary
culture;[98] and the contrast between the coastal towns and the
hinterland was seen by Europeans as one between civilization—albeit a rather decadent one—and barbarism: One observer wrote floridly of the coast as 'this thin line of civilisation
. . . unable to cope with the hordes of savages of the interior'.[99]
The sympathetic attitude to coastal culture of the first Commissioner of the Protectorate, Hardinge, has been noted
elsewhere,[100] and Eliot, Hardinge's successor, wrote that the
Swahili were distinguished from up-country Africans by
'civilisation and intelligence'.[101] The Mombasa Collector
noted angrily in 1906 that the Public Works Department was
leaving its trolleys in the charge of *wachenzi* (*sic*), up-country
Africans; and he demanded that this responsible job be reserved to Swahilis.[102]

Yet already by 1906, the word was being used in a new way.
The perception that Africans in an urban culture must be
immoral and decadent, as a corollary of their association with
a civilization that was seen as essentially alien to them, came
to predominate. Eliot's complimentary remarks were qualified
by the comment that 'their [Swahili] honesty is rarely above
suspicion'.[103] The Swahili were beginning to metamorphose,
in official perception, from civilized allies into the anti-social

---

[97] Letter 5/76, précis of mail to Mombasa, 24 Feb. 1893, IBEA File 53 (25).

[98] W. Taylor was the most prominent of these; see J. Knappert, *Four Centuries of
Swahili Verse* (London, 1979), 54. But Taylor too was suspicious of urban Africans,
as is suggested in his comparison of Swahili and Giriama languages, for which see
W. W. A. Fitzgerald, *Travels in the Coastlands of British East Africa and the Islands of
Zanzibar and Pemba* (London, 1970 (first 1898), 114–15.

[99] C. H. Stigand, *The Land of Zinj* (London, 1966 (first 1913)), 2.

[100] Salim, *Swahili-Speaking Peoples*, 75–6.

[101] C. Eliot, *The East African Protectorate* (London, 1905), 112.

[102] Collector, Mombasa to Ag. Sub-Commissioner, 12 Nov. 1906, KNA PC Coast
1/1/113.   [103] Eliot, *East African Protectorate*, 113.

dregs of Mombasa. The *East African Standard* began to describe as 'Swahili' almost anyone convicted or accused of a crime in Mombasa, and labour touts were similarly called 'Swahilis' or 'Swahili rogues'.[104] The police picked up this habit of classifying criminals as Swahili,[105] and the association of the word 'Swahili' with a lazy and criminal population that defied regulation came to dominate European attitudes. A European woman wrote of the Swahili in 1910 that 'their favourite occupations are eating, sleeping and loafing about the bazaar',[106] and in 1920 a visitor was told that *Swahili* meant 'those who cheat all alike'.[107] Ainsworth-Dickson, the District Commissioner of Mombasa in the early 1920s, who was happy to co-operate with the more powerful figures in the town for administrative purposes,[108] none the less had a low opinion of most of the Swahili population: 'The Swahili, lethargic and thriftless, is a striking example of self deception. The possessor of a bare mud hut, a bed and a faithless wife, he sees himself the lavish host of a hundred guests and the envied of men [*sic*].'[109] Presumably worried that he had not made his opinion clear, Ainsworth-Dickson later described Swahili youth as 'a generation of drunken, dangerous wasters'.[110]

It is in the context of the options offered by Swahili identity and by the mainland networks of credit and trade that the spread of the Singwaya story, and the beginning of the struggle over its significance, should be understood. It was in the first one and a half decades of this century that the story of Nyika migration from Singwaya became established. In these years, Singwaya was a projection back into history of shared interests with the Swahili, and the possibility of a shared identity. The link with the Swahili seems to have been explicit in the Singwaya stories of this period: various Nyika groups were

---

[104] See the *EAS* (D), 14 May 1912, 20 Apr. 1912.
[105] Police Annual Report (1905–6), in Donald, Inspector General of Police to HM Commissioner, 10 May 1906, PRO CO 533. 14; also Assistant District Supt. to PC, 24 Mar. 1910, KNA PC Coast 1/1/159.
[106] E. Younghusband, *Glimpses of East Africa and Zanzibar* (London, 1910), 43.
[107] H. Norden, *Black and White in East Africa* (London, 1924), 43.
[108] Ag. DC Mombasa to PC, 12 Aug. 1919, KNA PC Coast 1/12/196.
[109] Mombasa District Annual Report (1923), 2, KNA DC MSA 1/3.
[110] Ibid. (1925), 6.

said to have come from Singwaya with the Swahili, or even to have been led by them.[111] Morton associates the Singwaya story with a very particular set of circumstances, the relationship between the Giriama and some Arabs of Malindi, notably one Fadhili bin Omari.[112] This is, as has been argued, too narrow an explanation for such a widely diffused story,[113] although there is evidence that Fadhili's association with the Giriama was even closer than Morton suggested; in 1917 Fadhili tried to organize a legal action on behalf of the Giriama to prove their right to occupy the land north of the Sabaki.[114] A Giriama claim to origins north of the Sabaki would obviously have flourished under these conditions.[115] Yet there is no need to attribute the adoption and spread of the story to this one event: for this event was in itself part of a pattern of co-operation between individual Nyika, Swahili, and Arabs to evade the power of the colonial state.

This co-operation was not without tension, nor was it at the grand level of 'the Nyika' and 'the Swahili': it expressed itself in minor alliances and friendships, kin ties between groups, the movement of individuals from hinterland to town. All these minor alliances could themselves fuel wider conflict, and the tensions over dependants were to combine with the hostile attitude of the colonial state to produce a progressive reworking of the nature of these alliances—and of the meaning of the Singwaya story.

Already by 1912, some officials were moving beyond simple accusations of indolence, or concerns about the breakdown of

[111] 'Notes on the Origins and Movements of the Wachonyi and Wajibana', attached to Kilifi Station Diary, Mar. 1925, KNA PC Coast 1/1/443.

[112] R. F. Morton, 'The Shungwaya Myth of Mijikenda Origins', *IJAHS* 5 (1972), 397–423, 409–16.

[113] Morton himself notes the difficulty of explaining the 'motive' for the fabrication which he alleges ('The Shungwaya Myth', 415–16), and the point is made rather more forcefully by N. Chittick, 'The "Book of the Zanj" and the Mijikenda', *IJAHS* 9 (1976), 68–73; and by T. T. Spear, 'Traditional Myths and Historian's Myths', *HIA* 1 (1974), 68, 75–6.

[114] 'Minutes of Baraza Held at Kakoneni Station', 21 Feb. 1918, 2, KNA PC Coast 1/2/1.

[115] In this context, it is interesting to note that one of the *kaya*s which lay in this disputed area north of the Sabaki was called Singwaya. See the maps in Fitzgerald, *Travels in the Coastlands*, 1; and H. W. Mutoro, 'The Spatial Distribution of the Mijikenda *Kaya* Settlements on the Hinterland Kenya Coast', *Trans-African Journal of History*, 14 (1985), 78–100, 79.

tribal authority, to locate the problem of hinterland people's reluctance to work in their relationship with the coastal peoples, and the nature of the coastal labour market. In 1919, the District Commissioner of Nyika still saw the problem as one of reluctance to work, remarking that 'the Wanyika cling obstinately to idleness. The Kenya Mining Syndicate, which is prospecting at Vitengeni, has had to import all its labourers from Kavirondo'.[116]

But others had realized much earlier that people were only avoiding some kinds of labour: 'There were large numbers of natives living in Mombasa who would materially assist in augmenting the labour supply if they could be made to work, but they earned sufficient in one week to keep them for two months.'[117] From 1912, the administration began to institute measures designed to restrict the alternatives of African workers in and around Mombasa, to break down the networks which allowed them these alternatives and to force coastal groups into conformity with the state's image of African societies. Implicitly, they were restating a question: no longer asking why the people in the hinterland would not work, they were asking instead why they would not work *for them.*

[116] Nyika Reserve Annual Native Report (1919–20), 3, KNA PC Coast 1/12/279.
[117] Evidence of Mr Waller, *Native Labour Commission of 1912–13*, 91.

Part III

'Close contact with the coast residents is most prejudicial': State Intervention, 1900–1931

From 1912 a group of local officials led by Provincial Commissioner Charles Hobley began to perceive that the root of their problems with labour and administration on the coast lay within the relationships between the people of the coast and its immediate hinterland. They worked out their responses to these problems through the metaphor of contamination. The idleness and immorality with which they associated the 'Swahili' community were, in this imagery, a disease—a contagious disease. Arab and Swahili traders, with their allegedly deceitful practices, were vectors, as it were, of this disease.

The discourse on moral health was bound up with that concerning physical health and with urban planning in Mombasa. Here, the perceived spread of infection was, initially, in the opposite direction: the Swahili were seen as practised urbanites, whose separation from more recent newcomers to the town was necessary to their good health.

Policies on the coast, up to the 1930s, concentrated on preventing the spread of these contagions: quarantining the Swahili by sealing the permeable boundaries of ethnicity. This separation involved the division of land, and the nature and boundaries of administration; attempts to change the patterns of trade between coast and hinterland; and the physical reshaping of the town of Mombasa. Against the background of these policies, a series of measures aimed at the control of labour within Mombasa was instituted.

These measures reshaped the society and economy of the coast; but they did so in ways which the administration had neither desired nor expected. The state could force change, but it could not control the direction of that change.

5

The Creation of Administrative and Landowning Categories

The further they are removed from Swahili influence, the more industrious they become.

(Vanga District Annual Report, 1915–16)

The legal aspects of land ownership on the coast were confused by the ambiguous status of the area. Theoretically, the coast was the domain of the Sultan of Zanzibar, and it remained so after 1921, when the rest of Kenya became a colony. Muslim inhabitants of the area were governed according to Muslim law, a law which recognized the individual's right to possess and to alienate land on his own behalf. Elsewhere in East Africa, the British administration held that land belonged to no individual, but either to certain groups as a communal possession or to nobody at all. In either case, the British Crown claimed the right to dispose of such land. On the coast, the problems raised by private ownership were intensified by the imprecision of the boundaries involved. The Sultan's domain was described as a coastal strip ten miles wide, but the meaning of this was obscure: if it were ten miles measured from the median tide-mark, the creeks of the coast would push the Sultan's boundaries considerably more than ten miles inland. This issue was never resolved: the 'ten-mile strip' was never properly mapped.

After the declaration in 1895 of the British Protectorate, there was for several years no system of land registration or survey. This absence of registration coincided with a considerable boom in land sales. Initially, this buying, largely speculative in nature, concentrated on the projected line of the railway through

Mazeras and Mariakani, where land was bought up not only because of the transport advantages that the railway line would bring, but more simply because purchasers expected that the railway would have to buy the land from them.[1] After this, buying was mostly concentrated on potential plantation land at Changamwe, Miritini, Maunguja, and Nguuni—areas close to creeks or within reasonable distance of the railway line. Some buyers were speculators, others were themselves planters.[2] All these sales were recorded in the transactions register in Mombasa, without the land being surveyed, and often without evidence of ownership being offered or requested. The possibilities for fraud were tremendous, and some pieces of land were sold to several different people by competing vendors. Some were sold several times by the same person.[3]

These sales were frequently represented by European observers, official and unofficial, as frauds perpetrated upon hinterland people by unscrupulous Arabs and Swahili: 'In ways that are crooked and things that are dark, the simple Swahili is a specialist, and his talents are most prodigious when he wants to sell a shamba to which he has no title.'[4] Officials presented the process as a clash between the Nyika, with no idea of individual land tenure, and avaricious coastal Muslims anxious to sell land,[5] an analysis to which they gave historical depth by quoting Krapf's views on 'encroachment'.[6]

This view of the clash of two systems of land tenure, the possessors of one being able to exploit the other, simplified a

[1] Collector, Mombasa, to Sub-Commissioner, 30 Aug. 1906, KNA PC Coast 1/11/113; see also F. Cooper, *From Slaves to Squatters* (New Haven, Conn., 1980), 205.

[2] ADC Shimoni to PC, 8 Oct. 1913, KNA PC Coast 1/11/146; Registrar of Documents to PC, 14 Apr. 1913, KNA AG/4/2162.

[3] For some examples of frauds, or alleged frauds, see ADC Rabai to Land Officer, 25 Mar. 1914, KNA AG/4/2162; Application Cause 83 of 1920, KNA AG/4/1889; Land Officer to Attorney-General, 9 May 1916, KNA AG/4/1929; DC Mombasa to ADC Rabai, and ADC Rabai to Bowen, 17 Mar. 1908, Bowen to ADC Rabai, 4 Aug. 1908, in KNA PC Coast 1/11/9.   [4] *EAS* (W), 3 Aug. 1912.

[5] R. W. Hamilton, 'Land Tenure among the Bantu Wanyika of East Africa', *JAS* 20 (1920), 13–18.

[6] Hollis, Report No. 4 on Mile 7.2–9.5, 23 Dec. 1906, KNA AG/4/2055. The classic land case of this time was that concerning the sale of land near Kidutani to an Indian, Allidina Visram, by an Arab/Swahili, Ali bin Salim el-Mandhri. The sale was eventually disallowed in a case judged by Hamilton, who went on to fix Nyika land law in the article mentioned in n. 5: see Civil Case No. 60 of 1913, Mombasa High Court, KNA PC Coast 1/10/209.

complex situation in which individuals from all groups could exploit networks of patronage to their advantage. Land was plentiful in the nineteenth century, and the payments made to hinterland and Mombasa elders by those wishing to use land in the pre-colonial period[7] fitted into concepts of patronage rather than those of land tenure: these payments dealt in authority and obligation, not in access to land as such. On the mainland just around Mombasa Island, where land was a little more scarce, a market in land had developed,[8] as individuals employed Muslim law on private tenure to their advantage, but there were no clear-cut boundaries between one system and the other. Trees and standing crops could be, and were, sold both on the coast and in the hinterland: though it was more usual to mortgage them, as the establishment of relationships between people was generally considered as important as control over property.

The potential value of land rose enormously with the coming of the railway and of European plantation companies, prompting individuals from all groups into an intense negotiation on the nature of land tenure, each seeking his own advantage. It was a negotiation carried on through sales, deals over the division of the proceeds from sales, court cases, and the presentation of ethnographic material to administrators. Hinterland elders colluded with Muslims in selling land,[9] or themselves sold land, claiming that as elders they had the right to do so.[10] For all concerned, such sales were in part a defensive measure; faced with the possibility of someone else selling these lands, or of the government claiming them, they sought to turn their claims on people into claims on the land which

[7] Such payments are recorded for Nyika and Arabs/Swahili alike; Kayamba, 'Notes on the Wadigo', *TNR* 23 (1974), 80–96, 90; 'Native Laws and Customs of Takaungu Subdistrict' (1898), 1, KNA PC Coast 1/1/138; D. C. Sperling, 'The Growth of Islam among the Mijikenda of the Kenya Coast', Ph.D. thesis (London, 1988), App. 5, parts 2, 5, 6; DC Rabai to Ag. SNA, 30 June 1908, KNA PC Coast 1/11/9.

[8] Even here, there was usually a careful enumeration of the number of trees upon any land sold, suggesting that these were at least as important as the land itself; see e.g. Entry 983 A of 1906, in the Transactions Register.

[9] Bowen to PC, 3 July 1912, KNA PC Coast 1/11/89.

[10] Registrar of Slaves to Ag. PC, 30 Mar. 1910, KNA PC Coast 1/11/363; ADC Rabai to PC, 28 July 1913, KNA PC Coast 1/11/144; Sub-Commissionery Seyyidieh, Memo, 22 July 1904, KNA PC Coast 1/1/60; ADC Rabai to DC Mombasa, 11 Oct. 1909, KNA PC Coast 1/12/53.

they farmed.[11] When it was convenient, as with the purchase of land from Duruma elders for the railway, the government accepted the right of Nyika elders to sell.[12] Officials contributed to the growing literature on Nyika traditions by noting that the elders from whom they purchased land were the only ones entitled to sell it.[13]

Members of the Twelve Tribes were heavily involved in the renegotiation of concepts of land tenure: as officials sought to limit and control these concepts to their own advantage and gain possession of land for the government,[14] so members of the Twelve Tribes sought to define their rights as widely as possible, in their own interests or in that of their group.[15] One analysis has suggested that the Swahili system of land tenure was African in the way land was acquired, but Muslim in that it permitted alienation once land was acquired.[16] It might be more appropriate to argue that the laws of land tenure were not fixed, that individuals could and did innovate: where ethnicity was negotiable, so could law be.[17]

Arabs and Swahili had a clear advantage in selling land, having better access to the registration of transactions, which was carried out in Mombasa by a Muslim scribe, and having acquired more clients, through their superior access to credit,

[11] ADC Shimoni to PC, 26 Sept. 1913, KNA PC Coast 1/11/144; Salim, *The Swahili-Speaking Peoples of the Kenya Coast, 1895–1963* (Nairobi, 1973), 116. For an example, see the claims of two Swahili that they had received 'rent' from Rabai people for land which they then sold; Ag. DC Mombasa to ADC Rabai, 13 Nov. 1908, KNA PC Coast 1/11/9. [12] Document 553A of 1908, 4 June 1908, KNA PC Coast 1/1/341.
[13] Cf. document in n. 12 with the Political Record Book, 112, KNA DC MSA 8/2.
[14] Supplementary report by ADC Mombasa, 17 Mar. 1908, KNA PC Coast 1/11/9; Hollis, Report No. 4, Mile 7.2–9.5, 23 Dec. 1906, KNA AG/4/2055.
[15] Deed, dated 15 Aug. 1913, KNA PC Coast 1/11/197; Hamilton, Judgment, 23 Dec. 1918, in KNA PC Coast 1/11/24; evidence of Said bin Sheikh, quoted in Hamilton, Judgment, 23 Dec. 1918, ibid. The often conflicting nature of the evidence offered suggests the intensity of negotiation over this issue. The details of the Twelve Tribes system almost certainly underwent considerable elaboration and codification in this period, although the suggestion that the Twelve Tribes were created for the purpose of claiming land (Watkins, 'Report on Coastal Federations', 31 Dec. 1909, KNA DC MSA 3/1) is certainly incorrect. See also Cooper, *From Slaves to Squatters*, 193–5.
[16] Salim, *Swahili-Speaking Peoples*, 125–6.
[17] The ability of individuals to negotiate law and custom was revealed in other matters. In one inheritance case Magwayi, a Muslim Digo and a government headman, claimed certain property under Digo (matrilineal) law, having failed to have his claim upheld in a court of Muslim (patrilineal) law; Dundas, DC Mombasa to PC, 15 Sept. 1915, KNA PC Coast 1/11/267.

than had most hinterland patrons. But Nyika too took part in this process. The suggestion that the Nyika were the helpless victims of fraud was a distortion of reality; but it played an important part in shaping and justifying policy.

In 1908, the Land Titles Ordinance was passed by the government. The ostensible aim of this legislation was to guarantee titles to land within the unmapped ten-mile strip of the coast, for purchasers of land not infrequently found that their title was contested by someone else who had bought the same piece of land and it was feared that 'the insecurity of title to land at the coast does and will materially retard the economic development of the coast'.[18] The new ordinance required proper survey and proof of ownership. But it had a further intention: all landowners, not only those who were selling or buying, had to prove and register their title, and under section 17 of the ordinance all land to which title was not proven became the property of the Crown. The administration had been seeking possession of such 'waste' lands since the beginning of the Protectorate, but it was only with the 1908 ordinance that the legal basis for this control was established.[19] The term 'waste' was, however, something of a misnomer, since land to which no one could prove title was often wholly or partly occupied by Nyika or ex-slave cultivators.[20]

The government was anxious to secure this land, partly to encourage the establishment of European plantations on the coast. The problem with privately-owned land on the coast was not just that of insecurity, as the Sub-commissioner noted in 1906: 'At present all land within the 10 miles zone is more or less claimed by Arabs or Swahilis, many of whom own small plots for which they want exorbitant prices. It is therefore very difficult for intending settlers to acquire land in any quantity.'[21]

[18] Memo, Crown Advocate, 1908, KNA AG/4/2143.
[19] Article 2 of IBEA Concession, 24 May 1887; Waste Lands Regulations, 31 Aug. 1897; Notice, Hayes-Sadler, HM Commissioner, 18 May 1907, all in KNA AG/4/2162.
[20] See e.g. DC Mombasa to Ag. PC, 10 Sept. 1914, KNA PC Coast 1/11/197; Hollis, Report No. 4, 23 Dec. 1906, KNA AG/4/2055; SC to Crown Counsel, 21 Mar. 1924, KNA PC Coast 1/11/336.
[21] Lane, Sub-Commissioner Seyyidieh, quoted in EAS (W), 14 Apr. 1906.

If 'freed from native claims',[22] this land could be granted to settlers.

Acquiring this land for the government would bring other benefits. It would prevent numbers of hinterland people and ex-slaves from becoming permanently established on land which they had come to occupy, often as the clients of traders and planters who themselves had no effective title to this land. The Crown Advocate had stressed the necessity of this in asking for the passage of the ordinance:

Meanwhile, particularly in the neighbourhood of the larger towns, the number of squatters with the most shadowy claim of right, or with no claim of right at all, are extending and planting shambas to which, if the Government takes no steps, they will in course of time acquire a good holding title . . . It will shortly become impossible in many instances for the Government to affirm its right to its own property.[23]

The struggle in which this legislation was employed was not so much one between squatters on the one hand and Arab or Swahili landowners on the other: rather it was one between hinterland farmers and their trading or planting patrons on the one hand and the government and a body of large-scale Arab and other landowners, who had aligned themselves with the government, on the other.[24]

The 1908 ordinance effectively acted to bar Nyika and ex-slave farmers from claiming title, though it did not explicitly prohibit this.[25] Most had little idea that they were supposed to claim ownership, nor any idea of how to go about this.[26] Claims to ownership were 'proven' by amassing numbers of witnesses,

[22] An expression used in an appeal for the 1908 ordinance to be applied to the coast south of Mombasa; Memo, ADC Mombasa, 20 Dec. 1913, KNA AG/4/2160. The situation in this area was acute, as the administration had by 1910 approved the grant of more than 500 sq. m. to plantation companies, land to almost none of which the government had an existing legal claim. 'Waste' land acquired through application of the Land Titles Ordinance was to solve this problem. See also 'Report on Lands South of Mombasa', Watkins, ADC Mombasa, 2 Dec. 1913, KNA AG/4/2160.
[23] Memo, Crown Advocate, 1908, KNA AG/4/2143.
[24] Cooper, *From Slaves to Squatters*, 191–3 and elsewhere, notes the differentiation among landowners caused by the 1908 ordinance, but concentrates more on the question of the extent to which the state was willing to intervene to help landowners to control squatters.
[25] Cooper, *From Slaves to Squatters*, 196–200. [26] Int. 5*b*, 54*a*.

usually ex-slaves, and decisions as to the veracity of this evidence were left in the hands of certain local officials, notably those of a Baluchi called Abdul Wahid and of Ali bin Salim el-Busaidi, the Muslim governor of Mombasa.[27] These and other Arab officials, all the owners of considerable lands, tended to uphold the claims of the government and of other large-scale landowners. The extent to which this process could be abused was suggested in 1910, when all but one of the Arab officials on the coast refused point-blank an order to supply to the Provincial Commissioner a list of the property which they owned, on the grounds that, as one put it, 'if I write a list I am afraid they might think that we have taken other people's land'.[28] Under the 1908 Lands Ordinance, people claiming land had to pay a fee of 1 per cent of the value of the land, and those whose claims were disallowed were fined a further 2 per cent of the value for making a 'trivial' claim.[29] If the occupiers of land did not expect sympathetic treatment, such charges were powerful disincentives to making any claim at all. There was, instead, constant passive resistance to the process of title registration.[30]

For those hinterland people who managed to claim title despite these obstructions, there could be one final and insuperable obstacle. The Recorder of Titles sometimes ruled (it is unclear on what grounds) that a Nyika claimant, even a Muslim, was not legally capable of owning a freehold, and would in this case be granted a 'certificate of interest' in the land, not title to it.[31]

[27] See the Collector's Intelligence Diary, 1 June 1906, KNA PC Coast 1/17/33; PC to Chief Sec., 28 May 1914, KNA PC Coast 1/11/315.

[28] *Liwali* of Mambrui to DC Malindi, 16 Dec. 1909, KNA PC Coast 1/11/19.

[29] 'Report of Special Committee on the Land Titles Ordinance', 6 Mar. 1908, KNA AG/4/2143.

[30] Such resistance included refusal to turn up to point out plot boundaries, refusal to mark boundaries or pay survey fees, and the destruction or removal of survey beacons; PC to Attorney-General, 14 July 1913, KNA PC Coast 1/11/104; PC to Chief Sec., 4 Aug. 1913, KNA AG/4/2162; Memo on survey, 1914, 3, Recorder of titles, KNA AG/4/2162.

[31] Sperling, 'The Growth of Islam', 132. This was a policy established early in the Protectorate; HM Commissioner to Collector, Mombasa, 24 Aug. 1899, KNA PC Coast 1/12/98. A similar principle came into operation in the Bowen case. This concerned the sale by a member of the Twelve Tribes to a black American of land occupied by a number of Ribe. The Ribe received official support for their challenge to Bowen's title, only to lose this support, and the case, when they insisted in court that the Ribe,

This distinction between groups that could own land and those that could not was enshrined in law by a special ordinance in 1910.[32] Expressed as a measure to protect the hinterland people from fraud, this banned the sale of land by Nyika; should any manage to claim land, they would be denied the right to sell it. Any area gazetted as a 'reserve' was specifically excluded from the functioning of the 1908 ordinance: the Nyika were protected from exploitation by denying them title to land on the coast or in the hinterland: they were not even to be given a communal title to their reserves.[33] The Swahili of Mombasa were, on the other hand, denied a communal reserve, with or without the right to alienate the land thereof.[34] The Attorney-General argued that the Twelve Tribes were not a tribal entity and were not '*bona fide* agriculturalists',[35] and the Recorder of Titles agreed that 'it will also be found that the majority of members are residents of Mombasa and do not depend for a livelihood on their shambas'.[36]

There was, no doubt, some truth in this—many Twelve Tribes' members did not depend on their land for their livelihood. But numbers of their clients and other squatters, actually or potentially incorporated to the Swahili, did. Having denied Nyika and ex-slaves ownership of land on the coastal strip, officials were unwilling to let them gain access to this land through the permeable institutions of Swahili identity. They were acutely aware of the possibilities of this. The District Commissioner for Malindi claimed, in the aftermath of the expulsion of the Giriama from north of the Sabaki, that 'I understand that very considerable numbers of Wanyika since

not the government, owned the land; Chief Sec. to Ag. PC, 19 Sept. 1914, and Atkinson to DC, 7 Nov. 1914, KNA PC Coast 1/11/197.

[32] 'An Ordinance to Provide for the Protection of the Native Land Areas, Seyyidieh' (1910), in KNA AG/4/2160.

[33] Attorney-General to PC, 4 June 1913, KNA PC Coast 1/11/150; Attorney-General to PC, 16 June 1914, KNA AG/4/2162.

[34] Attorney-General to Ross (a solicitor), 31 May 1915, KNA AG/4/2111. The idea of an inalienable communal reserve for the Swahili had originally been supported by the Assistant Recorder of Titles; see comments of De Lacey, Recorder of Titles, in Application 25N, 26 May 1915; and Attorney-General to Chief Sec., 8 May 1916, KNA AG/4/2111.

[35] Monson, for Governor to Abdullah Rithiwani (of the Nine Tribes), 30 Dec. 1915, KNA AG/4/2111.

[36] Recorder of Titles to Chief Sec., 19 Nov. 1915, KNA AG/4/2111.

their removal from N of the Sabaki are daily being received into the Mohamedan faith in order that, being henceforth Mahaji, they may settle on "potential" Arab lands north of the Sabaki."[37]

The administration had thus divided the population of the area into discrete groups, one landowning and the other not, and allotted each its own area: the Nyika to the reserves and the coastal Muslims to a narrow coastal strip and the town of Mombasa. Hobley and his staff then tried to impose a corresponding physical separation. Several attempts were made to deport to the reserves those Nyika, particularly Giriama, who were not employed.[38] In 1914, the expulsion of all Giriama from Malindi District was begun. Only those with special permission from the District Commissioner were to remain.[39] When 'Arab and Swahili' landowners asked that some squatters be allowed to remain in the district,[40] Hobley's assistant, Hemsted, produced a form for the registration of these squatters; the landowners were required to hand over their squatters to the government for labour on request.[41] Hobley was firmly against the settlement of hinterland people on coastal lands for any purpose other than wage labour.[42] He argued that such people were essentially in the wrong place, and that they belonged in the reserve where there was land 'which the government is quite prepared to dedicate to the use of their tribe'.[43] Efforts continued to expel groups of Giriama who kept moving back into the district,[44] and in 1916 the Acting District Commissioner for Malindi reaffirmed that, 'Owing to the undisciplined state of the wa-Giriama the policy is to keep them inside their native reserve under tribal authority, and they may only settle outside as labourers on private lands or for private employment.'[45]

[37] DC Malindi to PC, 15 May 1915, KNA PC Coast 1/11/236.

[38] Officials had complained of their presence even before 1912; Registrar of Slaves to PC, 31 Oct. 1910, KNA PC Coast 1/11/363.

[39] DC Malindi to PC, 10 Dec. 1914, KNA PC Coast 1/12/68.

[40] DC Malindi to PC, 30 Nov. 1914, ibid.

[41] See form attached to DC Malindi to PC, 10 Dec. 1914, ibid.

[42] PC to Hemsted, 4 Dec. 1914, ibid.; see also DC Malindi to PC, 22 Oct. 1915, and Hobley's reply, PC to DC Malindi, 13 Nov. 1915, KNA PC Coast 1/11/236.

[43] PC to DC Malindi, 13 Nov. 1915, KNA PC Coast 1/11/236.

[44] DC Malindi to PC, 14 July 1915, KNA PC Coast 1/11/266.

[45] Ag. DC Malindi to PC, 10 Oct. 1916, Ag. DC Malindi to ADC Giriama, 28 Oct. 1916, and PC to DC Malindi, 4 Oct. 1916, KNA PC Coast 1/11/266.

Just as the Swahili and Arabs were being expelled from the reserves, accused of being too deceitful to live among the hinterland people,[46] so the Giriama were being expelled from the coastal strip, accused of being too wild to live among Muslims.

The expulsion of the Nyika from the coastal lands was never fully carried through, however: lacking sufficient coercive power the Provincial and District Commissioners could do little to enforce the policies which they had so boldly formulated. It was not only the Giriama rising of 1913–14 that made the administration reluctant to push the Nyika too hard,[47] for attempts to expel the Giriama continued after this time. It was the steady determination of the Giriama and others to keep returning after they were expelled which the administration were unable to counter, not the one-off explosion of violence in the revolt.[48] When, in the 1920s, the Resident Natives Ordinances were brought into operation in the rest of Kenya, the coastal administration decided not to try and enforce them to control squatting on the coast,[49] in tacit acceptance of the failure of this aspect of the policy of separation.

Yet the policy of separation had other effects. The division of the population into two groups with radically differing rights over land brought a sharp end to the renegotiation of concepts of land tenure. Arabs and Swahili could sell land, and Nyika could not—could not even claim land, in fact. Thus hinterland patrons were denied the ability to turn their claims on people into alienable claims on land. Instituting this legal divide to protect the Nyika, officials imposed the pattern which they had ostensibly been trying to prevent—the sale by Muslims of the land of helpless Nyika. As sellers adduced their ties of patronage and claims to kinship with the hinterland people as proof of their right to sell disputed land,[50] these ties became devalued. Among the Ribe, the allegedly deceitful character of the Arabs and Swahili is still illustrated by reference to these events.[51]

---

[46] See Ch. 6.
[47] This is the view of Cooper, *From Slaves to Squatters*, 224, and Spear, *The Kaya Complex*, 141.   [48] DC Malindi to PC, 15 May 1915, KNA PC Coast 1/11/236.
[49] Kilifi District Annual Report (1924–5), 8, KNA DC KFI 1/1.
[50] See Document, 15 Aug. 1913, in KNA PC Coast 1/11/197; see also SNA to PC, 24 Dec. 1907, KNA PC Coast 1/11/9.   [51] Int. 20*a*, 43*b*.

The pattern of separation, of distinct groups each with its allotted place, came to be reflected in administrative structures. Both the Company and the Protectorate employed coast people, mainly Arabs, in senior roles to supplement their European staff.[52] Combined with the legal status of the coast as a possession of the Sultan of Zanzibar, this produced a curious parallel administration: not a system of indirect rule, but a Muslim administration some of whose members had the same legal powers as colonial officials.[53] Though these officials were theoretically involved in administering the coast's Muslim population, they were in fact used more widely: a reflection of the initial British belief in the extent of Arab domination on the coast.[54]

These Arab officials, possessed of considerably more influence and local knowledge than their European counterparts, had markedly more success in the collection of tax than did European staff.[55] But they were used only briefly in this role: by 1908, they were being withdrawn from Mombasa's local hinterland, and the government had begun to downgrade their status.[56] Despite consequent difficulties in collection of tax, after this Arab officials were kept firmly out of Nyika areas.[57]

This change has been seen in the context of the general transfer of official interest way from the coast, which reflected increasing disillusionment with the economic potential of the area.[58] Yet this move was more than that: it came at a time when the labour problems of the coast were coming to be associated with the influence of coastal Muslims. The image of the Swahili and Arabs corrupting migrants to the town had

[52] Mackinnon to Mackenzie, 26 Feb. 1890, IBEA File 54; Salim, *Swahili-Speaking Peoples*, 76–9.   [53] Salim, *Swahili-Speaking Peoples*, 76–9.
[54] The IBEA, for example, attempted to secure its claim to the coast by signing a treaty with the Mazrui, who claimed to sign on behalf of the Nyika; Mackenzie to Directors, 1 Dec. 1888, IBEA File 1a.
[55] Collector, Mombasa, to Sub-Commissioner, 7 Aug. 1906, KNA PC Coast 1/1/138; Ag. Collector, Mombasa, to Sub-Commissioner, 17 Jan. 1905, KNA PC Coast 1/1/99.
[56] Ag. DC Vanga to PC, 18 Dec. 1907; ADC Mombasa to DC Mombasa, 14 Dec. 1908, KNA PC Coast 1/1/138; for the downgrading of the Arab officials, see Salim, *Swahili-Speaking Peoples*, 93.
[57] Hemsted briefly proposed reintroducing the use of Arab officials as tax-collectors following a fall in revenue, but the suggestion was not taken up; Ag. PC to DC Mombasa, 22 Jan. 1910, KNA PC Coast 1/1/159.
[58] Salim, *Swahili-Speaking Peoples*, 93.

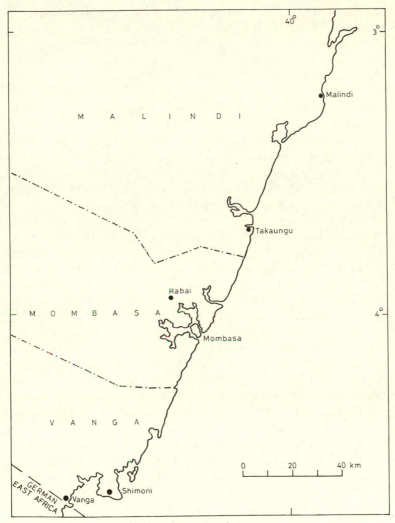

MAP 4. *District boundaries, 1912*

already been evoked by newspaper references to labour being 'contaminated by the evil example of the Mombasa loafer'.[59] Particularly after the Native Labour Commission of 1912, officials constantly asserted the need to separate people in the hinterland from the Swahili and Arabs of the coast. The District Commissioner for Vanga said of the Digo in 1916 that 'The further they are removed from Swahili influence the more industrious they become; close contact with the coast residents is most prejudicial and they generally appear to adopt the slothful inertia of the Mohamedan.'[60] In 1913 Hobley ordered that 'arrangements must be made by which no Arab official is to have dealings with the concrete tribes such as Digo, Duruma etc.'[61] The characterization of the Nyika groups as 'concrete' is a revealing one: the root of the administration's objections to the Swahili was that they were not sufficiently concrete to be controllable. Shortly after issuing this order, Hobley instructed a subordinate that 'It must be realised that it is not in our interest or in that of the people that the Mohamedan faith and the sheria [Muslim law] should spread among the aboriginal tribes.'[62] Islam was perceived as a symbol, and an agent, of the influence of the Swahili.

This separation, like that concerning land legislation, was presented in terms of the need to protect the hinterland people, a need projected back into history by reference to the slave trade. In 1913 a judge mocked the idea that Arabs or Swahili might have long been present in the Kidutani area, among the Jibana, saying that 'there was naturally little in common between the pagan Jibana and the Mohammedan Arab who brought [sic] and sold their children into slavery'.[63]

The withdrawal of Arab officials was followed by the establishment of separate structures of administration, marked off by new boundaries. Between 1913 and 1915, the councils of elders that operated in the mainland fringes of Mombasa—at

---

[59] *EAS* (W), 27 Oct. 1906.
[60] Vanga District Annual Report (1915–16), 7, KNA DC KWL 1/1.
[61] PC to ADC Shimoni, 2 Mar. 1913, KNA DC KWL 3/3.
[62] PC to ADC Shimoni, 12 Mar. 1913, ibid.
[63] Hamilton, Judgment, 23 Mar. 1914, in Civil case No. 60 of 1913, Mombasa High Court, KNA PC Coast 1/11/209.

Changamwe, Jomvu, and Mtongwe—were abolished. These councils were similar to those established by the administration among the Nyika, but in these peripheral areas, officials argued that they were corrupt, inefficient, and most of all inappropriate for the Swahili: 'The Swahili have been ruled by the Arab for so long, it is doubtful if they retain the capability of looking after themselves properly. It is certain that they remember nothing of their original native customs.'[64]

The people of the hinterland, on the other hand, were to be made to remember their 'native customs'. In 1915 the District Commissioner for Mombasa extracted from several groups of Digo elders south of Mombasa a series of signed documents, stating that they did not wish to be governed by Muslim law in any matter—although a number of them were Muslims. The Commissioner happily reported that 'the retention of a system of law common and acceptable to the whole tribe will do much to facilitate its administration'.[65] He asserted that the Digo were 'essentially Wanyika' and should be administered as such.[66] As a model for this administration he produced an account of Digo custom which, in dramatic contradiction to all previous and subsequent accounts, suggested that all the Digo had once been ruled by a council headed by a single executive.[67]

Between 1912 and 1919 administrative boundaries changed to reflect these new arrangements. Mombasa District, which had previously extended miles inland, beyond Mariakani, and had stretched a considerable distance north and south, was drastically reduced. Malindi and Vanga Districts took up much of the coastal land taken from Mombasa District, but inland the northern part of the Nyika Reserve (which came into legal existence between 1908 and 1912) was turned into a separate

[64] 'Memo on Native Councils at Changamwe and Jomvu Kwa Shehe', DC Mombasa, 30 July 1914, KNA DC MSA 3/4; see also 'Rabai District Boundaries', Pearson, 1 Sept. 1913, KNA DC KFI 3/2.

[65] DC Mombasa to PC, 1 July 1915, KNA DC MSA 3/4; see the 6 statements by elders, dated 19–29 June 1915, attached to this. The DC Mombasa at this time was Dundas, an old friend of Hobley from their time together in Ukambani; C. C. F. Dundas, *African Crossroads* (Westport, Conn., 1976 (first 1955)), 16.

[66] Political Record Book 127, KNA DC MSA 8/2.

[67] Dundas, 'Digo Custom', 1916, KNA DC MSA 3/4.

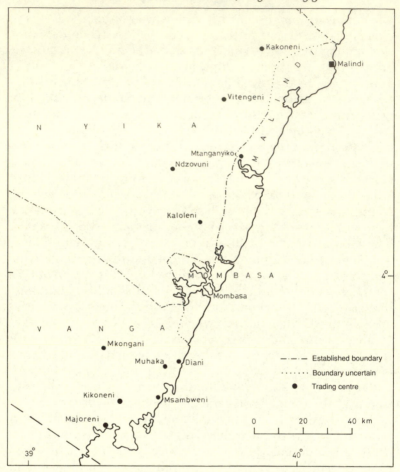

MAP 5. *District boundaries and trade centres, 1920*

administrative district. The boundary between this and the new
coastal districts, intended to be the new line between the Nyika
and the Arabs and Swahili, followed the edge of land to which
title had successfully been claimed.[68]

The corollary of this separation was an intensification of the

---

[68] Ainsworth-Dickson, Note, 20 Aug. 1919, KNA PC Coast 2/11/6; the *mudir*ship of
Mtwapa was abolished as part of these boundary changes, DC Malindi to PC, 16
Mar. 1915, KNA PC Coast 2/11/1.

official search for Nyika figures of authority.[69] Anxious to govern the hinterland by a political system entirely separate from that of the coast, officials sought to identify and perpetuate such a structure: even as their own attempts to force such figures to send young men out to work, and their interference in coastal networks of patronage, undermined some of the bases of authority. This search produced a mass of conflicting material, as different informants each described structures advantageous to themselves.[70] Among the Duruma, one individual was able to exploit the possibilities of this situation to great advantage.[71]

This search for traditional authorities failed to produce any satisfactory central authority, and the administration of the Nyika was carried on largely by District Commissioners and such homestead heads as they saw fit to appoint as headmen. By the mid-1920s, the search for a traditional underpinning to the system of administration was being abandoned,[72] and the administration turned instead to the use of Local Native Councils to bolster the power of approved elders. Half of the members of these councils were appointed by the District Commissioner, and were all headmen.[73] The separation of coast and hinterland was maintained in this system. Coastal administrators had originally thought the idea of Local Native Councils best suited to the Arabs and Swahili,[74] but when the Governor

[69] This had already absorbed much time and effort; ADC Rabai to PC, 4 Oct. 1907, KNA PC Coast 1/12/42; PC to MacDougall, Registrar of Slaves, 16 June 1907, KNA PC Coast 1/1/141; Political Record Book, I, 59, KNA DC KWL 3/5.

[70] Political Record Book, 127, KNA DC MSA 8/2, 127. Also of Dundas, 'The Wadigo', in KNA DC KWL 3/5, with the discussion of the titles of *zumbe* and *kubo* in 'Wadigo Laws', attached, District Clerk, Shimoni to PC, 16 Sept. 1913, KNA PC Coast 1/1/309; and with 'Notes on the Wadigo of Tanga', 19 Dec. 1928, KNA DC KWL 3/5. See also ADC Rabai to PC, 5 Oct. 1918, KNA PC Coast 1/9/52.

[71] After a long dispute ('Notes on Waduruma in Vanga District', n.d., Political Record Book, KNA DC KWL 3/5; 68; Assistant PC to PC, 18 July 1917, KNA PC Coast 1/3/114), Mwaiona wa Munga persuaded the PC to accept him as 'paramount head' of the Duruma (Minutes of Duruma Baraza, 16 Nov. 1923, KNA DC KWL 3/5), claiming that he alone could conduct initiations to produce a new set of elders. He then delayed the initiations indefinitely, and used his position to accumulate wealth (Digo Station Diary, Mar. 1924, 6; Digo Station Diary, Dec. 1924, 6, KNA DC KWL 5/1; also SC Office Diary, 12 Feb. 1924, KNA PC Coast 1/1/417).

[72] Digo District Annual Report (1925), 6, KNA DC KWL 1/11.

[73] ADC Kilifi to SC, 10 June 1925; DC Malindi to SC, 9 June 1925, KNA PC Coast 1/12/286. [74] Ag. DC Malindi to SC, 19 Nov. 1924, KNA PC Coast 1/12/286.

insisted that these councils should be established in the hinterland, the Swahili and Arabs were promptly excluded from
participation.[75] Thus officials sought to maintain the conceptual division between two discrete groups in the coast's population, who required very different forms of administration and
had very different rights.

[75] SC to all Coast DCs, 19 Jan. 1925, A. de V. Wade, for CNC to SC, 16 Feb. 1925,
KNA PC Coast 1/12/286.

6

The Control of Trade

... the ignorant native of the hinterland is at the mercy of any peddling coast native.

(Vanga District Annual Report, 1916–17)

Government interference in the trade networks of the coast took two distinct forms. The first was the attempt to limit participation in certain small-scale trades, notably that in palm wine, which were partly bound up with the clientship networks of Mombasa. These attempts led over time to the transformation of the kind of clientship through which these networks were constructed. The second form of government interference was an attempt to destroy the influence of Arab and Swahili traders in the hinterland.

The Palm Wine Regulations of 1900 were first introduced as a revenue-raising measure.[1] They required anyone selling palm wine to obtain a licence, at a cost of 15 rupees per annum.[2] By 1903 these regulations had been applied to the whole coast. The trade was clearly a profitable one, for hundreds of licences were taken out, and even the raising of the fee to 25 rupees (nearly three months' wages at the prevailing rates) did not dissuade sellers.[3] By 1906, the local newspaper was associating palm wine with the shortage of labour on the coast and with the corrupting influence of Mombasa:

The drink curse has the lower class of the natives in the Mombasa district in its grip ... The habit is most rife among the mainland

---

[1] See the reasons advanced for the widening of the regulations in 1903; Sub-Commissioner to Commissioner, 22 July 1903, KNA PC Coast 1/1/93.

[2] Palm Wine Regulations, 24 Nov. 1900, KNA AG/4/1579.

[3] *EAS* (W), 24 Feb. 1906.

natives who come over here to labour, probably with the intention of earning their hut tax and then returning to their shambas. They are however drawn towards the wine market.[4]

Officials were more concerned with the income which this trade offered to hinterland people, who then had little incentive to seek wage labour.[5] Officials were also worried by the arrangements with Arab and Swahili landowners by which Nyika worked for a payment in palm wine.[6] Effective controls on the trade began after the 1912 labour commission had reported. In Mombasa and Rabai, the administration drastically curtailed the issue of licences: in 1912, 198 Rabai held licences, but in 1913 only thirty-nine did.[7] In Mombasa, where the number of licences issued dropped from seventy-four in 1912 to ten in 1914,[8] the District Commissioner sought to fix and limit the trade by giving licences only to those who had permanent premises from which to sell their wine,[9] ending the previous dominance of hawkers who had operated largely from the area of the Mackinnon Market on Salim Road.[10] Hobley encouraged these changes, and indeed persuaded the Assistant District Commissioner for Rabai out of his initial belief that palm-wine legislation could not increase the labour supply.[11] Hobley was particularly concerned at the involvement of women in the trade, and he sought to deny them licences— clearly perceiving the role that the palm-wine economy of the town played in supporting newly arrived Swahili women in the town. Women marketeers responded by applying for licences in the names of their husbands.[12]

Additional palm-wine legislation was introduced in 1915, but never enforced. In 1921 a further ordinance was introduced

    [4] Ibid.
    [5] ADC Rabai to Ag. PC, 16 Oct. 1907, KNA PC Coast 1/1/130.
    [6] SNA to Sec. for the Admin., 28 Sept. 1907, KNA PC Coast 1/1/130. The arrangement was theoretically illegal (ADC Mombasa to DC Mombasa, 14 Dec. 1908, KNA PC Coast 1/1/138), but the administration was unable to enforce this law.
    [7] ADC Rabai to PC, 27 Jan. 1913, KNA PC Coast 1/10/54.
    [8] DC Mombasa to PC, 20 Nov. 1912, DC Mombasa to PC, 4 Jan. 1915, KNA PC Coast 1/10/54.   [9] PC to DC Mombasa, 18 Dec. 1912, ibid.
    [10] Collector, Mombasa, to Sub-Commissioner, 4 Jan. 1906, KNA PC Coast 1/1/113.
    [11] PC to ADC Rabai, 20 Feb. 1913, PC to DC Mombasa, 18 Dec. 1912, KNA PC Coast 1/10/54; for the initially contrary views of Deacon, ADC Rabai, see ADC Rabai to PC, 24 Dec. 1912, ibid.
    [12] Morrison (a solicitor) to PC, 17 Dec. 1914, ibid.

to control the trade. Unlike the earlier regulations, this ordinance sought to control not just the sale but also the production of palm wine: a tree owner who wished to tap had to
possess a licence to do so, and a tapper had to be licensed to
work for a tree owner.[13]

These measures curtailed the easy access to cash which many,
particularly Rabai, had enjoyed through the palm-wine trade.
A considerable illegal trade continued, though, in the hinterland[14] and in the town. The restrictions led to an increasing
Rabai involvement in paid labour: but not in contract labour
for Europeans. Instead, a new kind of casual labour developed: tapping palm wine in Mombasa and its suburbs. The
difficulties of preventing coconut theft encouraged landowners
in Changamwe, Kisauni, and Mtongwe, and on the island, to
turn their palm trees over to the production of wine rather
than of nuts.[15] The licensing regulations favoured those with
more trees (as only one licence was required per owner, whatever the output of wine), and this became the most profitable
use of palm trees, far more lucrative than supplying whole
nuts or copra.[16] Some took to renting plantations from others
and using them to produce palm wine, which they sold to
licensed club owners.[17]

These landowners relied on Rabai or Digo as tappers; a
reliance that began because it was members of these groups
who knew most about tapping, and which continued as a result of the system of recruitment.[18] Workers lived on the estate
of their employer, and were at first paid half of the proceeds
from the sale of the palm wine which they tapped. Later, they
were paid a flat rate for each gourd of palm wine they produced.[19] There was no fixed contract or requirement to work
each day, nor was there a definite term of employ, but workers

---

[13] Ag. Governor to SoS, 22 July 1921, KNA AG/4/1523.

[14] For evidence of continued tapping, see Affidavit, Paya wa Jabu, KNA PC Coast
1/14/189; also Int. 39a, 36a.

[15] Int. 61a. A tree tapped for palm wine will not bear good coconuts.

[16] Int. 61b; also see the comments of Ali bin Salim el-Busaidi in the minutes of
'Conference Convened to Discuss the Coconut Ordinances', 20 Oct. 1920, KNA PC
Coast 1/1/165.

[17] Int. 36a, 61a. After 1934, the Municipality had a monopoly of legal alcohol sales
in Mombasa but continued to buy supplies of palm wine from these producers; Int.
43b.

[18] Int. 43a.   [19] Int. 43a, 36a.

were expected to provide a replacement for themselves when they left. The replacement was usually a relative from their homestead in Rabai.[20] For, unlike other casuals, the tappers remained part of the homestead, and returned to it: 'I was living here in Rabai . . . for sleeping, I slept there [Changamwe palm plantation], at the end of the month when I left, my mate would come. End of the month, when you go, your mate comes, I come back here . . . at the end of the month, I went down and relieved my mate again.'[21] Most of these tappers returned regularly to their homestead, some interspersing a few months of work with months or even years in the homestead.[22] Unlike the casual workers on the docks, these were truly migrant workers: the networks through which they found employment were based on their membership of clan or homestead, not on involvement in the town. Rabai avoided other kinds of work, able to do so because they could tap.[23] They also derived a considerable independent income by keeping back some of the wine which they tapped and selling it on their own account, an activity which allowed them to demonstrate their commitment to the homestead by remitting most of their other earnings.[24]

The government restricted the possibilities of earning from other small-scale marketing in Mombasa. Contagion was again the dominant metaphor in official discourse concerning these new restrictions; existing market arrangements were condemned as insanitary, and new market facilities were provided, in which cleanliness was the corollary of control. The Pigott Market, which was in the old town of Mombasa and frequented by large numbers of casual marketeers who paid a daily fee each time they came to sell their goods,[25] was condemned as insanitary and a danger to public health, and was finally closed in 1919.[26] Extra accommodation was to be provided at the Mackinnon Market on Salim Road for those displaced, but the stalls there were built of concrete, and rented monthly rather than daily (and at considerably greater cost than any stalls at

---

[20] Int. 36a, 32a.   [21] Int. 32a, 2.   [22] Int. 36a.
[23] Int. 31a.   [24] Int. 43b.
[25] Superintendent of Conservancy to PC, 25 Oct. 1918, KNA PC Coast 1/14/97.
[26] Collector, Mombasa, to Ag. Sub-Commissioner, 9 Aug. 1906, KNA PC Coast 1/1/113; MOH to Sub-Commissioner, 19 June 1905, KNA PC Coast 1/1/99; Acting Supt. Conservancy to PC, 26 Apr. 1917, KNA PC Coast 1/12/76.

Pigott had been).[27] On public health grounds, Hobley pushed through the closure of Pigott Market, and the enforcement of monthly renting, rather against the will of the Superintendent of the Conservancy Department.[28] Shortly after the move was enforced, the overheads of those selling from Mackinnon Market were raised further by additional public health regulations.[29] The income which some Swahili residents of Mombasa's mainland periphery—Changamwe, Kisauni, and Likoni—had obtained from petty produce-marketing, was thus curtailed.[30]

Small-scale marketing did not become impossible, however: by the 1930s, Mackinnon and other public markets were unable to rent out their stalls due to the competition from 'private' markets. These were collections of insubstantial stalls, erected on private land by casual marketeers.[31] The Municipal Board, complaining that these markets 'befouled the town',[32] tried to force them to close down by imposing an enormous 'licence' fee (one hundred pounds) on the landowners involved.[33] It is not clear how successful this was.

Hawkers in Mombasa also had their lives made more difficult by measures introduced to improve public health. Before the First World War, water had been obtainable free of charge from the numerous wells on the island.[34] However, access to the water had not been entirely free: it was not physically

[27] Mombasa District Annual Report (Apr.–Dec. 1921), 10, KNA DC MSA 1/3; PC to Supt. Conservancy, 10 Aug. 1916; and Supt. Conservancy to PC, 1 Feb. 1917, both in KNA PC Coast 1/12/76.

[28] PC to Supt. Conservancy, 14 Apr. 1916, PC to Director of Public Works, 27 Apr. 1917; for opposition of the Superintendent, Sanderson, to the cost of stalls on the new market, see Supt. Conservacy to PC, 18 Apr. 1916, all in KNA PC Coast 1/12/76.

[29] Stallholders were required to clear their goods from the market completely each evening; PC to Supt. Conservancy, 7 Jan. 1919, ibid; Ag. MOH to PC, 9 Jan. 1919, KNA PC Coast 1/14/97.

[30] For a letter from one such small marketeer, see the letter of Salama binti Amani, EAS (W), 8 Sept. 1906.

[31] Minutes, Mombasa Municipal Finance Committee, 28 Feb. 1933, and Mombasa Municipal Health Committee, 3 Mar. 1933.

[32] Minutes, Mombasa Municipal Health Committee, 17 Jan. 1933.

[33] Ibid. 3 Mar. 1933; Minutes Mombasa Municipal Board, 8 Aug. 1933.

[34] For use of well water, see Int. 54a. For a list of the 140 wells on Mombasa Island in 1913, see KNA DC MSA 8/1. There had been constant worries about the supply and quality of water in Mombasa (EAS (W), 1 Dec. 1906; Report of Medical Department for 1904, 22 June 1905, PRO CO 533. 2), and water was piped in from the Shimba Hills at considerable expense; EAS (W), 5 Aug. 1911; Governor to SoS, 23 Mar. 1930, PRO CO 533. 399/1.

possible to draw water from most of the wells by hand, and networks of patronage had developed around those, mostly Hadhrami Arabs, who owned the beams and pulleys which were needed to hoist water up. They had as their clients a number of men who hawked the water through the streets of the town.[35] Following the completion of the Shimba Hills water pipe-line in 1918, a number of the wells were closed on public health grounds, and water was sold by the authorities from public kiosks at a price set to undercut the hawkers. None the less, people were still willing to pay to have water brought to their houses, so that although the hawkers now had to buy water before they could sell it, and previous patronage networks were disrupted, some could still make a living from hawking water.[36]

Those small producers who hawked their own goods in Mombasa suffered from these changes, but so too did the traders, the Swahili and others of Mombasa who dealt in the produce of other people. It was they who were the *tajiri*, in a small way, of Nyika who brought their goods along the creek trading routes and to the old port. The capital required to sell goods in Mombasa had been increased by the new markets, and thus so had the expense of playing the *tajiri*'s role as patron/agent of a producer. As patrons and clients were financially squeezed, the relationships between them became far less personal, losing the additional ties and obligations constructed around the actual or potential adoption of the client that had characterized earlier relationships.[37] A Duruma who sold chickens in Mombasa in the 1930s described a relationship with his Arab *tajiri* which, while excluding other buyers, was never expressed in terms of family:

These Shihiri, I don't know them, I don't know his name, no. When I arrived I was given my money and went home . . . I sold to him, never to another, just him. He would get used to you, who you are, so that if you come with your goods you don't sell to anybody else . . . he knew that 'this is my man, when his produce comes, he doesn't sell it to anyone else, he sells it to me'. So you go to his house,

---

[35] Res. Engineer, Mombasa Water Supply to Director of Public Works, 15 June 1915, KNA PC Coast 1/14/175.
[36] Ibid.; Memo, Hobley, 1 Oct. 1915, ibid.; Int. 43*b*, 49*a*.   [37] Int. 21*b*.

he welcomes you, you drink tea, and finish, then you count your produce, it's alright, it's alright, he pays you. You go home.[38]

The transformation in these relationships was not immediate or complete: the private markets survived, at least for a time, as outlets for the less capitalized trader, and in some forms of trade, notably that in fish, incorporative networks survived this period. Nyika coming occasionally to Mombasa to sell fish came to rely on town patrons in the fish-market (which had not been moved or improved) as business partners. Under the influence, and with the help, of these patrons some moved permanently to the town.[39]

In the hinterland, official policies in this period struck rather more directly at relationships of credit and clientage. They were policies framed in the idiom of moral corruption, rather than of physical contagion, and their major targets were the Arab and Swahili traders of the hinterland.

In 1909, the Assistant District Commissioner of Rabai had complained of the 'usury and other malpractices'[40] perpetrated by these traders and had proposed 'licensing every trader inside the Native reserve who cannot show that he is on the lands of his own tribe'.[41] Traders of whom officials disapproved could then be refused licences and expelled. The suggestion was not then taken up, and in 1913 the Assistant District Commissioner complained again of the 'Swahili invasion' of traders who controlled all the produce of the area so effectively that he had to buy food from the border of German East Africa, sixty miles away.[42] After 1915, in the context of the general policy of separation, the aim of expelling these traders was pursued more vigorously. Arguing for the creation of controlled trade centres, officials justified the policy as necessary to protect the hinterland people from being cheated.[43] Significantly, one of the complaints against these traders was that they enticed women away with them to town. It was this movement of dissatisfied women on which many of the coast's incorporative

---

[38] Int. 66a, 4–5.   [39] Int. 55a.
[40] ADC Rabai to DC Mombasa, 25 Nov. 1909, KNA PC Coast 1/12/53.
[41] Ibid.
[42] ADC Rabai to PC, 13 May 1913, KNA PC Coast 1/14/11.
[43] Vanga District Annual Report (1915–16), 8, KNA DC KWL 1/1.

networks were based, for these women provided initial contacts in Mombasa for other migrants from the hinterland. 'The
market system is not a popular one with the Arabs and wa-
Swahili who wish to be allowed to wander through the reserve
and trade wherever opportunity occurs. This latter method is
undesirable as the wa-Nyika are apt to be swindled. Further
one of the objects is to secure wa-Nyika women.'[44] In 1915, Arab
and Swahili traders were banned from the reserves, on the
grounds that it was illegal for them to occupy land in a reserve
without permission.[45] This attempt to separate the population
was the corollary of the attempts to force Nyika off coastal
lands. Over the next ten years, officials pursued a veritable
vendetta against these traders, constantly repeating the argument that their presence was a danger to the population of the
hinterland.[46] The traders, for their part, showed a considerable determination to maintain their presence.[47]

Where the government did displace them, these traders were
replaced by a system of gazetted and controlled 'trade centres', where plots were rented out under the watchful eye of the
administration. It was Hobley who insisted on the creation of
these centres, arguing (somewhat opaquely) that 'For administrative reasons I am desirous to found these centres for I am
convinced that it is the only way in which the natives will be
able to obtain a fair price for their produce.'[48] Hobley overrode
the hesitations of the Attorney-General on this question,[49] and
the District Commissioner of Vanga welcomed the establishment of the trade centres, writing that without them the 'ignorant native of the hinterland' was 'at the mercy of any peddling
coast native'.[50]

---

[44] Takaungu Subdistrict Annual Report (1916–17), KNA DC KFI 1/1.
[45] Vanga District Annual Report (1915–16), 8, KNA DC KWL 1/1.
[46] e.g. Notice to Quit, issued by DC Kilifi to Said bin Sheikh, 9 June 1922, KNA PC
Coast 1/14/177; Rabai Safari Diary, 22 Nov. 1918, KNA PC Coast 1/18/182; Kilifi Station
Diary, 30 Mar. 1926, KNA PC Coast 1/1/443; Kilifi Intelligence Report, Apr. 1924, KNA
PC Coast 1/17/13; and for the area south of Mombasa see D.C. Sperling, 'The Growth
of Islam among the Mijikenda of the Kenya Coast', Ph.D. thesis (London, 1988) 119–
20. For the determination of the traders, see Ag. DC Kilifi to SCC, 10 Aug. 1922, KNA
PC Coast 1/14/177.
[47] Kilifi Station Diary, 28 Mar. 1926, KNA PC Coast 1/1/443; Native Council minutes, 8 Feb. 1927, KNA PC Coast 1/12/281.
[48] PC to Chief Sec., 9 Feb. 1917, KNA AG/4/407.
[49] Memo, Attorney-General to Chief Sec., n.d., 1917, KNA AG/4/407.
[50] Vanga District Annual Report (1916–17), 27–8, KNA DC KWL 1/2.

As intended, these trade centres came to serve as hinterland markets outside the control of Arabs and Swahili. The capital requirements of paying a lease and building and stocking a new shop discouraged such men, many of whom were in debt anyway. Instead, Indian traders took up most of the leases in the new centres. Close official scrutiny in these centres threatened the illicit trade in ivory which had once been an irregular but useful source of income for traders in the hinterland.[51]

Events in 1919 revealed how very different the attitude of the administration was to Indian, rather than Arab or Swahili, traders. In that year the District Commissioner Kilifi noted that 'many natives, and especially the Headmen, were so deeply in debt that it was quite impossible for them to pay',[52] and he proposed an amendment to the Credit Trades Ordinance to limit the activities of traders.[53] The legislation was drafted, but never passed; aware that much of this credit trade was by then being carried on by Indian merchants in the trade centres rather than by Swahili or Arab traders, the Acting Provincial Commissioner recommended abandoning the legislation.[54] He did, however, agree to limit the use of Muslim courts, which Arab and Swahili creditors were using to uphold their claims over debtors.[55]

The essential difference between the Arab and Swahili traders who were expelled and the Indians who replaced them lay, in the administration's view, not so much in the problem of indebtedness; for debt to Indian traders seems to have increased as that to others decreased.[56] Rather, it was in the aspect of incorporative patronage that underlay indebtedness. Unlike the Arabs and Swahili, the Indian traders did not intermarry with the Nyika, nor did they encourage Africans to join their particular, usually Shi'ite, sects of Islam. There was no blurring

[51] Kilifi Intelligence Report, Sept. 1924, KNA PC Coast 1/17/13.
[52] DC Kilifi to Ag. PC, 17 June 1920, KNA PC Coast 1/19/1. Other administrators reported similar levels of indebtedness; Ag. DC Malindi to PC, 3 Aug. 1918, DC Malindi to Ag. PC, 7 May 1920, Ag. PC to CNC, 8 Oct. 1919; Attorney-General to CNC, 13 Apr. 1920, KNA PC Coast 1/19/1.
[53] Ag. DC Kilifi to Ag. PC, 28 Jan. 1920, KNA PC Coast 1/19/1.
[54] Ag. PC to CNC, 29 June 1920, ibid. For the Indian involvement in the credit trade, and official justifications of credit trade, see Ag. DC Vanga to PC, 3 Aug. 1918; Ag. DC Malindi to PC, 22 Sept. 1919; DC Malindi to Ag. PC, 7 May 1920; DC Malindi to Ag. PC, 17 June 1920, ibid.
[55] Ag. PC to CNC, 29 June 1920, ibid.
[56] Memo, 'The Development of the Coast', 1922, KNA PC Coast 1/1/165.

of ethnic lines here, no adoption of outsiders as junior family members. Forms of patronage did develop around some Indian employers in Mombasa,[57] but they did not incorporate these clients.

The expulsion of the Arab and Swahili traders, like the restrictions on the palm-wine trade and marketing in Mombasa, produced neither an upsurge in production for the market nor any immediate increase in the numbers seeking wage labour. Some of the Swahili and Arab patrons retained a position in the reserves through the use of surrogates,[58] and so continued their lending and patronage activities. Many producers were still bound by debt, if often now to new, Indian creditors. In the longer term, members of hinterland groups responded to the restrictions placed on their options by creating new alternatives; seeking still, in new ways, to decide for themselves how best they could get by.

[57] Int. 47a, 34a.   [58] Int. 26c.

7

Planning Mombasa

Government wanted the land for the location of natives
who go and work on the steamers, to avoid carrying
plague.

(Ali bin Salim el-Busaidi, 1931)

In the years after 1912, while the boundaries and the commerce of the hinterland were being altered by the administration, the town of Mombasa itself was similarly reshaped through
town planning. In Mombasa, as elsewhere in the world, authorities sought to remake urban physical space in order to
change social relationships.[1] As with the reshaping of the hinterland, official discourse around the planning of the town
invoked an imagery of moral and physical contamination, which
emphasized the importance of establishing proper boundaries
and preventing the incorporation of even more migrants into
the Swahili population.

For a number of reasons, the implementation of these plans
in the town was considerably delayed. While serious planning
had begun under Hobley in 1913, the remaking of the town
began only in the later 1920s, and came some time after the
peak of attempts to enforce the policies of separation in the
hinterland. Unable to impose their will on the hinterland,
the administration sought at least to control the town.

Mombasa presented administrators with kinds of problem that
were unusual in East Africa. It had long been a settlement of

[1] See e.g. G. Stedman Jones, *Outcast London: A Study of the Relationship between Classes
in Victorian Society* (Oxford, 1971); F. Cooper (ed.), *Struggle for the City: Migrant Labor,
Capital and the State in Urban Africa* (Beverly Hills, Calif., 1983).

considerable size, in which houses and roads had developed over a long period without planning or central control. Even more importantly, much of the land on the island was claimed as private property under a system of law which the administration was obliged to recognize, so that officials were unable to simply allocate and reallocate space to suit their purposes.[2] Mombasa was, as some Europeans commented, a 'native' town,[3] challenging the colonial notion of the city as a European area in which space must be controlled and ordered.[4] Concerned as they were with regulation and good order, officials felt the physical complexity of Mombasa's alleys and houses to be an affront. As with the replanning of Mombasa's markets, official disapproval of the complexity of society within the town found expression through reference to the insanitary nature of the physical structures of this society.[5]

The first major exercise in town planning had, in fact, begun before the relocation of the markets, but was similarly concerned with the location, and hence the control, of commerce. During the first three decades of colonial rule, Mombasa's main harbour was moved from the anchorage on the north side of the island, known as Mombasa harbour, to that on the south, which was known as Kilindini. The move was not as uncontroversial as has been implied;[6] for it was a move away from a harbour where land and warehouse accommodation were largely in Arab and Indian hands, and where labour was organized in ways over which the shipping companies had little influence. The major shipping companies and some officials went so far as to urge the administration to ban steamships

[2] Hobley regretted that the IBEA Company had not bought more land on the island, allowing the government to redesign the town at an earlier stage; C. W. Hobley, *Kenya: From Chartered Company to Crown Colony* (London, 1929), 71. Most of the land on Mombasa was in private hands; 'Memo on the Formation of the Land Titles Board', Hamilton, 27 Jan. 1906, PRO CO 533. 18; also K. Janmohamed, 'A History of Mombasa' c.1895–1939', Ph.D. thesis (Northwestern, 1977), 215.

[3] Janmohamed, 'African Labourers in Mombasa, c.1895–1940', in B. A. Ogot (ed.), *Economic and Social History of East Africa* (Nairobi, 1976), 172.

[4] Cooper (ed.), *Struggle for the City*, 18.   [5] See Ch. 6.

[6] Cooper treats the transfer of harbours as a natural consequence of the superior physical attributes of Kilindini; *On the African Waterfront* (New Haven, Conn., 1987), 27. In the long term this may have been the case, but Mombasa harbour could and did successfully accommodate steamers of the period; see Memorandum, Ainsworth, Military Commissioner for Labour, 18 July 1917, KNA PC Coast 1/9/42.

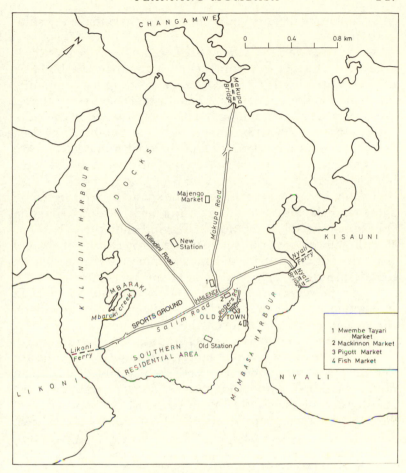

MAP 6. *Mombasa Island*

from using Mombasa harbour.[7] This was not done, but from
the time of the Company, the administration had seen Kilindini
as the future site of the harbour,[8] and they concentrated investment in infrastructure there, against considerable protest

[7] Smith Mackenzie and Co. to HM Commissioner, 3 Jan. 1906, PRO CO 533. 11;
Crown Advocate to Acting Commissioner, 24 Nov. 1905, PRO CO 533. 6. Smith Mackenzie and Co. was owned by the British India Steam Navigation (BISN) Co., which
was intimately involved in the IBEA Co. and the beginnings of colonial rule in East
Africa; J. Forbes Munro, 'Shipping Subsidies and Railway Guarantees: William Mackinnon, Eastern Africa and the Indian Ocean, 1860–1893', *JAH* 28 (1987), 207–30.
[8] Pigott, IBEA Administrator to IBEA Sec., 21 Jan. 1893, IBEA File 52 (20).

from Indian merchants and from Europeans outside the shipping industry.[9]

After 1924, the dominance of Kilindini over Mombasa was assured by further government investment, in the building of deep-water berths.[10] Two European shipping companies dominated Kilindini, having gradually taken control of almost all aspects of cargo-handling.[11] This consolidation of the shipping companies' position in the 1920s seems to have been associated with a renegotiation of their accommodation with the networks of patronage which controlled dock labour. Through this renegotiation, a man of Chonyi origins called Salim bin Ali came for a while to dominate the recruitment of shorehandlers, his powers as a patron being heavily reliant on the support of the companies.[12] Having shifted the harbour to Kilindini, away from the commercial networks of the old port, the administration and the shipping companies had in part transformed the networks of labour recruitment.

It was, however, in replanning the residence of Mombasa's population that officials were to have their greatest impact on the society of the town; even though the plans were never completed and the eventual effect was far from that intended.

The debate over town planning was begun by the Collector and the Director of Public Works in 1907. Their ideas, and an additional proposal from the Commissioner of Lands, favoured the division of the island into areas, and the separation of African from European housing.[13] The problems of any such

[9] For Indian and European business reaction to these policies, see Phirozsham Gimi, Ag. Hon. Sec., Mombasa Chamber of Commerce to HM Commissioner, 15 Oct. 1906, printed in *EAS* (W), 20 Oct. 1906; and the editorial in *EAS* (W), 11 Aug. 1906. The Chamber of Commerce similarly resisted attempts to force all traffic to Kilindini by use of the health regulations; Memo of Minutes, Mombasa Township Committee, 28 Aug. and 8 Oct. 1912, KNA PC Coast 1/11/377. For the concentration of investment at Kilindini, see also *EAS* (W), 7 Sept. 1912; Minutes of Mombasa Sites Board, 30 Dec. 1914, KNA PC Coast 1/11/377.

[10] For the expense of this programme, see e.g. *Kenya Colonial Report for 1929* (London, 1930), 40.

[11] The major companies involved were the Union Castle and the BISN, who, after 1927, controlled cargo handling at the port through a jointly owned subsidiary, the Kenya Landing and Shipping Company; see 'Report of the Port Commission of Enquiry', Dec. 1925, KNA AG/4/2941; and 'Agreement for Handling Cargo at Mombasa', 13 Apr. 1927, KNA AG/4/2937.   [12] Int. 71*b*.

[13] 'Report of the Town Extension Plan for Section of Mombasa Island', MacGregor Ross, Sept. 1907, Memo, Commissioner of Lands, 17 May 1909, KNA PC Coast 1/14/98.

scheme, particularly the enormous expense of buying the land involved, meant that the idea was dropped for several years.

In 1912, an outbreak of pneumonic plague in Mombasa killed a number of Africans,[14] and inspired town planning proposals from Hobley and other officials: proposals which revealed the depth of their frustration at the unmanageability of Mombasa, and the extent to which they associated problems of control with those of disease and infection. Hobley suggested that a line of soldiers be drawn up across the island, separating the largely African and Asian north and east of the island from the mainly European enclave in the south. The island would be sealed off from the mainland, and 'those Asiatics and Africans who wish to leave the island will have to remain 7 days under observance in an isolation camp'.[15] In order to feed this isolated island, '[markets] will be so arranged so that sellers from the mainland will be able to cross the various ferries, enter barbed wire bomas and sell their produce over the fence to natives of the island standing outside the same'.[16]

In was an extravagant fantasy, which the administration had no resources to support, and which came to nothing. Yet in identifying the population of the island as a source of contamination, controllable only by the most extreme measures, it reveals something of the preoccupations of local administrators in 1912—the year of the Native Labour Commission, as well as of the pneumonic plague.

1913 was something of a year for new policy initiatives, and it was in that year that Professor Simpson was despatched to East Africa by the Colonial Office. Combining the role of health expert and town planner, Simpson epitomized the approach to planning that has been called the 'sanitation syndrome'.[17] He was a founder of the School of Hygiene and Tropical Medicine, had worked on the planning of Cape Town, and was held in considerable awe by the Colonial Office.[18] He produced a long and detailed report on Mombasa which comprehensively

[14] 'Daily Bulletin', Medical Officer of Health (MOH), 15 Nov. 1912, KNA PC Coast 1/15/90.
[15] PC to Chief Sec. 12 Oct. 1912, ibid.   [16] Ibid.
[17] M. W. Swanson, 'The Sanitation Syndrome: Bubonic Plague and Urban Native Policy in the Cape Colony, 1900–1909', *JAH* 18 (1977), 387–419.
[18] R. W. Baldock, 'Colonial Governors and the Colonial State: A Study of British Policy in Tropical Africa, 1918–1925', Ph.D. thesis (Bristol, 1978), 326–7.

damned the town as a health risk, asserting that 'the condition of the greater part of the native town is so radically bad that ordinary measures to improve its sanitary state will not be effective'.[19]

Simpson set out in some detail the extraordinary measures which he therefore considered necessary. Like the planners of 1907, he proposed the division of the town into different areas for African and European housing, the two to be separated by a chain of parks and public places to prevent the spread of contagion; trees would take the place of Hobley's soldiers.[20] Simpson's plans went beyond those of 1907, however, for he sought to introduce another division in the population, beyond the simple one of colour.

Simpson, unusually for a European observer in this period, had some praise for the Swahili in his report: 'The western portion of the town consists principally of makuti huts inhabited chiefly by Swahilis and by Africans from the interior who have been Islamised and who have adopted the Swahili mode of life . . . on the whole they and their surroundings are kept in a comparatively clean condition.'[21] Simpson presented the obverse of the discourse of infection then current, changing the nature of the contamination—from a spread of laziness to a spread of disease—and reversing the direction of contamination. He wrote that 'The Swahili or coast people are cleanly in their habits, and it is of the highest importance that they should retain that virtue which is very difficult to practise when their dwellings are intermingled with lodging houses for primitive Africans who, cleanly in their villages, are unable to adapt themselves to the conditions of town life.'[22]

To safeguard the Swahili from this threat, Simpson proposed that land be set aside for the construction of 'a model town for the more permanent Swahili and African population'. For other Africans in Mombasa was needed 'a site for a native location where the labourers who are mostly engaged at the Kilindini Harbour can reside under healthy conditions and where the larger part of the floating population will find suitable accommodation'.[23] The view of the Swahili as a population

---

[19] Simpson, 'Report on the Sanitation of Mombasa', 13 Sept. 1913, 9, KNA MOH 1/1231.
[20] Ibid. 16.   [21] Ibid. 5–6.   [22] Ibid. 16–17.   [23] Ibid. 11.

somehow separate from the casual labour force was a fantasy—all other evidence shows very clearly that the 'floating population' was in fact rather firmly grounded in the Swahili community of Mombasa, and Simpson's concern with the idea of a floating population reflected thinking then current in the Empire, rather than a realistic assessment of conditions in Mombasa. Yet in the context of the official discourse of 1913, the notion of separation was an attractive one, and Hobley embraced Simpson's suggestions wholeheartedly.[24] Mombasa's labour force would be made more tractable if such a distinction were to be created, as it would break the influence of Swahili patrons on casual labourers and turn these labourers into purely temporary migrants. Simpson's proposal to 're-duce the overcrowding in the Old Town'[25] by moving people from there and dividing them between the model town and the location would do much to limit the incorporative power of Swahili identity.

Simpson's plan was strikingly similar to one that had been put forward by the Director of Government Transport in 1907: infuriated by the control which Swahili 'headmen' exercised, he had suggested that Africans coming to Mombasa be housed in 'a separate settlement, on the outskirts of the town, or a large shed erected to house them'.[26] The assumption, implicit in Simpson's plan, that Africans in controlled, officially supplied, housing were healthier, was questionable,[27] but it fitted well with the dominant discourse of the time: some Africans belonged in the town, but they should remain in the town, as a distinct and clearly separate group marked by their Muslim religion as well as by urban residence. All other Africans were unfitted for long-term life in the town and threatened public health by their presence in all but the most carefully controlled urban setting.

[24] PC to Chief Sec., 16 Sept. 1913, KNA MOH 1/1231; and Hobley, App. 2 to 'Report on the Sanitation of Mombasa', ibid. 5–6.

[25] Simpson, 'Report on the Sanitation of Mombasa', ibid. 13. This relocation would partly be achieved by strict building controls, to prevent the extension of houses to accommodate more dependants; Ibid. 19.

[26] Director of Transport to SNA, 16 Aug. 1907, KNA PC Coast 1/12/41.

[27] The 1912 plague began among some of the few workers who were housed by their employer, those of the Public Works Department; Confidential, MOH, 9 Sept. 1912, KNA PC Coast 1/15/90.

This was a policy clearly distinct from that pursued in Mombasa in the late 1930s and 1940s, when the concern of the administration had shifted to the development of a stable and regular working class in Mombasa.[28] To this end, the administration sought in those years to remove the threat posed by the 'residuum' of casual labourers whose contacts with the local hinterland allowed them to resist attempts to impose stricter work discipline upon them. The administration then sought to regularize these labourers, making them both permanent employees and settled residents, as part of a general plan to produce a work-force imbued with the right attitude to work. Yet such plans were laid in quite different circumstances to those of the early twentieth century: until the later 1920s, casuality and migrancy in Mombasa were not synonymous; the bulk of the casuals were long-term residents of Mombasa. It was this long-term residence, and the associated ability to lose themselves in the town, that gave people freedom from a system of control and identification based on the homestead: and this was the freedom that the administration sought to restrict. In 1913, employers and officials still wanted migrant labour, for the realization that 'cheap labour was expensive'[29] was yet to come. The concern of officials was, if anything, to create the 'floating population', not to abolish it.

In 1914, Hobley began acquiring the land necessary for the implementation of the Simpson scheme, buying and leasing more than one hundred acres of island land from the *liwali*, Ali bin Salim, and another landowner.[30] Ali bin Salim was later to claim that, as a favour, he had sold this land cheaply, in a phrase that encapsulates the association of uncontrolled casual labour with disease: 'Government wanted the land for the location of natives who go and work on the steamers to avoid carrying plague. It was for this reason we gave the land for much less than what the land was worth.'[31] Ali bin Salim made this claim as part of a demand for compensation for the land

[28] Cooper, *On the African Waterfront*, Intro.
[29] Cooper (ed.), *Struggle for the City*, 22.
[30] Crown Counsel to Commissioner for Local Government, Lands and Settlement, 25 June 1931, KNA AG/4/1736.
[31] Ali bin Salim to Commissioner for Local Government, Lands, and Settlement, 4 Mar. 1931, ibid.

some eighteen years later—for the land had not in fact been
used for the building of a location. Though Hobley had started
acquiring land, finance was not available to follow the plan
through. Hobley himself had estimated that the laying of roads,
the erection of new buildings, and most of all the compensation to displaced householders and landowners, would cost
well over £70,000.[32] The Berlin Treaty, which at that time still
limited British rule on the coast, effectively precluded the im-
position of a local property tax to finance this work.[33] With the
start of the First World War, demands on the official purse
increased, and the appallingly high death-rate among conscripted Africans in the Mombasa Carrier Corps hospital forced
the administration to use some of its scarce island land for
a new cemetery.[34] The administration temporarily shelved all
attempts at town planning, but the intention to implement the
Simpson plan was maintained.[35]

Housing in Mombasa, and the shape of the town itself,
continued to develop beyond official control, reliant instead on
personal contact, kinship, and clientship. Official criticism of
the condition of the town continued to locate the problem in
the Old Town and the mixed population there:

The housing of the Swahili in the older portions of the town, i.e. such
parts as lie between the Salim Road and Mombasa harbour is,
however, extremely bad. The ground is uneven and difficult to keep
clean . . . It may be of course that the best Swahili have migrated to
the areas first mentioned and only the poorer and lower-class natives
and communities such as the Washihiri to whom dirt does not seem
to be repugnant have remained.[36]

Kin and clientship were important in finding housing not only
in the Old Town of Mombasa, but in the growing western part
of the town. Here, most of the householders did not own the
land on which their houses stood, but rented it from Arab or
Indian landowners. It was this part of the town which housed
the bulk of the new arrivals in Mombasa in the first decades

---

[32] PC to Chief Sec., 16 Sept. 1913, KNA MOH 1/1231.
[33] Hobley, *Kenya: From Chartered Company to Crown Colony*, 150–1.
[34] PC to Principal Sanitation Officer, 31 Oct. 1917, KNA PC Coast 1/12/285.
[35] PC to Land Officer, 10 Feb. 1915, KNA MOH 1/3876.
[36] Mombasa District Native Annual Report (1919), 2, KNA PC Coast 1/12/279; see
also Labour Inspection Officer to CNC, 17 July 1919, KNA PC Coast 1/9/53.

of this century.[37] The householders had no security of tenure on their plots;[38] they could be evicted at any time, but rarely were, for the rent from these tenants was the only income the landowner earned from the land.[39]

The process of renting was already in transition in 1913; at that time householders paid an initial lump sum of two to five rupees for permission to build (similar to the payments made for use of land on the mainland) and then paid a monthly rental of between half and one rupee. The monthly payments, the amounts of which were steadily increasing,[40] were an innovation and were steadily displacing the lump sum payment and the clientship relationship which this had established. Landowners were beginning to look for a regular income rather than a one-off payment to establish their claims over their 'tenants'.[41] However, while the aspect of clientship in the provision of land for building was in decline, such relationships continued to be important for those seeking accommodation in someone else's house.[42]

Official laments at the uncontrolled nature of building by these householders—whose houses were, of course, called 'Swahili' houses[43]—continued through the early 1920s.[44] Problems of compensation and expense forestalled attempts to introduce a town plan until 1926 when, after the passage of appropriate enabling legislation and a lengthy period of consultation with landowners over the nature of compensation, a new town plan was published and attempts began to put it into effect.[45]

It has been suggested that official enthusiasm for planned segregation diminished in Kenya after 1921,[46] but Simpson's

[37] Int. 61a.

[38] For an example of the conditions under which land was occupied, see Entry 566A, in Transactions Register A17, for 1904. The terms of this arrangement were fairly standard.

[39] Hobley, App. 2 to 'Report on the Sanitation of Mombasa', KNA MOH 1/1231, 5–6.   [40] Simpson, 'Report on the Sanitation of Mombasa', ibid. 13.

[41] Hobley, App. 2 to 'Report on the Sanitation of Mombasa', ibid. 5.

[42] Int. 61a, 43a, 56a.

[43] PC to Supt. of Conservancy, 10 Sept. 1915, KNA PC Coast 1/14/134.

[44] Ibid.; see also Chief Sanitation Officer to PC, 30 July 1913, KNA PC Coast 1/11/104; and Mombasa District Annual Report (1920–1), 3, KNA PC Coast 1/1/412.

[45] The enabling ordinance was passed in 1919. The town plan was published as the *Mombasa Town Planning Scheme* (Nairobi, 1926); there is a copy in KNA AG/4/1348.

[46] Baldock, 'Colonial Governors', 338–9.

influence on the 1926 plan is clear. The town plan set aside a commercial area, banned trade from some residential areas, and proposed the driving of roads through some of the most densely populated areas of the town. The number of buildings per acre was limited to twenty, and new or modified buildings were not to cover more than one-half of the area of the plot on which they stood. The 'Southern Residential Area', south of the Fort, was set aside for exclusively European settlement. Most importantly, the scheme retained Simpson's suggestion that the African population be divided: one area was set aside for a 'Model Swahili Dwelling House Scheme' and another for the 'accommodation of African casual labourers'.[47]

The discourse in which this separation was situated had shifted, though: no longer was it one of Swahili suitability to urban life, and the dangers to public health that newcomers to the town posed. The concern in the mid-1920s was with the contaminating influence which the Swahili had on the morals of others: just as ten years before, it was such contamination in the hinterland that had been the central concern. In town too, the Swahili had come to be seen as the vectors of moral disease. The views of Ainsworth-Dickson, the Resident Commissioner of Mombasa in the mid-1920s and a man who had started his career as a junior official under Hobley, have already been noted. In 1925, he described Swahili youth as 'loafing through the days, contaminating every tribe in the country through personal example before those of its members temporarily residing in Mombasa'.[48]

The part of the scheme that had the most immediate effect on Africans and the poorer Arabs in Mombasa was the scheme of demolitions and clearances to make way for wider roads and public buildings. From 1926 many were evicted in such clearances.[49] The agreement of landowners to the 1926 scheme had been won by guarantees that they would be compensated, and that a board would be established to hear all claims for compensation. The negotiations leading up to this agreement revealed a split among Mombasan landowners. Opposition to

[47] Draft Order, dated 20 Mar. 1926, in *Mombasa Town Planning Scheme*, KNA AG/4/1348. [48] Mombasa District Annual Report (1925), 6, KNA DC MSA 1/3. [49] Ibid. (1926), 4; also R. Stren, 'A Survey of Lower Income Areas in Mombasa', in J. Hutton (ed.), *Urban Challenge in East Africa* (Nairobi, 1970), 97–115.

the possibility of forced land acquisition was initially general, but Ali bin Salim el-Busaidi, the *liwali*, persuaded most landowners to accept the plans.[50] These plans offered compensation to landowners, but not to the houseowners whose property stood on the land of others. Small landowners, who were more likely to own one or two houses on the land, as well as the plot itself, maintained their opposition to the town plan, as did those who owned only houses and not the land on which they stood. Correctly, these groups foresaw that, their houses destroyed without compensation, the cost of rebuilding would force them into 'recourse to money-lenders with payment of ruinous interest'.[51] The small landowners described themselves as the 'Arab, Baluchi and Swahili landowners'.[52]

Most of the larger landowners (that is, those with more than one acre of island land), whose relationships with those who had built on their land were primarily financial, readily accepted the town plan, but a small group, all Arab or Swahili, maintained their opposition.[53] At least two of this small group are still remembered as patrons and providers of land to Nyika and other immigrants to Mombasa:[54] it seems likely that these landowners were protecting the position of their client-tenants, who faced eviction and loss of property without compensation. Ali bin Salim, once himself a considerable patron in this way,[55] had made his own, highly successful accommodation with the colonial state, and no longer needed such clients.

The Town Planning Authority fought and won a court case over their refusal to recognize an obligation to compensate householders.[56] When the Authority offered *ex gratia* payments to some householders, of up to 50 per cent of the value of their dwellings,[57] there were accusations that landowners were evicting householders before the Authority took over the land; the householders had no security of tenure, and the landowner could expect better compensation if the Authority paid none to

---

[50] Mombasa District Annual Report (1924), 3, KNA DC MSA 1/3.
[51] Objection 3, 25 Oct. 1924, in *Mombasa Town Planning Scheme*, KNA AG/4/1348.
[52] Ibid. Objection 2, 15 Mar. 1924.
[53] Ali bin Salim to Res. Commissioner, Mombasa, printed in *Mombasa Town Planning Scheme*.
[54] Int. 72a, 26b.   [55] Int. 67a.
[56] Mombasa District Annual Report (1930), 3, KNA DC MSA 1/3.
[57] Ibid. (1929), 6.

householders. Ali bin Salim was himself accused of this practice in 1931.[58]

The bulk of these clearances took place in the 'western' town,
to the west of Salim Road, in the areas of Hailendi, Shehe
Jundani, and Mwembe Tayari. Kibokoni and Bondeni, both
in the 'Old Town', were also the site of a number of clearances.[59] It was to the western part of the town that many migrants from the hinterland first came, and Bondeni was the
area of Mombasa that the Ribe and Kauma claimed, and where
many of them found relatives with whom to stay.[60]

It began in Hailendi. Number one, Hailendi. Where the hospital was
built, the Lady Grigg. We had our houses, our *wajombas*, they were
all moved. You see, from there, where the 'Blue Room' [a restau-
rant] is, Shehe Jundani, up to Kilindini Road, there were houses.
Now where are they? Houses, like these ones, local houses. They
were knocked down. And there was nothing, no money. It was bad
in those days . . . There came an order, if the landowner wanted the
houses, you had to go . . . people weren't happy, some people had
built very good houses, they were told 'knock them down'. They
were dying . . .[61]

The town plan operated to separate the interests of landowners and their tenants in a new and dramatic way, and so
to undermine the networks that housed so many migrants to
Mombasa.[62] Even landowners who were not directly affected
by the clearances faced penalties for maintaining previous
systems of clientship. A punitive tax was imposed on those
with undeveloped land, and the definition of 'undeveloped land'
seems to have included that on which 'unauthorized dwellings' stood.[63]

Mombasa's population shifted further westwards in the face
of the clearances, to the new areas of Kaloleni, Sidiriya, and
Majengo. The change came swiftly, as the 1927 Annual Report
remarked:

[58] Mbarak Hinawy to Under-SoS, 14 May 1931, PRO CO 533. 411/6; see also
Janmohamed, 'A History of Mombasa', 309.   [59] Int. 71*b*.
[60] Int. 67*a*, 20*a*, 40*a*, 55*a*.   [61] Int. 71*b*, 9.
[62] In Cooper's terms, the town plan was intended to transform space, from 'illegal'
to 'legal' space; that is, from allocation through clientship to allocation through law
and money; Cooper (ed.), *Struggle for the City*, 31.
[63] Mombasa District Annual Report (1929), 1, KNA DC MSA 1/3.

The general trend of native housing of labour has been towards the Sidiriya, Kaloleni and Shimanzi areas, and this movement has been accentuated during the year by the demolitions under the Town Planning Scheme, and consequent establishment of Native Village Housing Schemes. It is estimated that the previously almost de-populated area to the northwest of Kilindini Road now has some 11,200 inhabitants whose numbers are increasing daily.[64]

Legal action was taken against those in the Old Town who tried to extend their houses to offer accommodation to family or clients,[65] further encouraging this relocation of the population.

In the new areas of the town, companies rather than indi-viduals owned much of the land—a large area of Majengo belonged to an estate company partly owned by the notorious European speculator, Major Grogan.[66] In 1930, a report noted some effects of the demolitions:

the Medical Authorities took the opportunity of insisting on the construction of houses of an improved type. The natives concerned foresaw the possibility of making money by letting rooms and readily fell in with the suggestion, but not having the necessary capital they borrowed from Indians at rates of interest from 50% to 120% ... The result is that rents of rooms range from Shs 10/- to Shs 25/- per month and, a still worse feature, numbers of houses are falling into the hands of Indian money-lenders.[67]

The renting of rooms under extremely cramped conditions was becoming common: 'five or more natives hire a room and each pays his proportion of the rent, but in some cases a native hires a room and sublets to any who may require a night's lodging, and as many as ten may sleep in one room'.[68] Houseowners were

[64] Mombasa District Annual Report (1927), 7, misfiled at KNA PC Coast 1/10/110.
[65] Ag. Governor to SoS, 18 Dec. 1930, KNA AG/4/3111.
[66] Janmohamed, 'A History of Mombasa', 200. Grogan's co-owner was Tannahill, a retired official of the Lands Office. He was not the only such official who acquired land and profited from it; for De Lacey's land, see Commissioner of Lands to Colonial Sec., 2 Apr. 1924, KNA AG/4/1889; and Janmohamed, 'A History of Mombasa', 197. Grogan, for his part, had already earned a reputation in Mombasa for profitable land speculation, particularly at Mbaraki, where he manoeuvred the government into buying back from him a lease which they had only recently issued: see Attorney-General to Ag. Chief Sec., 11 Feb. 1918, KNA AG/4/2947; and Colonial Sec. to Ag. Governor, 16 Mar. 1925, KNA AG/4/2949.
[67] 'Report on Native Affairs in Mombasa', Dec. 1930, 9, KNA DC MSA 3/3.
[68] Ibid. 10.

forced by debt to charge rent, and increasingly high rent, for
accommodation which might previously have been offered
through relationships of kin, as a kind of patronage, or in return
for occasional labour. Insecurity remained chronic, even in the
new areas: some houseowners suffered eviction several times
over as the clearances continued.[69]

The problems of indebtedness and rising rents were compounded by the administration's inability to carry through a
major part of the scheme: the construction of a location for
temporary residents and a 'model' housing scheme for the permanent population of the town. The 'Native Villages' granted
the official blessing of capital letters in the 1927 Annual Report
were private developments, and the 1926 plans for government
schemes never materialized.[70] Having found the money for
compensating landowners and building roads, the administration, particularly in the straitened circumstances of the late
1920s, could do no more.

After beginning the clearances, the administration effectively
lost control of the development of new housing to replace that
demolished. In 1928 the District Commissioner observed for-
lornly that 'it is impossible at present to predict the ultimate
position of the native residential area'.[71] There had been hopes
that the clearances would force Africans to live off the island,
in Miritini or Mtongwe[72]—the latter being described as 'a most
desirable area for housing and controlling the native population'[73]—but these came to nothing. The location of housing,
and the ways in which it was allocated, changed. But they
changed in ways unwelcome to the administration, and quite
beyond its control.[74] The population of the Mombasa area
continued to make the most of their options.

Yet the town plan had, to an extent, the desired effect. The
physical reshaping of residence was not enforced by the provision of housing, but financial pressures imposed by the

---

[69] Int. 71b.

[70] The 1930 Report noted and deplored this lack of action; 'Report on Native Affairs in Mombasa', Dec. 1930, 10–11, KNA DC MSA 3/3.

[71] Mombasa District Annual Report (1928), 3, KNA DC MSA 1/3.

[72] Native Affairs Department Annual Report, 1928 (Nairobi, 1929), 78.

[73] Res. Commissioner, Mombasa to Ag. Colonial Sec., 26 June 1925, KNA PC Coast
1/11/39.   [74] Int. 34a, 49a; see Part IV, below.

clearances contributed to a social reshaping. In 1929 the Native Affairs Department reported that 'The area between Makupa Road and the railway is developing rapidly as native quarters. This location houses large numbers of the floating population of Mombasa who work at Kilindini Harbour.'[75] By this time, the equation of the casual labour force with migrancy had some accuracy. Some at least of Mombasa's population had become a 'floating' population, as the incorporative potential of the town's networks declined in the face of house clearances, controls on trade, and other factors.[76] Town planning was, in a way, a victory for the administration, though it was a partial victory, and one that came late in the day. Ironically, only a few years later official efforts were to take a very different direction, towards the elimination of the floating population which the administration had struggled to create.[77]

[75] *Native Affairs Department Annual Report, 1929* (Nairobi, 1930), 78.
[76] See Part IV.   [77] Cooper, *On the African Waterfront*, 114–93.

8

Labour Legislation, Casuality, and the Cost of Labour

What use is a Mombasa wife? . . . they get there, they've
reached the land of luxury, they're lost

(Interview 43*a*)

While the policy of separation described in the preceding
chapters was conceived and implemented, direct efforts to
discipline Mombasa's labour force were continuing. The lack
of success which attended such measures in the years up
to 1912 had been the initial stimulus which brought forth
the separation policy. The continued lack of success of this
policy of separation, conceived by an administration ambi-
tious in its ideas but constrained in its resources, was revealed
by the continued expense of labour, and the difficulty which
officials encountered in enforcing new labour legislation. In
the later 1920s, when patterns of working and recruitment did
change significantly, these changes were due only in part to
the policy of separation, and they were beyond the control of
the administration.

Workers in Mombasa were, in theory, subject to a number of
coercive and restrictive laws and regulations. The 1903 Masters and Servants Ordinance, which made breach of contract
by an employee a criminal offence, was supplemented by special
Township Rules which required the registration of all porters,
messengers, and boatmen, so that even non-contracted employees in these jobs were subject to regulation. All of these
workers were required to carry badges of identification, and

faced deregistration and banning for any misconduct.[1] In 1910 a new Masters and Servants Ordinance outlawed the activities of the African 'labour agents' whom many coastal planters accused of stealing their labour by enticing workers away to the town to work under their patronage.[2] Yet officials and the police seem to have made little effort to enforce these laws, despite the complaints of irate employers:[3] whatever the law, desertion, 'crimping', and avoidance of registration continued to be common.[4]

Events at Kilindini harbour demonstrated the difficulty of enforcing such laws. An attempt there to enforce the registration of casual boat crews provoked a near riot, a strike, and then compromise on the part of the administration.[5] The official hand in this dispute was weakened by the government's own reliance on unidentifiable casuals: government boats were crewed by casuals, and while officials refused to allow private boats to work if their crews were not properly registered and controlled, they were unable to enforce this lock-out against the workers themselves, who could simply find work on the government's own boats.[6] Against the unidentifiable, the 'sanction of the sack' had no force; headmen, not employers, controlled recruitment, and a worker fired one day could be hired again the next.

It was the easy availability of casual labour, and the anonymity of the casual labour force, that made Mombasa's workforce so hard to discipline. When the First World War made these problems of discipline more acute, further attempts were made to control casual labourers, attempts which concentrated on the dock labour force.

[1] See 'Township Rules' and 'Registration of Boats', attached to Despatch 624, 28 Nov. 1906, PRO CO 533. 18.

[2] See *EAS* (W), 27 Oct. 1906; and the contents of file KNA AG/4/1612.

[3] See the comments on desertion in Part II, above. Also see Brand to Collector, Mombasa, 24 Feb. 1907, KNA PC Coast 1/12/41; *EAS* (D), 20 Apr. 1912; and J. Willis 'Thieves, Drunkards and Vagrants: Defining Crime in Colonial Mombasa', in D. Anderson and D. Killingray (eds.), *Policing the Empire: Government, Authority and Control 1830–1940* (Manchester, 1991), 219–35.

[4] 'Crimping' was the term used of the activities of labour touts. For the failure to enforce registration rules, see *EAS* (W), 24 Feb. 1912.

[5] See *EAS* (D) 21, 29 May and 21 June 1912, and *EAS* (W) 18 May 1912. For more details of this dispute, see Willis, 'Thieves, Drunkards and Vagrants', 223–5.

[6] Memo of Minutes of Mombasa Township Committee, 19 Sept. 1912, KNA PC Coast 1/11/377.

Before 1914 there had been occasional complaints of the slow speed of work in the docks,[7] but the war compounded these problems. Partly this was a result of the sheer volume of traffic, but it was also a product of the diversion of all non-military cargoes to Mombasa, rather than Kilindini, harbour:[8] the European shipping companies seem always to have been less confident about their control of labour on the Mombasa side.[9]

In 1916 the average daily need at the docks was for 386 workers only but although officials estimated that there were altogether more than 1,000 casuals who worked occasionally, there were often not enough workers on any given day. The Provincial Commissioner fulminated against the headmen who controlled the labourers,[10] but the employers[11] were too reliant on the *serangis* to challenge them directly by dispensing with their services. Dissatisfied with the employers' lack of action, the government instituted a registration scheme. By June 1917, only 791 porters retained their registration, the rest having been struck off for irregular working, and the District Commissioner wrote that 'the men now on the books are all genuine labourers and during the past month have worked an average of 10 days per month as against a previous average of less than two days'.[12]

It says much for the freedom which dock-workers had won for themselves that ten days labour a month was enough to earn the title of 'genuine labourer', at a time when other African workers found their months measured by thirty-working-day tickets. From the administration's point of view, worse was to come: by September, an average of only 100 workers a day were turning out,[13] and wages were higher than ever before.[14]

---

[7] PC to Chief Sec., 1 Aug. 1917, KNA PC Coast 1/9/42; for pre-war complaints on this subject, see also *EAS* (W), 8 July, 2 Sept. 1911.

[8] Memo, Military Commissioner for Labour, 18 July 1917, KNA PC Coast 1/9/42.

[9] See Ch. 7 for Smith-Mackenzie's attempts to enforce the use of Kilindini.

[10] PC to Chief Sec. 9 Feb. 1917, KNA PC Coast 1/9/42.

[11] At this time, two shipping companies, Union Castle and the British India Steam Navigation Co. (of which Smith-Mackenzie was an offshoot) employed most of the stevedores through subsidiary companies, while the shorehandlers were employed by the Railway; see *EAS* (W), 24 June 1911, and 'Agreement for Handling Cargo at Mombasa', 13 Apr. 1927, KNA AG/4/2937.

[12] DC Mombasa to PC, 18 June 1917, KNA PC Coast 1/9/42.

[13] DC Mombasa to PC, 12 Dec.1917, ibid.

[14] A. Clayton and D. Savage, *Government and Labour in Kenya, 1895–1963* (London, 1974), 98.

In February 1918 the Provincial Commissioner reported that 'although there are about 800 hamals registered on the books of the Port Labour bureau, the average number of days which each man has worked on cargo during the last few months is only four per month'.[15] The companies themselves had undermined the registration scheme by employing unregistered labour.[16] This was not necessarily a wilful contravention of the law; as the dispute with the boatmen in 1912 had shown, registration was not easily compatible with a system whereby the daily recruitment of labour was left to networks completely outside the employers' control. The registration system was quietly forgotten again, as the urgency of the demand for labour lessened with the end of the war.

Irregularity and the evasion of systems of registration continued to characterize Mombasa's labour force in to the 1920s. The Senior Commissioner wrote in 1924 that 'Mombasa labour is largely "kibarua" and Personal Servants. I have no idea of the numbers but it is impossible to state what labour in Mombasa is permanently employed'.[17] Employers continued to complain about the shortage of labour on the coast, and about the impossibility of obtaining labour from the local hinterland.[18] The inability of the administration to control workers and fix their identities was shown again in the mid-1920s, after the introduction of the *kipande*, or Native Registration Certificate.

The Natives' Registration Ordinance was passed in 1915, but remained unenforced throughout British East Africa until after the war.[19] Under the Ordinance, Africans who left the reserves were required to carry with them a certificate, the *kipande*, which bore their name and an identity number and carried details of their employment record. Africans could be arrested for not carrying such a certificate, and the details on it allowed the authorities to identify and punish those who had deserted from their last employment. Used in conjunction with

[15] PC to Chairman, Famine Committee, 14 Feb. 1918, KNA PC Coast 1/2/6.
[16] Hodges, *The Carrier Corps: Military Labour in the East African Campaign, 1914–1918* (London and New York, 1986), 97.
[17] Ag. SC to CNC, 1 Apr. 1924, KNA PC Coast 1/9/52.
[18] See e.g. Kilifi District Annual Report (1920–1), 12, KNA PC Coast 1/1/412.
[19] Clayton and Savage, *Government and Labour*, 131; S. Stitchter, *Migrant Labour in Kenya: Capitalism and African Response* (London, 1982), 46.

the Vagrancy Ordinance of 1920, which made it an offence for Africans to be outside the reserves 'not having any visible means of subsistence',[20] the *kipande* provided a new legal framework for the control of casual and informal labour, which might have seemed particularly suited to the needs of employers in Mombasa. Yet, despite the continuing complaints from employers on the subject of labour shortages, and the clearly perceived link between the demand for casual labour and the shortage of other kinds of labour, a meeting of coastal District Commissioners and the Senior Commissioner in 1924 agreed to suspend the operation of the Ordinance on the coast.[21]

The decision was presented as a generous administrative concession, either in recognition of the strains which the war had placed upon the Giriama and others,[22] or because of the resistance of some of the Twelve Tribes' Swahili to being classified as 'natives'.[23] It was, however, rather more an admission of defeat. Officials elsewhere on the coast had complained that the situation in Mombasa rendered the Ordinance unworkable:

It is useless for me to enforce the Ordinance in this district unless steps are taken to see that Mombasa comes into line. In every single instance where a Mombasa native comes to my office or into the district he leaves his certificate in Mombasa, as he states he never carries it in the town, and did not know it was obligatory elsewhere.[24]

The provincial administration's decision was not welcomed in Nairobi, but a special representative despatched by the Chief Registrar of Natives decided, to the dismay of his superiors, that enforcement of the law within Mombasa was indeed a hopeless task.[25] His judgement was not accepted and, after prodding from Nairobi, registration on the coast began again from 1926, but evasion continued to be common, and enforcement patchy.[26]

[20] Memo on the Vagrancy Ordinance, n.d., PRO CO 533 389/9.
[21] SC to CNC, 18 Dec.1924, KNA PC Coast 1/10/120B.   [22] Ibid.
[23] Mombasa District Annual Report (1924), 4–5, KNA DC MSA 1/3.
[24] DC Kilifi, quoted in Chief Registrar of Natives to SC, 27 Mar. 1922, KNA PC Coast 1/10/120B.
[25] Department of Native Affairs to SC, 29 Sept. 1924, ibid.
[26] For some details of the continuing evasion of the *kipande* law, see Willis, 'Thieves, Drunkards and Vagrants', 226–8.

This new legislation had not changed the basic problem: several of the major employers in Mombasa were unwilling to meet the long-term costs of supporting a full-time labour force, and in this situation the state lacked the resources to discipline labour effectively. In 1924, the East African Lighterage Company was convicted of employing as a casual a worker who was absenting himself from his contracted work for the railway.[27] Temporarily unnerved by this, the shipping companies agreed to the establishment of a register of casual labour, but only on condition that the state should run (and therefore pay for) the scheme and that registered casuals would be legally obliged to work if offered employment.[28] When the lighterage company's conviction was overturned on appeal, on the grounds that they had no knowledge of the worker's status, the Mombasa District Commissioner withdrew the registration scheme.[29] If the dock companies were not willing to discipline their own labour, neither was the administration willing to do it for them.

Mombasa's small industrial sector also preferred casual labour, presumably because of the costs of feeding and housing labour in Mombasa, and the difficulty of getting permanent workers.[30] Quarrying, building, and portering concerns similarly relied on casuals.[31] In these occupations, as in dock labour, certificates, numbers, and laws were not the means of organizing workers, and could not be in a situation where personal contact and recognition were the basis of employment. Within such arrangements, there was no point at which the identity of an individual worker could be checked by his employer. Employers were not willing to co-operate in enforcing the *kipande* law, for the individual checking of cards involved would have destroyed the system of employment through gangs on which they relied, and would have been enormously time-consuming and costly. The shipping companies and others

[27] Minutes, Special Meeting of Port Advisory Board, 23 June 1924, KNA AG/4/2968.

[28] Memo, Frudd, Union Castle Mail Steamship Co. Ltd., n.d.,'Casual Labourers' Employment Bill', draft; Fazan, Res. Commissioner and Chair of District Committee to Colonial Sec., 17 Oct. 1924, all ibid.

[29] Ainsworth-Dickson, Res. Commissioner and Chair of District Committee to Ag. Colonial Sec., 13 Aug. 1925, ibid.

[30] See *EAS* (D), 26 Nov. 1936, which refers to a case brought against a coffee-curing company who had long used casual labour. Casual work for this company is also referred to in Int. 74a.   [31] Int. 71a, 20a, 47a.

continued to employ large numbers of casuals, some of whom were deserters, others of whom were moonlighting, and most of whom used the casual labour system to survive by doing as little waged labour as possible.

There were changes in the networks which organized this labour, though; changes which grew out of the changing nature of work and which gave opportunities to new patrons. On the docks, the growing importance of Kilindini at the expense of Mombasa and the reorganizations of companies in the 1920s were associated with the rise of one *serang* in particular, a man called Salim bin Ali. For a number of years this man dominated the cargo-handling force at Kilindini through a number of lesser *serangs* and *tindals* organized in the Sadla dance society.[32] He was, by origin, a Chonyi,[33] from Junju, one of the creek-head areas where planters and traders had been most active.[34] He became very much a man of the town, to the extent that many no longer remember his original identity.[35] His earnings were invested in property in Mombasa, around Mwembe Tayari,[36] and his status as head *serang* was recognized by his employers, who according to one account went so far as to assist him in making deductions from workers' wages.[37]

Salim bin Ali, incorporated into the Swahili community as he was, was of a rather different group to earlier patrons of casual labour within Mombasa. Previously, those able to organize and market the labour of subordinates had been traders or planters with some established wealth in property; men such as Rastam bin Talasam, of the Basheikh clan, who was the head of the Kingi dance society.[38] Colonial rule had offered these men, already established patrons, new opportunities to benefit from the labour of their followers. Changing conditions allowed others, lower down the social scale, to build followings of clients who relied on these new patrons' knowledge of the town and

[32] Int. 71*b*, 26*b*, 67*b*.   [33] Int. 71*b*.

[34] D. C. Sperling, 'The Growth of Islam among the Mijikenda of the Kenya Coast', Ph.D. thesis (London, 1988), 52–4; Int. 9*a*, 9*c*.

[35] Informant 26, himself a Chonyi and who had known Salim bin Ali, did not identify him as a Chonyi, unlike other informants.

[36] Int. 26*b*.   [37] Ibid.

[38] For Rastam and the *Kingi*, see Int. 5*a*; for *Kingi*, Rastam, and dock labour see Int. 53*a*, 71*b*, 55*a*.

relationships with employers, rather than on their personal wealth. The challenge which these new patrons presented to more established figures fed into tensions over status which were played out in the intensification of the debate over Swahili ethnicity in the 1920s.[39]

In the mid-1920s, administrative action had failed to close off the options which migration to Mombasa or involvement in rural networks of trade and credit offered to coastal Africans, though access to these options had been made more difficult. As a result of this failure, the level of wages in Mombasa stayed relatively high into the 1920s;[40] for people still avoided long-term wage labour, and were able to resist attempts to coerce them into more regular employment.

At the same time, the cost of living, the cost of the daily reproduction of labour, was higher in Mombasa than elsewhere in Kenya.[41] Workers in Mombasa, casual though they were, were not generally migrants in this period, and their reproduction was not subsidized by the rural homestead.[42] Instead, the task of caring for and servicing those in waged employment fell upon the considerable army of concubines, hawkers, cooks, wood-cutters, and water-drawers in the town. Employers, of course, benefited from the labour of these people, who kept their employees fit for work without direct payment.[43] 'Work?

[39] See Part IV, below.

[40] Though lower in real terms than before the war (F. Cooper, *On the African Waterfront* (New Haven, Conn., 1987), 32–3), casual earnings in Mombasa in 1929 still compared favourably with wages elsewhere in Kenya; App. A, 'Minimum Rates of Wages', *Native Affairs Department Annual Report, 1929* (Nairobi, 1930), 134; see also K. Janmohamed, 'A History of Mombasa, c.1895–1939', Ph.D. thesis (Northwestern, 1977), 332–3.

[41] Janmohamed, 'African Labourers in Mombasa, c.1895–1940', in B. A. Ogot (ed.), *Economic and Social History of East Africa* (Nairobi, 1976), 156–79, 174; 'Report on Native Affairs in Mombasa' (1930), 13–14, KNA DC MSA 3/3.

[42] Administrators noted this of some Mombasans in the 1940s (see Janmohamed, 'African Labourers in Mombasa', 170–1), but it seems clear that it had been true long before the new concerns of administrators in this period directed attention to it. There is a considerable literature on the importance of the subsidy which reproduction of the labour force within the homestead has provided to capital, a seminal piece being H. Wolpe, 'Capitalism and Cheap Labour Power in South Africa: From Segregation to Apartheid', *Economy and Society*, i (1972), 425–62.

[43] See G. Chauncey, 'The Locus of Reproduction: Women's Labour in the Zambian Copperbelt, 1927–1953', *Journal of Southern African Studies*, 7 (1981), 135–64, who argues that it was women in towns rather than in rural homesteads whose unwaged work subsidized the reproduction of labour for the mines.

The work was young men,' as one woman put it.[44] Yet they did not work for nothing, and their ability to evade official control and the level of demand for their services gave them considerable earning power. For women from the local hinterland in particular, such work in Mombasa was more remunerative than work in the homestead could ever be. As reproducers of male waged labour, women who lived as concubines in Mombasa were subordinated to the interests of capital, but they could demand and receive cash payments for their work, and they refused to perform all the work expected of women within the homestead: 'what use is a Mombasa wife? . . . . she's a lazy woman who runs away and is taken in Mombasa, because she just wants to cook and eat, she doesn't want lots of work . . . they get there, they've reached the land of luxury, they're lost.'[45]

Many women in Mombasa avoided cultivation, fetching water, cutting firewood, and grinding grain. Those who did perform such tasks generally had more chance of controlling the product of their labour than did women in the hinterland. Like other migrants to Mombasa, women had evaded the control of the homestead, and thus the control of the state through the homestead. As such, their subordination was less complete than that of women in the homestead, and the cost of their labour higher. This was, after all, why women went to Mombasa—it allowed them to renegotiate the terms of their participation in the domestic economy, and so to do less work. A permanently urban male worker cared for by an urban wife might have been cheaper for an employer than a permanently urban worker without a wife, but he was certainly more costly than a migrant worker with a wife and family in the hinterland. Mombasa's labour force earned more because of the options which their position as townspeople offered, but they needed to earn more to be townspeople.

It was this, in the end, that was to be the crucial cause of change in the nature of participation in Mombasa's labour market, combined as it was with new tensions and divisions between people on the coast which administrative policies had introduced. The separation of coast and hinterland did not

<hr>

[44] Int. 59a, 3.   [45] Int. 43a, 4–5.

immediately affect the supply of labour on the coast, for the administration failed to fully enforce this policy. Yet the legal framework laid down to enforce separation began a more subtle process of differentiation. By redefining, and fixing, the rights and proper positions of Swahili, Arab, and Nyika, this legislation put the people of the hinterland *as a group* in a position where their interests could easily conflict with those of Swahili and Arabs.

PART IV

'Other dances': Mombasa and the Mijikenda, 1925–1934

Hobley finally left the coast in 1919, but his influence continued to be felt after this, both through the measures which he had introduced and through those officials still on the coast who had worked under him. Not all of the innovations which he had introduced were to last: in 1921, at a time of general administrative reorganization, Malindi District expanded to take in the hinterland once again: the division of Nyika and coast areas into separate districts ended. However, distinctive styles of administration were maintained in each area, and Mombasa District remained shorn of its hinterland, covering only the island and its mainland suburbs. Other schemes of Hobley, particularly town planning and the control of trade, were more enduring and more important.

New patterns of migration from the local hinterland to Mombasa emerged during the 1920s. Numbers of men from hinterland groups who worked in Mombasa became 'migrant labourers', sending money to their homesteads and planning to return there. This shift in the nature of involvement in wage labour was partly a result of the numerous official measures enacted to change the relationship between Mombasa and the local hinterland. The effect of these measures was exacerbated by the intensification of the debate over ethnicity in the 1920s, a debate in which these measures themselves played an important part. In changing economic circumstances men adapted previous patterns of migration, seeking to make the best of their limited options.

The new patterns of involvement did not entirely displace earlier ones, but the changing nature of the relationship between the people of the hinterland and those of the coast had profound repercussions on the way people defined themselves and presented their history. To understand history on the coast in the period up to the 1920s, it is necessary to disaggregate, to look behind the group titles; but from the 1920s, understanding is reliant on an appreciation of a new, partly imposed, process of aggregation. To speak of the relationships of 'the Mijikenda' with 'the Swahili' before this time is unhelpful, for neither group was discrete or homogeneous, and the complex history of the coast was built on this heterogeneity. But by the late 1920s this was changing. The ethnonym 'Mijikenda' was not yet in use, but as a group defined by a separate area of residence, and separate rights, the Mijikenda were being created.

9

New Networks of Labour

I'd be asked, 'Hey, in Giriama, in your place, are there people who can work?' So now I'll become a person who goes out there and tempts the youngsters.

(Interview 34a)

In 1920, the District Commissioners in Vanga (Digo) and Kilifi Districts remarked, just as their predecessors had regularly done, on the reluctance of people in their districts to engage in waged labour for Europeans. 'A few go to Mombasa in search of work, but the number is so small that it cannot really be taken into consideration'.[1] The evidence discussed in previous chapters makes it clear that, in fact, numbers of people from the hinterland lived and worked in Mombasa at this time, but they did so as Swahili, not as 'Nyika'. The 1920s were to see a change in this pattern.

In 1923, the District Commissioner for Kilifi noted for the first time that 'large numbers of Wanyika do casual work at the harbour and elsewhere in Mombasa'.[2] In 1925, the District Commissioner for Digo noted a similar change: 'The Waduruma are working much more than previously and prefer to go to Mombasa and engage in daily work. They can thus earn a few shillings and return home again.'[3] For the first time, people from the hinterland were regularly finding casual work in Mombasa *as* Nyika, and were taking their earnings back to

[1] Vanga District Annual Report (1920–1), 11, KNA PC Coast 1/1/412; see also Ag. DC Kilifi to Ag. PC, 7 Feb. 1920, KNA PC Coast 1/9/52; Digo District Annual Report (1924), 5, KNA DC KWL 1/10.
[2] Kilifi District Annual Report (1923), KNA PC Coast 1/1/418.
[3] Digo District Annual Report (1925), 17, KNA PC Coast 1/1/347; and also Kilifi Intelligence Report, June 1924, KNA PC Coast 1/17/13.

the homestead with them: '50% of the 1923 tax is now in. The money appears to have been earned entirely by a great increase in the numbers going out to work on the coast and particularly at the Mombasa Harbour Works where the high rate of wages and the system of casual labour suits the Wanyika.'[4] In 1927 it was even reported that Duruma were going to work on the docks in response to famine;[5] a dramatic change from the situation in 1918 when temporary migrants fleeing famine were excluded from dock labour and other more lucrative forms of casual work. None the less, though migrant Nyika were working in new occupations, these workers maintained their resistance to strict discipline, and continued to avoid contracts. The District Commissioner for Kilifi noted in 1925 that 'they have a rooted objection to signing on for any length of time'.[6]

This partial transformation of the casual labour force of Mombasa involved the development of new networks, organizing labour in rather different ways; for the previous networks of labour had been constructed through institutions which ensured the urban identity of the casual labour force. Until the 1920s, people moving to Mombasa had often relied for initial support on townspeople to whom they had some blood relationship, men and women who had migrated to the town and stayed there. Some informants described such people as 'those who went before'.[7] Yet, generally, they could not rely on these people alone. To survive in the town they had to seek other help, making claims which were based on membership of a town community, not on a shared ethnicity outside the town. A migrant found casual work in the town not by being a Giriama, or a Kauma, but by attachment to a town patron. Such patrons, *serangs*, found people work because they were their friends, debtors, or clients in the town, not because of their identity outside the town.

During the 1920s, some casual labour came to be organized on different principles, which allowed temporary migrants to

<hr>

[4] Kilifi Intelligence Report, Feb. 1924, KNA PC Coast 1/17/13; Kilifi District Annual Report (1923), KNA PC Coast 1/1/418.
[5] Digo Station Diary, Feb. 1927, 3, KNA PC Coast 1/1/251.
[6] Kilifi District Annual Report (1924–5), 12, KNA DC KFI 1/2.
[7] Int. 44a, 34a, 26b, CHONYI/2.

work as casuals without commitment to life in the town. The gang system of hiring remained, but the means through which some *serangs* gathered their gangs changed; ethnicity as defined by descent and blood relationships came to be the organizing factor in these networks. This could lead to the use of what officials would call 'labour recruiters'—African agents working under the control of European employers—a group very different in official eyes from the 'touts' or 'crimps'.[8] These gang-leaders were a new brand of 'those who went before':

> ... it's like, if I went before, I'd work, I'd be asked, 'Hey, in Giriama, in your place, are there people who can work?'. So now I'll become a person who goes out there and tempts the youngsters, I'll tell them, 'Let's go!' ... So when I take them back to the *serangi* who sent me, 'Thank you very much,' he'll thank me. Now he'll take me as a senior, I'll be more important than the casuals, I'm sent to find people, like a *serangi* ... and the senior one is a Giriama like me, who came a long time ago, he's important now.[9]

If they were to be successful, these recruiters themselves needed to maintain links with their own homestead, and to encourage those who went to work with them to do the same, so that future attempts at recruitment would meet with co-operation from elders, homestead heads, and officials. Some of these *serang*s had built their knowledge of the town and employers through participation as townspeople, but had then returned to the hinterland and re-established their position in their homestead, returning to the town again only as temporary migrants.[10]

Not all workers were recruited in the hinterland: many continued to find their own way to the town, where they would seek out the *serang* from their own area and thus find work.[11] Sometimes such individual migrants were housed by relatives, or occasionally still in return for domestic labour;[12] but in town households these migrants remained unincorporated outsiders, their lower status clearly marked: 'they didn't rent,

---

[8] When 'touts' were banned, an amending ordinance exempted from the law those who acted to recruit new workers, rather than encouraging desertion by already contracted workers: Memo, Barth, Attorney-General, 4 Feb. 1915, KNA AG/4/1614.

[9] Int. 34a, 2; see also Int. 73a.   [10] Int. 54a.

[11] Int. 34a, 45a.   [12] Int. 40a, 56a, CHONYI/1.

not at all . . . your sweat is taken instead, he [house-owner] had a wife, she'd cook food, his wife, whether it's in a clay pot or a saucepan, in the morning she tells you, "Here's some food, eat and then wash out the pots".[13] Some of the new *serang*s found housing for those who worked in their gangs, in the houses of townspeople whom they knew. The *serang*s arranged the rent and, on occasion, themselves collected this rent; doubling up as housing agents and labour agents.[14]

The new gangs developed particularly in expanding areas of casual labour, on the harbour construction works and in the wave of demolitions and rebuildings that accompanied the town plan.[15] These gangs did not displace the previous system— which was by its nature well-entrenched and exclusive—but developed alongside it, usually in different areas of the labour market. However, at least one Giriama gang was involved in shore-handling by around 1930, indirectly recruited through a Baluchi married into a Giriama family.[16] The town plan, described by one informant as the start of Mijikenda involvement in Mombasa's labour force,[17] was a particularly significant event. On the one hand, it offered a greatly expanded field of employment, not yet dominated by networks of labour controlled by town patrons. On the other the destructive effects of the town plan on networks of patronage encouraged a system whereby people from the local hinterland could come to Mombasa without reliance on town patrons.

The emphasis on hinterland contacts and ethnic identity inevitably led to the development of minor specializations for different hinterland groups, or even different clans. Just as the Rabai had earlier developed a near monopoly of palm-wine tapping in Mombasa through recruiting friends and relatives, so by the late 1920s the Chonyi had established an exclusive little niche at Kilindini harbour, cleaning the rust off lighters.[18] In the 1920s the expansion of Kilindini was accompanied by a considerable expansion in work at the coaling and oiling terminal at Mbaraki. Giriama, Kauma, and Digo

---

[13] Int. 47a, 2–3.   [14] Int. 47a, 34a.
[15] Pauling and Co., the major contractors on the dock expansion, employed 1,300 casuals in 1924: Labour Inspection Reports (1923–4), KNA PC Coast 1/9/53. Domestic labour could also be employed through new networks; Int. 30a.
[16] Int. 54a.   [17] Int. 71a.   [18] Int. 25a, CHONYI/1.

*serang*s predominated here,[19] and the unskilled casual work-force seems to have become almost exclusively Nyika for a while: 'Coaling and discharge of oil is principally recruited from the wa-Digo and Giriama—the bulk of the former living on the mainland. Work is certainly hard but the pay is high.'[20] By contrast, the winch-men at Mbaraki, the more skilled casuals who operated the machinery, were drawn from the Swahili: people who learned their work and were accepted as winch-drivers through people they knew in the town. One man of Digo origin, who had become incorporated into the urban community of Hailendi, used his contacts in the town to move from basket-carrying, the unskilled work at Mbaraki, to winching:

I started off as a *kibarua*, I was carrying baskets, then I got tired, I made friends with the winch-men in the boats. I made friends, I got used to the winch, until I knew it . . . So I was tired of labouring, I gave up baskets, and I lined up [in the search for work each morning] with the winch-men. The winch-men were here, the labourers here . . . So I stood there, and the late Salim bin Ali asked the winch-men, 'What about this lad?' They told him, 'He's a winch-man'. I was taken on.[21]

Basket-carrying was the ultimate casual labour: payment was not even by the day, but for each basket of coal carried, and so the work was named *kikapu-senti*, 'cent-a-basket'. The work was unpleasant and unreliable,[22] and not as lucrative as some officials suggested,[23] but was still more rewarding than contract labour—and less restricting.[24] The gangs were clearly organized around ethnicity, as one Chonyi informant explained: 'Others were Kauma, and they had their people, and Giriama had their *serang*s. He takes you, because he knows you are an *ndugu* . . . And the Giriama goes and takes from his side . . . We

[19] Int. 20*b*, 48*a*, 45*a*.
[20] Mombasa District Annual Report (1926), 10, KNA DC MSA 1/3.
[21] Int. 67*a*, 4.   [22] See particularly the vivid description in Int. 25*a*.
[23] In 1927, the DC suggested that some earned 6s. a day carrying coal (Mombasa District Annual Report (1927), KNA PC Coast 1/10/110). Informants put the figure at around 1s. 50c., which is still a considerable amount, for carrying 150 baskets of coal (Int. 25*a*).
[24] The railway at this time paid 14s. a month; Labour Inspection Reports (1923–4), KNA PC Coast 1/9/53.

[Chonyi] go and wait, for our *serang* to come, "You, come here, you, come, you come!".'[25] There was a degree of cross-over between these hinterland-based gangs, as intermarriage between Nyika groups and the mobility of individuals who left one group and were incorporated by another had given many people kin in other hinterland groups. Thus, a Giriama could find work in a gang headed by a Kauma *serang*.[26] On one level the new gangs were particular, of one group, but they could draw on the idea of the unity of local hinterland groups, a unity based on kin ties and a shared interest in maintaining their identity and position as members of homesteads in the hinterland.

As some areas of casual work expanded, others, associated with systems of patronage based on urban identity, fell into decline. The passenger boats of the harbour, the crews of which had been the militant casuals of 1912, were rendered largely obsolete by the opening of the deep-water berths at Kilindini between 1925 and 1929.[27] The opening of the Nyali bridge, linking the island to the north mainland, similarly disrupted the networks of patronage and incorporation that had operated on the boats which had provided a ferry service.[28]

Just as the *beni* societies had given structure to earlier patterns of labour recruitment, new dances gave structure to these new patterns of recruitment. Appearing first in Mombasa in the second half of the 1920s,[29] these new dance societies were dramatically different from the *beni*.[30] Where *beni* had stressed identity as townspeople, and had been specifically

---

[25] Int. 25*a*, 2.   [26] Int. 45*a*.

[27] Int. 49*a*; some boatmen survived, offering tourist trips of the harbour; Int. 44*a*.

[28] H. Kindy, *Life and Politics in Mombasa* (Nairobi, 1972), 88–9. Unlike other crossings to the island, Nyali had never been a monopoly held by a single concessionaire (see the contents of KNA AG/4/3599). The bridge was affected by some acts of sabotage (Manager, Nyali Bridge and Development Co. Ltd. to District Surveyor, 18 Apr. 1935, KNA AG/4/2068). Intent on making a profit from tolls, the bridge company eliminated continuing competition from boats by fencing off the old ferry-landing site (District Surveyor to Commissioner for Local Govt., Lands and Settlement, 2 July 1935; Manager, Nyali Bridge and Development Co. to District Surveyor, 18 Apr. 1935; Attorney-General to Colonial Sec., 28 Sept. 1936, KNA AG/4/2068).

[29] Int. 34*a*.

[30] One informant described them as 'African dances', in contrast to *beni*; Int. 44*a*, 8.

non-ethnic,[31] the new societies were explicitly based on membership of ethnic groups which were not of the town. Most of the new societies in these years drew their membership from local hinterland groups. Like the *beni* leaders, the prominent figures in these new societies were noted *serangs*.[32] One informant described how Kenga wa Mwana, a Giriama *serang*, met those seeking work through the *namba* dance:

This dance drew people from far away, they came from Vitengeni, from who knows where! When they got there, 'Ah, we've come to look for work.' 'How many of you are there ?' 'There are six of us.' 'All right! Tomorrow, come to Kenya [Landing and Shipping Co.]'. The next day, he'll see a long line of people, queueing.[33]

Migrants seeking work had to know the *serangs*—and the ethnic dance societies offered the necessary contact, just as the *beni* had for a different group of workers.[34]

These were dances that had already existed outside the town. In the hinterland, dance societies seem often to have had a role in organizing loyalties within the group; one informant described a dispute between his father and some of his neighbours in terms of membership of different Digo dance societies, *kayamba*, *sengenya*, and *gonda*.[35] In Mombasa, dances were apparently identified with the members of particular groups, rather than being expressive of smaller loyalties within the group. Thus, in the town, the *kayamba* was a Duruma dance, the *namba* Giriama, the *mavunye* Chonyi, and the *sengenya* Digo.[36] The ethnic associations were not absolute, however, as cross-cutting kin ties brought Jibana and Kambe, for example, into the *namba*.[37]

The outward forms of these societies distinguished them from the *beni*. These dances were danced to drums alone, not

---

[31] A fact which caused considerable anxiety among officials nervous at the prospects of Pan-Africanism; Major Muggeridge to Commissioner of Police, 29 July 1919; Ag. DC Mombasa to PC, 12 Aug. 1919; Ag. DC Mombasa to PC, 1 Dec. 1919, KNA PC Coast 1/12/196.

[32] Int. 73a.   [33] Int. 34a, 4.   [34] Int. 54a.   [35] Int. 9c, 9d.

[36] Int. 22a, 23a, 34a. *Kayamba* should not be confused with a spirit dance of the same name. That the kind of identity manifested through this kind of dance of ethnic solidarity was somewhat different in the urban to the rural area is noted also in J. C. Mitchell, *The Kalela Dance: Aspects of Social Relationships among Urban Africans in Northern Rhodesia* (Manchester, 1956), 29–31, 42–4.

[37] Int. 30a; see also Int. 45a.

to the variety of European instruments which the *beni* employed,[38] and dancers sang in Nyika languages, not in the
Swahili heavily laced with English that characterized the *beni*.[39]
The *beni* members dressed in extravagant parodies of military
uniforms and other styles drawn from an urban, colonial en-
vironment, but the *namba* and other dances were attired very
differently: 'I used to wear a *shuka* [single cloth], you just dance
in a *shuka*. A *shuka*, then you have beads, you oil yourself, comb
your hair, and put the beads on. Then, just like that, your
chest bare . . . '[40] The new dances served to emphasize the
identity of dancers as members of groups based outside the
hinterland.[41] The words of the song, while maintaining the
competitive, boasting tradition of *beni* songs, had very different
themes to those of the Sadla or Kingi: they emphasized the
importance of not becoming 'lost', and of remitting earnings
to the homestead.[42]

The interest of the homestead head in such arrangements,
through which homesteads benefited from the earnings of people
working in Mombasa, can be clearly understood. Restrictions
on the palm-wine trade and on the activities of some lenders
had made cash more difficult to come by other than through
wage labour, while at the same time the demands on the population of the hinterland for cash were increasing. Taxes had
risen enormously by the mid-1920s, the rate of taxation doubling
between 1911 and 1922.[43] The efficiency of tax collection seems
also to have increased—takings of Hut and Poll Tax in Vanga
District in 1923 were *six* times what they had been in 1911.[44]
Those who could do so met the demand for cash by increasing
sales of livestock, and the price of cattle seems to have fallen

[38] For *beni*, see Int. 44*a*, 12*b*; T. O. Ranger, *Dance and Society in Eastern Africa, 1890–
1970: The Beni Ngoma* (London, 1975), 21. For *namba*, see Int. 54*a*.

[39] For the use of English and Swahili in *beni*, see Int. 7*a*, and Ag. DC Mombasa to
PC, 12 Aug. 1919, KNA PC Coast 1/12/196; for *namba* songs, see Int. 21*b*, 54*a*.

[40] Int. 21*b*, 17, Informant 30 talking.

[41] Cf. Mitchell, *The Kalela Dance*, 42–4.   [42] Int. 21*b*, 17.

[43] A. Clayton and D. Savage, *Government and Labour in Kenya, 1895–1963* (London,
1974), 139–46; see also Hobley's comments in C. W. Hobley, 'Some Native Problems
in East Africa', *JAS* 17 (1922–3), 287–301.

[44] See the record of tax revenues, 1910–26, in KNA DC KWL 10/1. The population of
the District had increased considerably with boundary changes, but the increase is
still startling.

considerably as a result.[45] The District Commissioner at Kilifi observed that 'Native stock is noticeably decreasing owing to their habit of selling it to pay Tax. Unless the Wanyika soon develop the habit of going out to work they will become very impoverished indeed.'[46] In these circumstances, though wage labour still threatened the homestead with the possibility that the labourer would not return, it had none the less become essential to many homestead heads that some of their juniors should seek waged work.

Yet, whatever the needs of the homestead, young men seem to have seen little improvement in their position within the homestead, or in the returns from homestead production generally, which might have encouraged them to maintain their ties and keep their stake in the homestead. The concentration of trade in Trade Centres had not improved producer prices,[47] the export trade in grain suffered from both the introduction of maize-grading[48] and the general decline in the dhow-borne trade consequent on colonial licensing requirements and the change of currency from rupees to shillings.[49]

It has been argued that young men would have found it easier to escape from the control of the homestead head and establish their own homesteads in the colonial period, given that colonial rule offered a form of security that was not dependent solely on membership of a large homestead, and that the dangers of kidnapping and cattle-theft had diminished.[50] This may be true to some extent, but it offers too rosy a view of the impact of the *pax britannica*. Law and security under British rule were largely administered through elders and headmen, and young men without protectors might find themselves exposed to new and peculiarly colonial dangers—notably to

---

[45] At Rabai, prices fell, from between 35 and 75 Rs. in 1912 to 20s. (10 Rs) in 1922; Rabai Subdistrict Annual Report (1911–12), KNA PC Coast 1/1/185, and SC to SC Kismayu, 21 Sept. 1922, KNA PC Coast 1/2/95.

[46] Kilifi District Annual Report (1923), KNA DC KFI 1/1.

[47] 'Coastal Trade', SC, 11 May 1923, 3, KNA PC Coast 1/1/165.

[48] F. Cooper, *From Slaves to Squatters* (New Haven, Conn., 1980), 263; exports of grain to the Benadir were, however, excluded from these restrictions; 'Précis of Meeting to Consider Commitments by CNC in Respect of Coast Trade', KNA PC Coast 1/1/165.

[49] ADC Kilifi to DC Malindi, 27 June 1923, KNA PC Coast 1/1/165; Sect. XIV, Malindi District Annual Report (1923), KNA PC Coast 1/1/418.

[50] A. Champion, *The Agiryama of Kenya* (London, 1967), 10.

demands for compulsory labour under the Native Authority Ordinance.[51] The British had, after all, determinedly tried to use the power of elders against their juniors,[52] and the system of Local Native Councils acted to bolster the power of government-approved elders and headmen.[53] The elder men who dominated the LNCs were forced into further conflict with young men through a number of measures pushed on them by the administration; the banning of the drinking of palm wine by young men, the introduction of a further poll tax, and the use of forced labour in officially approved building schemes.[54]

Elder male homestead heads thus still had considerable power over younger men, whether they were within the homestead or attempting to establish their own, independent homestead. Conflict within homesteads over bridewealth—essentially, over whether the homestead head used his wealth to buy wives for himself or for his juniors—continued to be intense. In 1937 a Malindi LNC motion outlawed marriage between a son and any of the wives of his deceased father since: 'It was alleged by most of the African members of the council that patricide is not uncommon locally, and is usually committed by an unmarried son on account of a desire for one of his father's younger wives.'[55]

Clearly, struggles over the control of wealth within the homestead continued to be intense. That young men from the hinterland were increasingly trying to maintain their identity and position as members of the homestead was a result of greater insecurity within Mombasa, not of improved terms of involvement in their rural homesteads.

[51] Int. 22a.

[52] e.g. in labour recruitment, see Part III, above; for co-option of Giriama elders to assist in relocation, see PC to DC Malindi, 4 Oct. 1916, KNA PC Coast 1/11/266.

[53] Half of the representatives were government headmen, and the representatives of the younger age-grades were selected by the elders; ADC Kilifi to SC, 10 June 1925 and DC Malindi to SC, 9 June 1925, also DC Kilifi to SC, 3 Apr. 1925, KNA PC Coast 1/12/286.

[54] For details of these motions, and government pressure to have them passed, see Minutes, Malindi LNC, 1 Nov. 1925, KNA PC Coast 1/12/244; Minutes, Digo LNC, 15 Oct. 1927; and DC Digo to SC, 25 Jan. 1926 and Ag. SCC to Ag. DC Kwale, 28 Apr. 1926, KNA PC Coast 1/12/281. 'Young men', it should be noted, included men whose own children had not yet married.

[55] Resolution No. 4 of 1937, Kilifi LNC, KNA PC Coast 2/16/11.

10

The Twelve Tribes and the Mijikenda

Sudi bin Ali claimed that they could point out who was a real member of the Twelve Tribes and who was a follower

(Governor's meeting with Afro-Asian Association, 1932)

The reassessment by young men of the opportunities which life in Mombasa offered in the 1920s was partly prompted by a considerable drop in real wages. In dock labour, the major form of casual labour, wages in 1911–12 had been about Rs 1/25 a day.[1] By 1918 these had risen to Rs 2/55 a day,[2] but this increase was not maintained after the war. Inflation and the change in currency from rupees to shillings allowed employers to reduce real wages all over Kenya,[3] and in the 1920s daily dock wages were 2s. to 2s. 50c. a day,[4] the equivalent of 1R to Rs 1/25, but with considerably less buying power than the same wage had had in 1912. By the end of the decade, dock wages were down to 1s. 50c. to 2s. per day.[5] Other casuals fared even worse: on the dock construction, daily wages in 1924 were 1s. to 1s. 50c.[6] The root of this progressive drop in wages was the end of the labour shortages that had once dogged all forms of casual work—as Mombasa's population swelled, workers were finding it harder to get work, and their previously strong bargaining position was undermined.[7]

While figures on Mombasa's population are hard to

---

[1] F. Cooper, *On the African Waterfront* (New Haven, Conn., 1987), 27.
[2] A. Clayton and D. Savage, *Government and Labour in Kenya, 1895–1963* (London, 1974), 98.
[3] Ibid. 143.   [4] Cooper, *On the African Waterfront*, 32; Int. 25a.
[5] *Native Affairs Department Annual Report for 1929*, App. A, 134.
[6] Labour Inspection Reports (1923–4), KNA PC Coast 1/9/53.
[7] Cooper, *From Slaves to Squatters* (New Haven, Conn., 1980), 244.

interpret,[8] the figures do make it clear that the population grew rapidly between 1913 and 1931. The total population of the island went from an estimated 19,600 in 1913 to an equally estimated 30,000 in 1922, and to 41,000 in the 1931 census.[9] The African population of the island was growing even faster than the total population.[10]

Much of this population growth was due to immigration from up-country. Wages in Mombasa were falling, but were still significantly higher than those elsewhere in Kenya, and they drew migrants from all over East Africa. Rates of labour migrancy throughout Kenya grew significantly in the 1920s,[11] and it has been suggested that it was these up-country migrants whose competition for jobs forced down casual wage rates in the 1920s.[12] The assumption that up-country workers dominated Mombasa's labour force in the 1920s is almost certainly mistaken, however.[13] Up-country workers did form the majority of the contracted labour force in Mombasa,[14] but informants rarely mention up-country workers in casual employ at this time.[15] The way in which casual labour was

---

[8] Sometimes these figures are for the District, sometimes for the island, and they were generally guess-work anyway; Mombasa District Annual Report (1928), 5, KNA DC MSA 1/3.

[9] Political Record Book, 27, KNA DC MSA 8/2; Mombasa District Annual Reports: (1922), KNA DC MSA 1/3; (1931), 3, ibid. 1/4.

[10] From 14,265 in 1921 to 21,352 in 1931: Mombasa District Annual Reports: (1922), 1, KNA DC MSA 1/3; (1931), 3, ibid. 1/4.

[11] G. Kitching, *Class and Economic Change in Kenya: The Making of an African Petite Bourgeoisie, 1905–1970* (London and New Haven, Conn., 1980), 249.

[12] Cooper, *From Slaves to Squatters*, 244.

[13] Cooper (ibid. 249) and K. Janmohamed ('A history of Mombasa, c.1895–1939', Ph.D. thesis (Northwestern, 1977), 358) both cite a 1925 report (*Native Affairs Department Annual Report for 1925* (Nairobi, 1926), 81) suggesting that only 17% of Mombasa's work-force were of coastal origin. Yet these figures are based on registration statistics, and compulsory registration did not apply in coastal districts, so that large numbers of coastal workers would have gone unrecorded. This may explain the discrepancy between these figures and those given by Wilson, who suggests that coastal participation in Mombasa's labour force dropped from 38% in 1947 to 19% in 1957 (G. Wilson, 'African Labourers in Mombasa', in G. Wilson (ed.) 'The Social Survey of Mombasa' (1957), typescript in KNA library, i. 218).

[14] In 1919, 468 of 492 contracted employees of the Conservancy and the Public Works Department were from up-country (Labour Inspection Reports (1919), KNA PC Coast 1/9/53) and in 1924 only 99 out of 1,087 were not from up-country, and 60 of these were Taita (Labour Inspection Reports, 1923–4, KNA PC Coast 1/9/53).

[15] See also Cooper, *On the African Waterfront*, 32, where he suggests that coastal workers dominated dock labour until the late 1930s.

recruited was inherently restrictive: while the Nyika were able to establish new casual labour networks, this was only possible because of the access to existing networks which some individuals had enjoyed. The increased competition for casual work was not principally a result of up-country migration; rather it was a product of increased migration from the local hinterland, as alternative sources of income for the rural homestead dried up.

The decline in the value of real wages consequent on this increased migration was itself enough to encourage young men to keep in touch with their homesteads. The economic dictum that labour whose reproduction was subsidized by the rural homestead was cheaper did not affect Mombasa's work-force through the schemes of cunning and all-powerful capital. Rather, this truth was realized through workers' own experience of increasing insecurity and poverty in the town. Labour migrancy was the workers' response to these conditions. In the circumstances of the 1920s, claims made on young men's wages by homestead heads may have been unwelcome, but those made by town wives were even more so:

If you keep a woman in the house, your father can't get any money. You use it all, it's comfortable, there's no hardship. Then you say to her, 'I'm going to work'. She goes to the shop, she buys doughnuts. The husband's late, she buys a massive load of doughnuts, she takes them and gives them to her friends, and at the end of the month it's you who pays . . . better to live on your own.[16]

The essential difference between these two potential claims on income lay in the security which they offered. 'Swahili marriages' were often unstable, and resulted in few children: and so offered little security.[17] While workers with wages in their pocket could find women to cook and wash for them and sleep with them, men who were getting too old to work had more difficulty: 'when you're old, those women don't want you any more'.[18] With the cost of housing, and of living generally, rising,

---

[16] Int. 47a, 6.

[17] See Int. 24a, 26c, on 'Swahili' marriages. Children to care for one in old age were and are of considerable importance to Mijikenda (Int. 40a). Officials commented on the low fertility of the Swahili population of Mombasa ('Population', Mombasa District Annual Report (1905–6), draft, 8 May 1906, KNA PC Coast 1/1/113).

[18] Int. CHONYI/2, 2.

those unable to earn had increasing difficulty in claiming support. Some old men did live off the rent from houses they had built,[19] but the insecurity of tenure in Mombasa after 1926 made this an unreliable option.[20] As informants said, *Mombasa yapapasa*, a phrase perhaps best rendered as 'Mombasa lulls one into a false sense of security'.[21] Sending money back to the homestead, and maintaining a family there, provided a much more effective form of security for the future: 'If you work in Mombasa, you must remember where you came from. In Mombasa you will plant nothing, what can you plant in Mombasa? If you are at your home, you can plant crops which tomorrow will benefit you.'[22] The planting was a literal as well as a figurative one. Intensive planting of coconut palms spread northwards along the ridge from Rabai in the first half of this century.[23] In Jibana, this is a development explicitly connected with investment by Jibana who had worked on the coast.[24] Palm trees were, importantly, a form of wealth that could not be appropriated by the homestead head; money sent to the homestead could be used by the homestead head as he liked, but trees were the property of whoever had planted them, or paid for their planting.

It was not only those living outside larger households in Mombasa, in a series of temporary marriages and short-term arrangements, who found their security threatened in the 1920s. Those who had become incorporated by town patrons, virtually as family members, could suddenly face exclusion and denial of their claims to support. This was partly a result of the rising cost of supporting such dependants; hardship exposed their marginality and broke down networks of patronage.[25] Yet

---

[19] Int. 40a, 43b.
[20] This is in contrast to Dar es Salaam, where there were a number of old men, the *fadhahausi*, with some security of tenure on goverment land, who relied on house rents for support in their old age; J. Iliffe, *A Modern History of Tanganyika* (Cambridge, 1979), 385. In Mombasa, the use of house rents as a sort of pension was noted in the 1940s; 'Social and Economic Survey of Mombasa' (1947), 56, 69, PRO CO 533, 545/4.
[21] Int. 8a, 1.   [22] Int. 27a, 1.
[23] Herlehy sees this as a 19th-c. development (T. Herlehy, 'Ties that Bind: Palm Wine and Blood Brotherhood on the Kenya Coast during the Nineteenth Century', *IJAHS* (1984), 285–308, 288–9), but informants suggest that the current superabundance of palms is a product of planting in the 1920s and 1930s: Int. 22a.
[24] Int. 29a, 30a.
[25] D. A. Johnson and D. M. Anderson, *The Ecology of Survival: Case Studies from North-East African History* (London and Boulder, Col., 1988), 6–10.

it was also a result of the devaluation of the term 'Swahili' through a colonial discourse which identified the Swahili as the idlers and cheats of the coast population: as the wealthier and more powerful attempted to secure their status and identity, they excluded the marginal members of the group.

In the nineteenth century, claims to Arabian origins had already carried some prestige, though they were by no means universal among the Twelve Tribes,[26] and in the early years of British rule reliance on Arab administrators had tended to increase the prestige attached to such claims.[27] The British soon sought to define firmly the category of 'Swahili', ensuring that it had a lower status than Arab identity. Swahili were 'natives' for the purpose of the 1910 Hut and Poll Tax Ordinance,[28] and the implication of lower status was confirmed in the wording of an amending ordinance on the subject, which put on the individual the onus 'to prove that he is not a Swahili'.[29] The increasingly precise definition of status by descent, and the concomitant danger of losing status by marriage or association with those of inadequate pedigree, pushed the Twelve Tribes and Arab communities of Mombasa into an increasingly tense and violent relationship by the 1920s.[30] Arabs claimed special treatment on the grounds that they had once been the rulers of the coast,[31] and others took up this theme. One Bajun, demanding special status, argued that 'your petitioner is a member of the Bajun tribe of Arabs, one of the earlier of the Arab colonizing tribes on the Coast of East Africa'.[32] While this renegotiation of the boundaries between

---

[26] R. Pouwels, *Horn and Crescent: Cultural Change and Traditional Islam on the East African Coast, 800–1900* (Cambridge, 1987), ch. 5. The Nabahani of Pate, for example, already claimed descent from Arabian settlers; see 'History of Pate', in G. S. P. Freeman-Grenville, *Select Documents of the East African Coast* (Oxford, 1962), 241–96. However, in a 10% sample of Transactions Register A4, for 1895–7, only 17 out of the 41 occurrences of Swahili clan names are Arabicized.

[27] Whereas Arab officials of the Busaidi and other Omani clans had been confirmed in their posts by the British, clan heads of the Twelve Tribes were refused the stipend that the Busaidi had paid them; see F. J. Berg, 'Mombasa under the Busaidi Sultanate', Ph.D. thesis (Wisconsin, 1971), 103; Letter 5/44, Précis of Mail to Mombasa, 27 Jan. 1893, IBEA File 52 (23); also 'Memo on Coast Land Difficulties', Watkins, 11 Oct. 1913, 7, KNA DC MSA 8/2.

[28] Sect. 2, Native Hut and Poll Tax Ordinance, KNA AG/4/798.

[29] Sect. 2, Ordinance No. 15 of 1910, KNA AG/4/798.

[30] H. Kindy, *Life and Politics in Mombasa* (Nairobi, 1972), 35–9.

[31] Petition to Governor, May 1930, PRO CO 533. 411/6.

[32] Petition to Secretary of State, n.d. 1930, KNA AG/4/3111.

Arab and Swahili went on, it provoked an equally significant, and intense, renegotiation of the boundaries of the Swahili and other African groups.

Though some Twelve Tribes leaders inveighed against Arab discrimination against them, they themselves sought to redefine Swahili identity through a use of the Twelve Tribes as an exclusive category, from which poorer Nyika, ex-slave, and other recent immigrants would be excluded. The administration, anxious to see Swahili identity made less permeable, encouraged this differentiation with offers of improved status for the Twelve Tribes: 'It was agreed that members of those families who were able to prove that they were of such grade in the Tissia Taifa or the Thelatha Taifa that they would have been recognized by the Zanzibar Government as Arabs, should also be accorded the status and treatment of Arabs by this government'.[33] The implication was clear: that the Twelve Tribes should themselves take on the task of separating out the population. Officials argued that 'the majority [of the Twelve Tribes] have so intermingled and intermarried with the natives that they are hardly distinguishable from them'.[34] Some Twelve Tribes members were eager to accept the deal: 'those who were present recognized that all members of the twelve tribes were not of the same status, and that the privileges asked for would only be accorded in part and not as a whole'.[35] Arabicized clan names within the Twelve Tribes were increasingly used to separate the Swahili into upper and lower classes, with the implication that the lower class were not true Swahili, but hangers-on: 'It is not really difficult for anyone with any knowledge of the coast people to differentiate between real members of the twelve tribes and followers of the same. The former can personally give Arabic clan origin whereas the latter can only show Nyika origin'.[36] Some Twelve Tribes members even offered to 'point out who was a real member of the Twelve Tribes and who was a follower'.[37]

[33] Ag. CNC to PC, 9 Dec. 1920, KNA PC Coast 1/14/160.
[34] From a description of a meeting between the SC and prominent Twelve Tribes members, given in SC to Governor's Private Secretary, 28 June 1924, KNA PC Coast 1/14/160.
[35] Ibid.   [36] SC to CNC, 13 May 1925, KNA PC Coast 1/10/120B.
[37] Minutes of Governor's meeting with the Afro-Asian Association, 22 Apr. 1932, PRO CO 533. 425/20.

Significantly, after 1920, officials stopped using 'Swahili' as a blanket term for all the African inhabitants of Mombasa, and instead began to use it selectively of 'real' Twelve Tribes members, encouraging the population to differentiate itself.[38] Clearly, it was generally the wealthier members of the group who survived the process of differentiation. In 1930 it was said of the Twelve Tribes that 'they are the owners of considerable property and the majority of them pay non-native tax'.[39]

Official concern about the 'demoralization' of Swahili youth[40]—which was essentially a concern about the presence of a large, permeable, and uncontrollable urban population—was taken up by some of the élite of Mombasa. Uncomfortably aware of their declining economic position and social status, these men turned their wrath on the *beni*, the great vehicle of incorporation,[41] and the coincidence of their interests and those of the administration led to increasing restrictions on the *beni* societies, which were virtually banned from performing by 1934.[42]

Claims to an origin in the Gulf became general among the Twelve Tribes. The adoption of Singwaya as a place of origin had spread among the people of the hinterland as a historical explanation of their closeness to many Swahili, and of their claims upon one another. Yet, only a few years after this story had become current among the people of the hinterland, the perceived need for the Twelve Tribes to distance themselves from the people of the hinterland meant that Singwaya was largely dropped from Twelve Tribes stories of origin.

[38] The Swahili population of Mombasa District dropped from 18,000 in 1917 to 1,063 in 1921, according to official definitions; PC to Military Commissioner for Labour, 25 July 1917, KNA PC Coast 1/1/328 and Mombasa District Annual Report (1921), 1–2, KNA DC MSA 1/3.

[39] 'Report on Native Affairs in Mombasa', Dec. 1930, 4, KNA DC MSA 3/3.

[40] For the use of this term, see *Native Affairs Department Annual Report, 1929*, 7.

[41] For opposition to the *beni*, see Petition to the Governor, published in the *EAS* (D), 22 June 1927; also M. Strobel, *Muslim Women in Mombasa, 1890-1975* (New Haven, Conn., 1979), 168–72; also see A. I. Salim, *The Swahili-Speaking Peoples of the Kenya Coast, 1895-1963* (Nairobi, 1973), 162–5; Int. 71*b*; and R. Pouwels, 'Sheikhal-Amin b. Ali Mazrui and Islamic Modernism in East Africa, 1875–1947', *International Journal of Middle Eastern Studies*, 13 (1981), 329–45.

[42] For offical hostility, see Handing-Over Report, Mombasa District (1931), KNA DC MSA 2/1; for the increasing restrictions on *beni*, see T. O. Ranger, *Dance and Society in Eastern Africa, 1890-1970* (London 1975), 88; and Strobel, *Muslim Women*, 169.

This redrawing of boundaries was to have a dramatic effect on many people from the hinterland, who had become incorporated to Swahili or Arab households but who suddenly found themselves excluded. One Ribe man was converted to Islam by his Arab employer, who became his father; but then found his claims on his patron's family denied:

I stayed in Changamwe nine years, I even married there, a Digo woman, the old man paid the bride price. Then, when the old man died, Nasoro [the Arab's natural son] said, 'You're not an Arab, you're just following the religion, you inherit nothing', and I got angry and left, I even left my wife. Then he stole all the wedding things, the bed, everything. 'You've just come as a religious follower, you're not an Arab . . . I left and I came back here, here to my father.[43]

This exclusion of the marginal did not take place everywhere or simultaneously: but it was an increasingly general pattern, made possible by the redefinition of ethnicity and usually prompted in individual cases by some crisis, such as a dispute over inheritance.[44]

It was not only those of Nyika origins who sought, in these circumstances, to re-establish a rural base in the 1920s. 'Detribalized' Africans of other origins were being absorbed by hinterland homesteads,[45] and ex-slaves were being given wives and adopted by Duruma homesteads.[46] For the most marginal members of the Swahili community, Mombasa was losing its attraction as a long-term home.

The development of networks of Giriama, Digo, Jibana, and others within Mombasa, and the redefinition of Swahili identity, played a crucial part in the construction of a new ethnic identity for these people. While shared origins are now presented as the root of this identity, it was an identity constructed through migration and through changing relationships with other groups, rather than through origins; a product of recent rather than distant history.[47]

---

[43] Int. 39a, 2.

[44] For other examples of rejection in the face of some crisis, see Int. 20c, 58a.

[45] PC to CNC, 15 Feb. 1928, KNA PC Coast 1/11/46.

[46] Ibid., DC Digo to Ag. SCC, 7 Dec. 1927.

[47] The Kru of Liberia may provide a comparison; members of several separate

The first known use of the term Mijikenda is from 1924, when a council of elders in the Digo area adopted *Midzichenda*, 'nine towns' as its title.[48] It was a very accurate title—the elders in question were drawn from nine settlements in the area. Not until the 1940s, when a group of workers in Mombasa founded the Mijikenda Union,[49] did the term become generally used to describe nine of the peoples who had previously been called the Nyika:[50] the nine involved being, usually, those living in closest proximity to Mombasa.

The development of this new identity, if not the new term for it, had begun in the 1920s, in response to changes in the nature of migration and of Swahili identity. The previous complementarity between Swahili and Nyika identity had been disturbed by the newly exclusive nature of Swahili identity and by the migration of Giriama, Digo, and others to Mombasa as members of their groups, rather than through incorporation to the Swahili community. As the 'Nine Tribes' and the 'Three Tribes' labels were used to change the nature of Swahili identity, so Nyika identity was changed, a change which was given a label by the use of the term Mijikenda from the 1940s. Where ethnic identity had been negotiable, constructed through claims on and obligations to others, now it became defined through descent; from the Gulf for the Twelve Tribes and, ironically, from Singwaya for the Mijikenda. An origin story that had expressed commonality came instead to signify distinction.

communities, with some similarities, they created a new identity as Kru through labour migration; F. D. McEvoy, 'Ethnic Realities among the Grebo and Kru Peoples of West Africa', *Africa*, 47/1 (1977), 62–79; J. Martin, 'Krumen "Down the Coast": Liberian Migrants on the West African Coast in the Nineteenth and Early Twentieth Centuries', *IJAHS* 18 (1985), 400–23. Ranger has similarly argued the importance of labour migration and urban networks in the creation of Manyika identity, in 'Missionaries, Migrants and the Manyika: The Invention of Ethnicity in Zimbabwe', in L. Vail (ed.), *The Creation of Tribalism in Southern Africa* (London and Berkeley, Calif., 1989), 118–50.

[48] Digo Station Diary, 5 Apr. 1924, KNA DC KWL 5/1.

[49] Int. 71*b*; Mambo suggests that the Mijikenda Union was founded in Nairobi, on archival evidence—possibly it started in both cities at the same time. R. M. Mambo, 'Nascent Political Activities among the Mijikenda of Kenya's Coast during the Colonial Era', *Trans-African Journal of History*, 16 (1987), 92–120.

[50] One informant claimed that the term had long been in use (Int. 38*a*), but this conflicts with all other evidence.

The confusions and ambiguities surrounding this redefinition persist. The Mijikenda Union is said by some to have been secretly funded by Muses Muhammad,[51] a Mombasan businessman whose leading role in the Swahili Nine Tribes seems unquestioned by many,[52] but who is said by many others to have been a Kauma incorporated to the Kilifi clan of the Swahili Nine Tribes.[53] Muses was a prime example of an incorporated member of the town community who had made good. Having established himself in Mombasa as a ship-chandler, he used his kin ties in the hinterland to work as a trader and to obtain land through mortgages. Muses' covert support for the Mijikenda Union is said to have been prompted by the refusal of the *liwali* of Mombasa to grant him 'non-native' status[54]—though wealthy enough to avoid exclusion, even Muses was threatened by marginality.

The overlap in the terminology used by informants for the Swahili Nine Tribes and the Mijikenda[55] may grow from the way in which the development of the one identity mirrored that of the other: Twelve Tribes to Mijikenda replaced Swahili to Nyika, though the relationship between the two had changed. It is even possible that the significance of the number nine was simply transferred; the number of Nyika groups had not been fixed at nine,[56] and like members of the Swahili Nine Tribes,[57] Mijikenda informants may differ in their listing of the constituent nine groups, selecting them from twelve or thirteen possibilities including Pokomo, Segeju, Taita, and Kamba.

While the name and origin stories of the new Mijikenda identity drew on relationships with the Swahili, a set of historical clichés

---

[51] Int. 68*a*.

[52] Berg's informants suggested that Muses Muhammed, more properly Ali bin Muhammed al-Kilifi, was the *Tamim* or leader of the Nine Tribes; 'Succession of *Tamims* in the nine tribes of Mombasa', Berg, n.d., typescript in Fort Jesus Library, Mombasa.

[53] Int. 50*a*, 5*c*, 68*a*. For Muses' successful use in business of his Mijikenda connections see Int. 26*c*, 68*a*.

[54] Int. 72*a*.   [55] Int. 71*b*.

[56] See J. L. Krapf, *Travels and Missionary Labours during an Eighteen Years' Residence in Eastern Africa* (London) 1968 (first 1860)), 159; and cf. Champion, *The Agiryama of Kenya* (London, 1967), 3, 5.

[57] See the list in KNA DC MSA 3/1; also H. E. Lambert, 'The Arab Community and the Twelve Tribes of Mombasa', in Wilson (ed.), 'The Social Survey of Mombasa', i. 81–92.

developed around this identity which expressed hostility to and separation from the Arabs and Swahili of the coast. The Mijikenda stories of residence on Mombasa island have become the first episode in a history of dispossession at the hands of coastal people:

> At that time, it was a forest, all of Mombasa, it was a forest, people went to hunt animals. Went to kill animals. Their house, they slept at the place called the Fort. That's a rock, it was a rock, lived in like a house . . . that was the house of the Mijikenda. They hunted and brought meat home. When they saw this, they saw this was a good land to farm, they began to clear it and farm. They farmed and prospered there, when they were beginning to prosper, the Arab came . . . The Arab came, when he came, he came as a guest like you, you have been given a seat to sit on. Me, the owner, I sit on the ground. I have sat on the ground because you're on the chair. So then a stranger comes, and asks 'Who is the owner of this place?' I say, 'I am.' You say 'No, the one sitting up here on the chair, they own the country!' And so I'm chased off; in giving the Arab the chair, you've given him the country.[58]

The Swahili occupy a nebulous middle ground in these stories, sometimes described as shameless Mijikenda turncoats denying their origins[59] and at other times dismissed as being the same as Arabs, unrelated to the Mijikenda.[60] Clichéd, timeless figures play a major role in this history of dispossession; Arab planters in Mijikenda areas, accused of stealing Mijikenda land[61] are usually identified simply as 'Sere Ali'—Ali bin Salim el-Busaidi.[62] In modern Kenya, education is widely perceived as the key to wealth, and informants may also present their dispossession in terms of schooling—accusing the Arabs of discouraging Mijikenda from attending mission schools, while secretly sending their own children to school.[63]

Slavery too is woven into these tales of dispossession. Arabs are accused of enticing Mijikenda on to boats with offers of gifts or easy jobs,[64] then taking them to sea to disorient them:

> . . . they were taken, they were put in a dhow, they said 'We're going to *Madzimare* ["deep water"]' Well, it's there, up there near Lamu, they called *Madzimare*. They were turned round in the boats, brought

---

[58] Int. 43a, 2–3.   [59] Int. 5a, 5b.   [60] Int. CHONYI/2.   [61] Int. 20a, 20b.
[62] Int. 44a, 40b.   [63] Int. 22a.   [64] Int. 46a.

here, you don't recognize the place where you were born, you just see the sea, going on and on, without beginning or end, well, you don't know your home.[65]

It is a powerful metaphor for the way in which Mijikenda migrants to Mombasa became 'lost' and failed to return. A similar story was that of the *mumiani*, blood-sucking creatures who inhabited the town and turned the living into zombies who were under their control and never returned from Mombasa.[66] The chief *mumiani* of the 1930s is said to have been Muses Muhammad:[67] the Kauma migrant turned Swahili, the 'lost' Mijikenda whose incorporative networks of credit stretched into the hinterland.[68] The image is even more striking than that of the slaves on the boat.

The *beni* too have been woven into this history of dispossession, accused of being Arab and Swahili devices which impeded the economic development of the coast.[69] As instruments of incorporation to the Swahili community, they too have become colourfully associated with enslavement:

They used to capture them and take them to sell, no one knows where—they had their houses, I don't know—they had a dance, if someone was captured they cried out, and they played the dance. So that the cries wouldn't be heard . . .

Yes, they made a noise, they played a dance . . . they called it *gwaride*.[70]

These are the fundamentals of history as presented by Mijikenda men. As part of this presentation, informants sometimes insist that their ancestors never went to Mombasa voluntarily,[71] and that women in particular have always stayed away from the island.[72] Yet this presentation of hostility and separation is not constant. One informant presented this history of hostility, and said of his own move to Mombasa that it had been easy since he was a Ribe, and the Ribe are the true

---

[65] Int. 46a, 6.
[66] *Mumiani* is, in Swahili, a medicinal herbal preparation which may have been believed to have contained blood. Stories of *mumiani* as blood-suckers became widespread in East Africa in the colonial period.
[67] Int. 66a, 62a, 47a.   [68] Int. 47a.
[69] Int. 20b. See also the comments of Mkangi, drawn from Ribe informants, in Ranger, *Dance and Society*, 152.
[70] Int. 21b, 7–8, informants 30 and 21 talking.
[71] See Int. CHONYI/1, 47a, 4b.   [72] Int. 21a.

owners of Mombasa.[73] But in a later interview, where Mijikenda history generally had not been discussed, he revealed that he had actually moved to Mombasa to live with his Arab 'father'.[74] Another informant, anxious to supply me with the details of Arab and Swahili oppression of the Mijikenda, only later told me that he had been brought up in Mombasa by his Swahili aunts.[75]

Most strikingly, women informants made little of this dispossession theme, nor were they so anxious to talk to me of the history of the Mijikenda as a group.[76] This may reflect their rather different historical experience: for women, unlike men, the 1920s saw no shift in the nature of migration. Those who went to Mombasa went to stay,[77] and complaints from Mijikenda men on the subject continued unabated.[78]

For women, while life in Mombasa may have become harder, the options in the homestead were worse. It was not generally practicable for women to invest earnings from a period of life in Mombasa in the homestead, for they could rarely expect to control the use of property. Young men could look forward to being elders, but women would still be women when they were old.

Indeed, the conditions of life for women in homesteads in many cases became worse in these years. The withdrawal of young men's labour—and those young men who maintained their position in the homestead expressed their obligations through remittance, not through seasonally combining wage labour with work in the homestead[79]—increased the work-load on women, as did the dispersal of cultivation consequent on the planting of palm trees.[80]

Women were intentionally excluded from the new networks which brought Mijikenda men to town in the 1920s and 1930s.

---

[73] Int. 20a.   [74] Int. 20c.   [75] See Int. 5a, 5b, 5c.

[76] With the exception of Int. 74a, where the presence of two men anxious to talk of Mijikenda history initially led a woman informant to talk of Singwaya and the Mijikenda.

[77] Lambert, ADC Digo, Note, 30 May 1924, KNA DC KWL 3/5.

[78] e.g., through the LNCs; Minutes, Malindi LNC, 6 Feb. 1927, KNA PC Coast 1/12/244.

[79] A pattern noted elsewhere in Kenya; Kitching, *Class and Economic Change*, 253.

[80] Int. 35a.

For men to be temporary residents in the town, women had to be kept outside the town, maintaining the homestead; for women were themselves, through the bridewealth system, a form of investment in the homestead. No pattern developed of women going to the town but remitting to the homestead, for women's subordination within the homestead was not easily compatible with the opportunities for independence which Mombasa offered.[81] Women continued to make independent lives as concubines in Mombasa,[82] and in old age lived off the rent from houses or eked out a precarious living as sellers of cooked food.[83] The history of the Mijikenda as told by the men avers that women never went to Mombasa,[84] and in seeking informants I was several times told by men not to talk to women, as they knew nothing of Mombasa.

The change in the nature of migration to Mombasa by Mijikenda men was not complete or immediate, and networks of clientage and incorporation in the town continued to function, as a 1930 report suggested:

Natives from neighbouring districts are usually in Mombasa in greatest numbers at about the time of Hut Tax Collection in their Reserves and they are constantly coming and going. A few of these become Mohammedans and remain as casual labourers but most return to their homes if and when they consider they have made enough money.[85]

Islam continued to be important as a means of incorporation to the town community; asked if his parents had converted to Islam before leaving Mombasa, one informant remarked 'if they had converted, they would have stayed there'.[86] Only among the Digo did a non-Swahili Muslim identity really develop, which may explain why some Mijikenda Muslims on the coast north of Mombasa, anxious to assert both their

---

[81] Some women did manage to return to the homestead from Mombasa: one a Giriama woman who repaid her bride-price to free herself from the husband she had deserted (Int. 34a); and another a Digo woman who, as a Muslim, had inherited wealth (Int. 59a).

[82] Mombasa District Annual Report (1935), KNA DC MSA 1/4.

[83] Int. 24a, 5b, 59a.   [84] Int. 21b.

[85] 'Report on Native Affairs in Mombasa', Dec. 1930, KNA DC MSA 3/3, 6.

[86] Int. 54a, 7.

identity as Mijikenda and their religion as Islam, have adopted Digo identities.[87]

Incorporation could still offer advantages to migrants, despite the danger of later rejection. One Giriama converted to Islam under his employer's tutelage, and thus achieved instant promotion, escaping life as a cement-mixer: 'Ah, I had no more *kibarua*, now I had become a boss! No more work. My job was being sent, to the plantations, he [the patron] had many plantations, even here in Kanamai. . . . I was the overseer'.[88]

The administration had worked hard to break down the incorporative networks of Mombasa, and the decline in their importance brought some gains for the administration and for European employers. Mijikenda working in the new networks often lived, while in Mombasa, in far worse conditions than had the urbanized casual labour which preceded them—some of the coal carriers slept in disused sheds at Mwembe Tayari and cooked their own food after a day's work.[89] The steady reduction in wages of the 1920s was both cause and effect in relation to these new patterns of migration: lower wages made it harder to live as a permanent townsman, while the increasing role of migrants in the work-force made these wage reductions sustainable. Supported by the homestead, and living poorly within the town, the cheapened reproduction of these workers allowed the considerable decline in real wages that took place between 1920 and 1930.

Yet these workers were only a little more amenable to regular discipline and control than were the 'Swahili'. The *kipande* laws were reintroduced, but continued to be evaded by many.[90] New casual labour rules were again proposed in 1928, but the idea was again abandoned.[91] Tax evasion and the numbers of 'unemployed' Africans on the island continued to alarm the

[87] See Field Notes, 10 July 1988, and Int. 48*a*; also D. Parkin, 'Being and Selfhood among Intermediary Swahili', in J. Maw and D. Parkin (eds.), *Swahili Language and Society* (Vienna, 1985), 247–60, for a rather different analysis of this group.

[88] Int. 54*a*, 9. See Int. 50*a* for a similar tale of improved conditions through adoption.

[89] Int. 45*a*.

[90] Evasion through the use of temporary registrations was particularly common in Mombasa; *Native Affairs Department Annual Report, 1929*, 134.

[91] Commissioner for Local Govt. to Chair, Mombasa District Committee, 14 Feb. 1928, KNA AG/4/1319.

administration.[92] Attempts were made in 1932 to expel 'unemployed' Africans, using the vagrancy and registration laws,[93] but these attempts were, apparently, soon abandoned.[94]

The Mijikenda successfully avoided certain kinds of employment, just as the Nyika had done. Despite the failure of several plantation companies[95] there was a continuing demand for labour for sisal estates in particular;[96] but the Mijikenda formed a small proportion of the work-force: 'The Wanyika are still disinclined to work on the Coastal Estates, and the shortage of labour continues to delay coastal development. Wanyika prefer going to Mombasa where wages, particularly at the harbour works, are high.'[97] Digo workers signed on for plantation labour and then disappeared after one or two days' work, a practice made all the easier by a 1923 ruling that workers could not be compelled to attend work if only engaged for a one-month ticket.[98] Such engagements had considerable attraction for Mijikenda, as the Senior Commissioner noted with annoyance; 'It is a common practice for natives residing in the vicinity of European plantations to apply for work thereon, obtain a work ticket to do two or three days' work on it and then keep it as evidence that they are actively employed by a European when called on for District road work.'[99] The Mijikenda were, to a degree, able to exercise choice, and so to avoid work which they disliked. In 1926 the District Commissioner for Kilifi glumly remarked of the sisal plantations: 'It has proved impossible to interest the Wanyika in this kind of work.'[100]

---

[92] For tax, see 'Report on Native Affairs in Mombasa', Dec. 1930, 19, KNA DC MSA 3/3; for unemployment, see Mombasa District Annual Report (1933), 12–13, KNA DC MSA 1/4.

[93] Mombasa District Annual Report (1933), 26, KNA DC MSA 1/4.

[94] Ibid. 27.

[95] For the rubber plantations, see J. F. Munro, 'British Rubber Companies in East Africa before the first World War', *JAH* 24 (1983), 369–79. The East African Estates Ltd., despite its large land grant, had only 2,000 acres under cultivation in 1916, most of it with coconut palms; Vanga District Annual Report (1915–16), KNA DC KWL 1/2.

[96] Prices for sisal fell in the 1920s, but demand remained fairly strong; N. Westcott, 'The East African Sisal Industry, 1929–40: The Marketing of a Colonial Commodity during Depression and War', *JAH* 25 (1984), 445–61.

[97] ADC Kilifi to SC, 3 Oct. 1925, KNA PC Coast 1/19/124.

[98] Digo District Annual Report (1924), 4, KNA DC KWL 1/10; Supreme Court Case 105/23, 13 Dec. 1923, KNA AG/4/1640.

[99] SC to Paton, Manager of Maunguja Estate, 21 Mar. 1924, KNA PC Coast 1/9/52. Those signed up to an employer were not liable to compulsory labour on public works.

In avoiding these kinds of work, and maintaining their independence from the state's desire to record and control them, Mijikenda still made use of the opportunities which Mombasa offered. Those who went to work in Mombasa as migrants paid a price—continued subordination within the homestead, and a low standard of living in the town. A bleak picture has been painted of the 'culture of poverty' in which a similar workforce, taking no part in town institutions, lived at this time.[101] Yet the Mijikenda in Mombasa were not hopeless or helpless. The colonial state had narrowed their options, and restricted their freedoms, but, through adaptation and renegotiation of identity, Mijikenda young men, women, and elders each maintained some ability to decide for themselves how they would live.

[100] Kilifi Subdistrict Annual Report (1926), KNA DC KFI 1/2; see also Int. 39a.
[101] J. Iliffe, A Modern History of Tanganyika (Cambridge, 1979), 386, 388.

Conclusion

The meaning of identity, and the nature of history, changed dramatically on the coast in the twentieth century. A previous system, whereby identity had been intensely negotiable and had been defined by attachments, the nature of obligations and claims, came into direct conflict with the colonial vision of an Africa peopled by distinct and fixed ethnic groups, defined by descent, each with its separate and traditional form of government. Official concern over this conceptual conflict and the administrative problems which it generated was intensified by the perception that the labour problems experienced by European employers on the coast were a result of the influence of Arabs and Swahili over the population of Mombasa's local hinterland, and of the ease with which Africans could move to Mombasa and become part of an urban culture that was regarded as work-shy and dishonest.

Official attempts to push the Nyika into particular forms of wage labour were resisted with some success. But the form of this resistance, and the behaviour of some Arabs and Swahili who manipulated colonial perceptions of ethnicity to their own advantage, led to a redefinition of identity that was rather more consonant with official perceptions of ethnicity. Ethnic identity became itself an institution through which networks of claim and obligation were constructed. Based now on ideas of origins and descent, ethnic identity lost much of its negotiability; and the possibilities for incorporation were diminished. History, as the foundation of identity, was remade in a framework of separation and hostility. United by the experience of exclusion and by participation in new urban networks which emphasized their shared distinctness from Arabs and Swahili, the people of Mombasa's local hinterland reworked a history that had once expressed their commonality with the Swahili, to make it instead an expression of their own unity, and of a shared experience of dispossession.

While the unity of the Mijikenda was somewhat shaky

during the 1940s,[1] it was to be reinforced in the 1950s through the debate over coastal autonomy.[2] Many Mijikenda, aware of the way in which Arabs and Swahili had exploited identity to their advantage in the colonial period, opposed autonomy, fearing a low status in any such autonomous state. Some Twelve Tribes members, fearful of domination by a non-Islamic state in which up-country people held most of the power, argued in turn that the Mijikenda were recent arrivals on the coast, who should have no say in the matter.[3] The continuing intense dispute over land on the coast, in which disputants frequently seek historical backing for their claims through stories of dispossession, has kept the issue of Mijikenda history very much alive.[4] Now, a Mijikenda historiography which bases the unified and discrete Mijikenda identity in a history of shared migration from Singwaya is an accepted truth, taught in schools and widely published, its veracity confirmed by constant repetition. Yet it is a history, and an identity, of recent origin; a truth whose ambiguity is constantly reflected in historical presentation.

---

[1] The Mijikenda Union broke down soon after its formation in the 1940s, to be superseded by other societies based on more particular identities, such as the Giriama Welfare Association: Int. 71b.

[2] Identity may still be expressed through reference to these events; one informant referred to Arabs and Swahili as *wale Mwambao-mwambao*, 'those Mwambao people'. 'Mwambao' was the name of the independent or autonomous coastal state sought by some.

[3] Several informants raised this issue, unprompted; see Int. 61a and 61b for the attitude of a Twelve Tribes member active in arguing for the Mijikenda views to be ignored, and Int. 5a and 5b for a Digo perspective.

[4] Int. 5a, 5b, 55a.

Appendix: Biographies of Informants

As some informants requested anonymity, all are identified by number only. Transcripts of interviews are deposited at the University of Nairobi and at the British Institute in Eastern Africa, Nairobi.

Informant 1: member of the Kilindini clan of the Three Tribes, born in Hailendi about 1910. He said that his grandfather had come to Mombasa from Pemba, having previously come from Oman. His grandfather's land in Mtongwe was cultivated by 'Swahili' without land, whom he also referred to as Duruma and Jibana. Informant's father had bought Duruma cattle and sold them in Mombasa, and had a number of Digo wives. Informant had been a merchant seaman most of his life.

Informant 4: a Duruma man, born around 1930. A seller of medicinal plants in Makupa market, he first came to Mombasa in 1960.

Informant 5: a Digo man, born in 1915 in Likoni. His grandfather and several great-uncles had moved to Mombasa from elsewhere, having converted to Islam. His father was brought up in Mombasa. When 5 was 2 years old he was sent to Mombasa to live with his father's sister, who was a Swahili, and from there he went to live with his great-uncle, who was also a Swahili. In 1938, 5 moved from Mombasa back to the mainland as a result of house demolitions.

Informant 8: a Duruma man, born in Kinango in about 1933. He left home at the age of 9 to live with his *wajomba* in Changamwe, and has since remained in Mombasa.

Informant 9: a Digo man, born around 1910. His great-great-grandfather was born in Magodzoni, but moved to Junju and converted to Islam. His great-grandfather lived in Junju and kidnapped people to sell as slaves. He was imprisoned in Fort Jesus as a punishment for this, but he and his wife escaped from there and went to live with his wife's relatives near Ng'ombeni. From there they went to Pungu. His grandfather lived in Pungu and worked buying cattle from Duruma and Zigua and selling them to his *tajiri*, Khonzi, a Digo Swahili who lived in Mombasa. He also helped a Swahili/Digo woman relative run a coconut plantation. His father followed the same business in cattle, selling to a Mombasa Arab who had a matrilineal kin tie with him. His father fell out with his neighbours in Pungu, was imprisoned for fighting, and after this went with other members of his dance society to found a new village, Shikaadabu. Informant 9 ran away to Mombasa as a child, and joined the Kingi *beni*, whose leader was a Three Tribes man of Digo origins; he then lived in town and performed as a stunt-man for this *beni* before tiring of life in the town and returning to Shikaadabu.

Informant 10: a Digo man, born about 1914. His father died in the Carrier Corps, and he went to live with his father's brother, who tapped and sold palm wine. He worked at Mbaraki as a coal-carrier in the 1930s, and his uncle gave him the wealth to marry.

Informant 12: a Digo man, born in 1911. His grandfather converted to Islam and came to Mombasa, and 12 and his father were both born in Mombasa. His father lived on the land of an Arab friend in Shimanzi until this house was demolished in the 1920s. After this they rented land in Majengo. Informan 12 worked first as an office messenger for Smith-Mackenzie, then on the docks, where he became a *serang* and an officer in the Sadla *beni*. In the 1940s he started working for the Navy, and in 1945 he moved to Likoni.

Informant 13: a Digo man, born around 1915. His father was born in Bombo, and left there when 13's grandfather died, dissatisfied with his uncles' treatment of him. He went to Likoni, to a relative of his mother. Informant 13 was born here, and his father paid the bridewealth for him to marry. He started working on the Likoni ferry in 1930, and found jobs there for two of his brothers.

Informant 15: a Digo man, born in 1925. His grandfather was a Digo who moved to Mwakirunge and converted to Islam. His father was born in Mwakirunge, and he was born in Kisauni, where they lived on the land of an Arab woman from Mwakirunge. His father died when he was young, and he lived as a fruit-hawker. He married a Rabai wife and paid the bride-price with his own money.

Informant 16: a Giriama man, born around 1918, His great-grandfather was a slave from Malawi, who was freed and settled at Kwa Jomvu Mission. He married into a Giriama clan, and the family stayed on mission land for several generations until 16, who worked as a clerk, bought land of his own as he wanted to plant trees.

Informant 18: a Duruma man, born around 1910. His maternal grandfather was a Muslim who lived at Changamwe and herded cattle, and who married a slave from the area which is now Tanzania. He moved to Mariakani to find better grazing for his cattle. His mother married a Duruma from near Mariakani, then left him and fled to her mother, who still lived in Changamwe. Her eldest son worked as a hawker to pay back the bridewealth which his father had paid for his mother; having done so, this son then became the head of the family. In Changamwe the family lived by selling tobacco, hawking fruit, and herding stock for others.

Informant 20: a Ribe man, born around 1900. He was born near Mtanganyiko, and his mother was a Ribe from Mwakirunge. In the 1918 famine the family moved to Mwakirunge, and 20 went to stay with his father's sister who had married an Arab in Mtanganyiko and lived with him in Mombasa. He worked as a casual at the docks and as a healer. He married in Mombasa. When his aunt and her husband died, 20 went to live with their children in Junda, but his wife fell ill and these cousins would not help her, so he and his wife moved back to Mwakirunge, to his natural father. His wife died, and he went back to Mombasa to work as a court interpreter and as a member of the Native Tribunal, until he retired back to Mwakirunge.

Informant 21: a Jibana man, born in 1920. He was born at Mgamboni, in Jibana, and as a young boy he went to Mombasa, where he lived in the house of an Arab woman in Bondeni, hawking perfume which the woman made. He danced with the Scotchi *beni*. He left Mombasa in 1937 (when there was an outbreak of fighting between Luo and Hadhrami Arabs in Mombasa), because a group of Arabs mistook him for a Luo. He never returned.

Informant 22: a Jibana man, born around 1926. His father was a Christian, who came to Tsunguni in Jibana in 1914, having been expelled from the Sabaki area, where he had lived among the Giriama. His father died when he was young, and he went to Mombasa because his uncles did not care for him. He worked as a domestic for an Arab in Bondeni, but left because the wages were so bad. He worked briefly in a shop, then as a building labourer, employed by a Giriama *serang*. In 1946 he returned to Jibana, and his uncle paid for him to marry.

Informant 23: a Jibana man, born in 1923. His father was a Christian. He was taken for forced labour in 1941, and after this he went to Mombasa to stay with a Chonyi relative in the house of this relative's uncle, who had converted to Islam and lived in Mombasa. He found a job as a building labourer, rented a room, and himself became a *serang*. He remitted wages to his father and maintained a wife in Jibana. In Mombasa he danced the *mavunye* and after five years of intermittent labour he retired to Jibana to live off the income from palm trees planted by his wife.

Informant 24: a Ribe woman, born around 1905. She was born in Mwakirunge. Her father was a Giriama convert to Islam who had been living in Mombasa. When she was 2 years old her mother left her father and went to live in Mombasa with her sister and brother. She was given to a Three Tribes family to be raised, as the head of this family had originally converted her mother. Her mother was taken back to Mwakirunge by her husband, but fled again when he was conscripted for the Carrier Corps. Her mother returned to Mombasa and lived in Kilindini selling fruit. Informant 24 married once but quickly separated, and lived by selling cooked food outside her house. She earned enough to build a house and live off the rent from this.

Informant 25: a Chonyi man, born around 1908. His father farmed rice and maize and planted coconuts at Mwarakaya. Informant 25 left Mwarakaya as a boy, his father not having enough money to support him, and went to stay with Chonyi relatives in Kuze, Mombasa. They were renting the house from a Swahili. There were no women in the house, and the men shared all the housework. He worked first cleaning lighters at Kilindini and then at the coal wharf, where his father's brother was a *serang*. After three years he left and went back to Chonyi, where his grandfather paid for him to marry, his father having died. In the 1930s he and his wife went briefly to hawk firewood in Mombasa, to earn tax money.

Informant 26: a Chonyi man, born in Mwarakaya around 1918. He left because of his parents' poverty and went to live in Mombasa at the house of his father's brother, who worked at Kilindini. He worked first at the Regal Cinema and then at Kilindini, where his *serangi* was Salim bin Ali. In Mombasa he lived for a while at a house where another Chonyi was staying, this house being the property of the other man's aunt, who was married in the town and had plantations in Changamwe on which the other man worked. He married in the town, and paid the bridewealth himself. He danced in the Sadla. In 1959 he left Kilindini for a monthly job with Shell Oil, and in 1973 he returned to Mwarakaya to live alone, his wife having left him.

Informant 27: a Chonyi man, born around 1911. He was born in Mwarakaya, and in 1928 worked briefly at Kilindini cleaning lighters. In Mombasa he stayed with his father's cousin, who lived in the town, having been taken there as a child.

Informant 30: a Jibana man, born around 1918 near Kilulu, Jibana. He was taken to Mombasa as a boy by his father's brother. This man worked in Bondeni, having found a job as a domestic through an aunt converted to Islam who lived in Kisauni. He lived as a child/domestic servant in the house of a Swahili family in Kibokoni. He left this job and his aunt found him another in Kisauni, where he lived as a domestic, eating separately. He danced in the *namba* at

Kisauni, which dance was led by a Giriama water-seller. In the 1930s he returned to Kilulu and tapped palm trees for his father. In 1945 he moved on to Muses Muhammad's land on the coast, and there married a Jibana woman. He returned to Kilulu when his father died.

Informant 31: a Rabai man, born around 1925 at Mgumowapadza, Rabai. In the 1936 famine he worked in Mombasa as a domestic servant, and his father collected his wages every month. In 1938 he returned to work as a tapper for his father.

Informant 32: a Rabai man, born about 1910. His father died in the Carrier Corps, and he was brought up by his father's elder brother. In the 1918 famine, he was sent to Mombasa to sell chickens and buy grain. In the later 1920s, he started working as a tapper in Majengo, his younger brother having worked there already. He worked inter-mittently there for nine years, renting a room in Majengo from a Duruma.

Informant 35: a Rabai woman, born in Mgumowapadza in about 1920. As a married woman, she earned money for herself by cutting firewood in Rabai and taking it to Mombasa to hawk. She also car-ried her father-in-law's copra to Mombasa for sale, but received no payment for this.

Informant 36: a Rabai man, born around 1906. He was taken by his father to work as a tapper on a plantation in Changamwe in the 1920s. He lived on the plantation, and sent his earnings to his father, who paid for him to marry. Informant 36 also found other Rabai to work on this plantation.

Informant 37: a Rabai woman, born in about 1898. She was married in 1916, but her husband was taken for the Carrier Corps, and his younger brother took her as his wife. He tapped palms, and she made ghee from the milk of her father-in-law's cattle, the earnings from which she gave to her father-in-law.

Informant 38: a Kambe man, born in 1918 at Pangani (north of Mombasa, between the ridge and the sea). His father sold rice to itinerant Arab traders and transported copra and bananas through Mwakirunge to Mombasa. His father became a Muslim, but he himself went to mission school and became a Christian. In the 1930s he went to work on a sisal estate with an older Kambe man, against the wishes of his father to whom he did not remit his wages. He returned to his father after this work, however.

Informant 39: a Ribe man, born around 1920, near Chauringo. He disliked having to farm for his father, and ran away while still a boy.

He worked first in Rabai, as a domestic for the Arab clerk of an Indian trader. The father of this Arab adopted him and took him to Mombasa, where he paid for him to marry and employed him on a coffee-stall. When this man died, his son chased him away. He returned to Ribe, then went to work as a policeman at Kilifi, where he lived well on bribes.

Informant 40: a Ribe man, born in 1917 at Kinung'una. His father was a Christian, and had worked briefly as a building labourer in Mombasa. Informant 40 went to Mombasa in 1932, to work as a domestic for a European family, alternating this with periods of casual labour pushing a hand-cart. He stayed in Bondeni, in the house of some Ribe who had gone to Mombasa and never returned. He always remitted money to his father, and in 1938 returned to stay with him. His father paid for him to marry.

Informant 41: a Giriama man, born around 1920 at Vuga, in Jibana. His father was a Jibana by birth, but left Jibana in anger as a young man because his sisters were sold as slaves. He joined a Giriama homestead near the Sabaki. In 1914 he returned to Vuga. In 1918–19 he and his wife went briefly to Kisauni as building labourers. 41 herded his father's cattle as a child, then learned to tap. In about 1934 he went to Mombasa with some other Giriama and worked with them for a Swahili building contractor who employed only Giriama labour. He was adopted by this Swahili and taken into his house, then he rented his own room, living with a succession of women. In the second year of this his natural father came and took him back to Jibana, and paid for him to marry. He never returned to Mombasa. In 1936 and 1944 he was sentenced to forced labour for tax default.

Informant 43: a Rabai man, born in Buni, Rabai, in about 1908. In 1923 he went to work as a tapper in Changamwe. All the tappers who worked with him were Rabai. After a period back in Rabai, he went to Mombasa briefly as a casual builder, to earn tax money. After a further period in Rabai he went to work at the coaling wharf. He then returned to marry in Rabai, going back to Mombasa in the mid-1930s as a tapper for a brief period to earn the price of a second wife.

Informant 44: Kambe man, born around 1910. He was born in Mereni, but moved with his father to live in *kaya* Kambe. His father died there, and he then had no one to care for him and so went to work on a sisal plantation. He left there, as the work was hard, and got a job on the Nyali bridge construction, 1928–9. He then returned briefly to Mereni, but quickly went to Mombasa to stay with his

father's younger brother who had converted to Islam and married a
Swahili, paying the bride-price with his own money. He was then
adopted by a Mombasan of slave origins who converted him to Islam
and for whom he worked crewing a tourist boat. They lived first in
Hailendi, and then in Kisauni. Both he and his patron danced in the
Sadla *beni*, of which his patron was an official. In 1933 he rejected all
this and returned to Kambe to live.

Informant 45: a Giriama man, born in Godoma about 1908. His
father lived in Mombasa during the 1898–9 famine, staying with a
sister who had married there. He and his wife left when his wife fell
ill. After the 1914 rising, the family moved to Mariakani to avoid the
fine imposed by the British. From there, troubled by disease in their
herds, they moved to Mibani, to a homestead where one of his sisters
was married. In the 1920s he went to work at the coaling wharf,
finding work through a Kauma *serang* who was related by marriage
to his mother's brother. He danced *namba* in the town and returned
to his father's homestead to marry.

Informant 46: a Giriama man, born at Godoma before 1913. Father
and mother moved to Kisauni, to mission land, during the 1898–9
famine, then moved to Gotani, near Mariakani. In the 1920s, 46 was
given a wife by his father, but she died, and he worked for the Public
Works Department for several years before marrying again and
returning to Gotani.

Informant 47: a Giriama man, born in Gotani in 1912. His family
moved to Mwamleka in 1915 to plant palm trees, for which Gotani
is too dry. In 1929 he went to Mombasa with other Giriama, hoping
to earn bridewealth. In Mombasa his father's younger brother introduced him to the Giriama overseer of a quarry near Changamwe.
The overseer found him work and a room to rent in the house of a
Digo Swahili. He sent his wages to his father, who paid for him to
marry, and his wife stayed on his father's homestead. In 1944, he
was moved to a new quarry near Mtwapa, and he brought his family
to live there too, on the land of a Digo.

Informant 48: a Digo man, born near Mtwapa around 1909. (Other
informants insisted that this man was a Kambe.) His father converted to Islam in Mtongwe and then came to Mtwapa. He went to
Mtongwe as a young man, and worked at Kilindini, where his father's
elder brother was a *serang*. He sent his earnings to his father, who
invested them in goats and paid for him to marry. He returned to live
in Mtwapa at his father's homestead.

Informant 49: a Swahili man, born in Shariani about 1908. His
grandfather was a Nyasa slave, who farmed maize at Shariani for his

master. Informant 49 said 'we are the real Swahili'. His father lived on the same land as his grandfather, and one of his father's brothers bought a portion of this land after working for the IBEA Company. He went to Mombasa in 1918 to stay with his mother, who had run away from his father and lived unmarried in a house in the Old Town with many other people. The house was owned by a Swahili of Giriama origins. His mother's brother found him a job on the boats carrying people to and from the steamers. In 1925 this work ended, and he took a monthly job with the Railways, which he kept until 1957. In 1933 he married a Swahili of Digo origins, paying the bride-price with his own money. He played trumpet in the Sadla as a young man, his mother's brother being an official of this *beni*.

Informant 50: a Digo man, born about 1920. His father was born in Matuga and converted to Islam there, living as a fisherman and planting palms. He was born in Matuga and went to Mombasa in the later 1930s, staying first with friends. He worked as a casual porter at the station at this time, and rented a room in the house of a Chonyi Muslim who found him work in an eating-house owned by an Arab. The Arab trusted him, promoted him, and paid the bride-wealth for him to marry, and in 1945 he moved to Mtwapa as the overseer of this Arab's land.

Informant 51: a Duruma man, born in Rabai about 1920. His father was Duruma and his mother half Duruma and half Giriama. His mother ran away to Mombasa, where she lived in the house of a Chonyi Muslim woman and converted to Islam. She hawked water in the town. His father died when he was about 7 years old, and his mother took him to Mombasa, where he worked as a domestic in the house of the Chonyi woman. His mother then married a Giriama man, and moved to the Sabaki. She took 51 part of the way, but left him at the homestead of some of her relatives in Vitengeni. He ran away from there to join the Public Works Department. His mother left her new husband after a few months and went to Changamwe, where she married again and remained until she died. Informant 51 was laid off from his work and went to live at Majengo-Mtwapa, on Crown Land. Here he was arrested for tax default. An Arab paid his taxes for him, and he converted to Islam and worked for this Arab carrying water to the mosque.

Informant 53: a Hadhrami man, born in Shariani about 1905. His father had come to Mombasa from the Hadhramaut and set up shops in Shariani and around Mtanganyiko, where he bought grain from local farmers for shipment to Mombasa. He married several Mijikenda wives. Informant 53's mother was a Kauma, a lineage which he recites with as much pride as his Arab lineage. His mother's father was killed in a fight with some Duruma over slave-raiding, and his children fled to 53's father for protection, as some of them had already converted to Islam under his influence. As a boy, he worked at Kilindini and danced in the Scotchi *beni*. He then returned to Shariani and sold water, paying others to farm land there for him. His father's shops went bankrupt, a fate which he attributes to his elder brother having struck and abused his mother because she was an 'Mnyika'. He himself divorced his first wife, an Arab, because she mistreated his Kauma mother. He then ran a shop for an Arab in Shariani, married a number of Mijikenda wives, and finally moved to Kidutani, to the land of one of his fathers-in-law, whom he had converted to Islam.

Informant 55: a Digo man, born around 1910 at Jumba la Mtwana. His father was a Muslim who had moved to the area from south of Mombasa. In 1926 55 went to Mombasa, worked as a fisherman, and danced in the Scotchi. Before going to Mombasa he had sold fish, which he and his father caught, to a Digo at Mombasa fish-market, and when he went to Mombasa he stayed with this man, whom he referred to as his 'father' and *tajiri*. He worked on this man's boat. He spent almost all his money in Mombasa, on women and dancing, but did occasionally send some to his father. He stayed in Mombasa until 1950 without marrying. His Mombasan father then died, and he returned to Mtwapa, where he married and stayed in his father's homestead.

Informant 56: a Rabai man, born in Jitoni, near Miritini. His father was a drunkard, who mortgaged his palm trees to buy another wife for himself. His father also bought him a wife, but she died and there was no money either to buy another wife or to feed the child of his first marriage. In 1929 he went to Mombasa, where he found work at Kilindini. When he missed work he scavenged crabs and fruit to eat. In Mombasa he rented part of an unfinished house to sleep in, and sent wages back to his mother to support his child. Then a friend found him a job as a hire-purchase hawker for an Indian, but in 1935 he left this job, fearing that he would grow old in Mombasa with no place of his own, 'like an ex-slave'. He went to Jitoni, and started growing sugar-cane. He joined the Seventh-Day Adventist Church, which lent him the money to marry again. Then the land at Jitoni, to which he had no claim, was taken by the Veterinary Department, and he moved to Buni to plant palm trees.

Informant 58: a Digo man, born in Waa about 1915. He lived with his father, the then chief of Waa, and his father bought him a wife; but in the early 1930s resenting his dependence on his father, he went to work in Mombasa. He lived first at Likoni in the house of a great-aunt, sharing a room with seven or eight other Digo men, and then he moved to Majengo to rent his own room. He worked as a casual at Kilindini and danced in the Sadla. Another Digo then found him a job working as a hawker for an Arab. In this job he worked with Digo, Giriama, and Taita, but he joined another *beni* group (possibly a subgroup of Sadla) called MP. He became very close to his employer, adopted an Arabic genealogy and cut off contact with his wife in Waa. The special treatment he received inspired the enmity of his colleagues, who persuaded the employer's business associate, another Arab, that 58 had seduced his wife. He was fired sometime in the late 1930s, and returned to Waa.

Informant 59: a Digo woman, born in Ukunda about 1915. Her parents were Muslims, and died when she was young. She moved to her father's brother at Magodzoni, and was then taken by her elder sister to Changamwe, to stay with another brother of her father. He was living on the land of a Swahili, guarding it but doing no other work and paying no rent. The land was worked by migrant Duruma. Her sister was married, and her sister's husband worked as a coconut harvester, while 59 worked in the household for her sister. They then moved to her sister's father-in-law's house in Mtongwe. Informant 59 was married here. Her husband soon died, and she moved to Mombasa in the 1930s and lived there for three years in a house owned by a woman of Digo origins. Informant 59 lived with a succession of young men, and was a member of a spirit-possession society. Then she moved to Waa, where her sister's husband had land and she had palm trees, and she married again.

Informant 60: a Digo man, born in Matuga about 1920. His father was a drunkard, and, as a boy, he worked helping his mother carry charcoal to sell in Mombasa. He then ran away to a relative of his mother who was an ex-slave of Ali bin Salim el-Busaidi. She lived in Hailendi and still worked for Ali bin Salim. Through her he found work with other Arabs as an errand-boy, but his mother's brother persuaded him to go back to Matuga. He and his mother then lived as petty traders: he earned money picking coconuts, which money they invested in chickens to sell in Mombasa. They sold chickens and charcoal to Hadhrami traders in Mombasa, and brought to-bacco and dried fish back to Matuga to sell. This precarious capital accumulation was twice disrupted by 60 marrying and then leaving his wife. In 1946 he made a brief foray into Mombasa market, lending money to a Digo stall-holder at Mwembe Tayari to buy more goods, but they abandoned the stall in the 1947 strike and could not get another.

Informant 66: a Duruma man, born in Mlafyeni around 1918. His father died when he was young and he was brought up by his father's brother. As a boy he herded goats, until his uncle lent him money to start trading in chickens. He gave the profits from this trade to the homestead head, who bought him a wife. He walked to and from Mombasa in this trade, but avoided sleeping on the island, where he feared muggers and *mumiani*. When his uncle could not afford to pay tax for him, he worked as a casual agricultural labourer for Digo or Duruma farmers. He set up his own homestead on the death of his uncle.

Informant 67: a Digo man, born in Dar es Salaam about 1910. His father had gone there from Mombasa. In about 1918 his parents returned to Mombasa, but he went to Tanga and was found work as a servant to a European elephant hunter. This man was killed by an elephant near Moshi, and 67 went to Mombasa to stay with his parents in Hailendi. His father died very shortly after this; 67's elder brothers were in Mombasa, and took care of him. He worked at the coaling-wharf, then as a winch-man, and then at Kilindini into the 1950s. He danced in the Sadla. In later life he started to farm at Ukunda, on the land of his mother's clan, where he grew annual crops for the Mombasa market. In old age he returned to Mombasa, renting out the land at Ukunda.

Informant 71: a man who refused to claim membership of any group. He was born in Takaungu about 1910. His father worked as a ship's captain in Takaungu, and when his father died in 1920, he went to Mombasa and stayed with his elder brother in Mwembe Kuku. His elder brother worked at Kilindini, and he himself found work there, through a *serang* who had known his mother's brother. This man became his adoptive father. Informant 71 stayed on the docks until 1973.

Informant 74: a Digo woman, sister of informant 67. She was born in Dar es Salaam in about 1912. Unlike 67, she said that their father was a Yao slave who had run away from Mombasa and married a Digo woman in Ukunda; their move to Dar seems to have been connected with the flight there of some Mazrui after they launched a brief revolt in 1895. She came back to Mombasa with her parents and was brought up by a Duruma woman in Hailendi, who was part of a spirit-possession group. This woman had been taken to Takaungu as a slave, then had been taken from there by an Arab who married her to a convert to Islam. She later left this husband and went to farm at Tsunza. Informant 74 was brought up by this woman and by her *mama wa kumwosha*, who taught her correct behaviour at puberty and for whom she did domestic work. This woman was in the same dance society as the Duruma woman who raised her. Informant 74 was married to a Pemba man, whom she managed to leave. She was then married to a Mazrui man, who took great care of her. When he died she left his house, though she could have inherited it, because she thought his relatives had murdered him by witchcraft and they might kill her too. Then she lived by casual work at the coffee factory and by food-selling, remaining in Mombasa until now.

Bibliography

ALLEN, J. DE V., 'Swahili Culture Reconsidered: Some Historical Implications of the Material Culture of the Northern Kenya Coast in the Eighteenth and Nineteenth Centuries', *Azania*, 9 (1974), 105–38.
—— 'Traditional History and African Literature: The Swahili Case', *JAH* 23 (1982), 227–36.
—— 'Witu, Swahili History and the Historians', in Salim (ed.), *State Formation in Eastern Africa* (London and Nairobi, 1986), 216–49.
—— (trans.), *Al-Inkishafi: Catechism of a Soul* (Nairobi, 1977).
AMBLER, C., *Kenyan Communities in the Age of Imperialism: The Central Region in the Nineteenth Century* (New Haven, Conn., 1988).
ANDERSON, D. M., and KILLINGRAY, D., *Policing the Empire: Government, Authority and Control, 1830–1940* (Manchester, 1991).
ANON. Typescript translation of extract from Botelho, *Memoria estatistica sobre os dominos portueguezes na Africa oriental*, in Fort Jesus Library, Mombasa.
—— Typescript translation of extract from Bocarro, *Decada XIII da historia da India*, in Fort Jesus Library, Mombasa.
ARENS, W., 'The Waswahili: The Social History of an Ethnic Group', *Africa*, 45 (1975), 426–38.
AUSTEN, R. A., 'Slavery among Coastal Middlemen: The Duala of Cameroon', in S. Miers and I. Kopytoff (eds.), *Slavery in Africa: Historical and Anthropological Perspectives* (Madison, Wis., 1977), 305–33.
—— 'The Metamorphoses of Middlemen: the Duala, Europeans and the Cameroon Hinterland, *c.*1800–*c.*1960', *IJAHS* 16 (1983), 1–25.
BALDOCK, R. W., 'Colonial Governors and the Colonial State: A Study of British Policy in Tropical Africa, 1918–1925', Ph.D. thesis (Bristol, 1978).
BARNES, S., *Patrons and Power: Creating a Political Community in Metropolitan Lagos* (London, 1986).
BAUMANN, O., *Usambara und seine Nachbarsebiete* (Berlin, 1891).
BEECH, M., 'Slavery on the East Coast of Africa', *JAS* 15 (1915–16), 145–9.
BERG, F. J., 'Mombasa under the Busaidi Sultanate', Ph.D. thesis (Wisconsin, 1971).

BERG, F. J., 'The Coast from the Portuguese Invasion', in B. A. Ogot (ed.), *Zamani: a Survey of East African History* (Nairobi, 1974).

—— 'Succession of Tamims in the Nine Tribes of Mombasa', n.d., typescript in Fort Jesus Library.

BINNS, H. K., 'Recollections in 1898 of Experiences in 1878', manuscript in KNA H. K. Binns Collection.

BOTELER, T., *Narrative of a Voyage of Discovery to Africa and Arabia* (London, 1835).

BOXER, C. R., and AZEVEDO, C., *Fort Jesus and the Portuguese in Mombasa, 1593–1729* (London, 1960).

BRANTLEY, C., 'Gerontocratic Government: Age-Sets in Pre-Colonial Giriama', *Africa*, 48 (1978), 248–64.

—— *The Giriama and Colonial Resistance in Kenya, 1800–1920* (Los Angeles, 1981).

BROWN, W. T., 'Bagamoyo: An Historical Introduction', *TNR* 71 (1970), 69–83.

—— 'A Pre-Colonial History of Bagamoyo: Aspects of the Growth of an East African Port Town', Ph.D. thesis (Boston, Mass., 1971).

BRYCESON, D. F., 'A Century of Food Supply in Dar es Salaam: From Sumptuous Suppers for the Sultan to Maize Meals for a Million', in J. Guyer (ed.), *Feeding African Cities: Studies in Regional Social History* (London, 1987), 155–97.

CASHMORE, T. H. R., 'A Note on the Chronology of the Wanyika of the Kenya Coast', *TNR* 57 (1961), 153–72.

—— 'Kaloleni Diary', KNA MSS 225/2.

CHAMPION, A., *The Agiryama of Kenya* (London, 1967).

CHAUNCEY, G., 'The Locus of Reproduction: Women's Labour in the Zambian Copperbelt, 1927–1953', *Journal of Southern African Studies*, 7 (1981), 135–64.

CHITTICK, N., *Kilwa: An Islamic Trading City on the East African Coast* (Nairobi, 1974).

—— 'The "Book of the Zanj" and the Mijikenda', *IJAHS* 9 (1796), 68–73.

CLAYTON, A., and SAVAGE, D., *Government and Labour in Kenya, 1895–1963* (London, 1974).

COHEN, D., *Womunafu's Bunafu: A Study of Authority in a Nineteenth-Century African Community* (Princeton, NJ, 1977).

—— and ATIENO-ODHIAMBO, E. S., *Siaya: The Historical Anthropology of an African Landscape* (London and Nairobi, 1989).

CONSTANTIN, F., 'Condition Swahili et identité politique', *Africa*, 57 (1987), 219–33.

—— 'Social Stratification on the Swahili Coast: From Race to Class', *Africa*, 59 (1989), 145–61.

COOPER, F., *Plantation Slavery on the East African Coast* (New Haven, Conn., 1977).

—— *From Slaves to Squatters: Plantation Labor and Agriculture in Zanzibar and Coastal Kenya, 1890–1925* (New Haven, Conn., 1980).

—— *On the African Waterfront: Urban Disorder and the Transformation of Work in Colonial Mombasa* (New Haven, Conn., 1987).

—— (ed.) *Struggle for the City: Migrant Labor, Capital and the State in Urban Africa* (Beverly Hills, Calif., 1983).

CORY, H., 'The Sambaa Initiation Rites for Boys', *TNR* 58–9 (1962), 2–7.

DALE, G., 'An Account of the Principal Customs and Habits of the Natives Inhabiting the Bondei Country', *Journal of the Anthropological Institute*, 25 (1895), 181–239.

DUNDAS, C. C. F., *African Crossroads* (Westport, Conn., 1976 (first 1955)).

EASTMAN, C., 'Who Are the Waswahili?', *Africa*, 41 (1971), 228–36.

ELIOT, C., *The East African Protectorate* (London, 1905).

EMERY, J., 'A Short Account of Mombasa and the Neighbouring Coast of Africa', *JRGS* 3 (1833), 280–3.

EPSTEIN, A. L., *Politics in an Urban African Community* (Manchester, 1958).

—— 'The Network and Urban Social Organisation', in J. C. Mitchell (ed.), *Social Networks in Urban Situations* (Manchester, 1969), 77–116.

FEIERMAN, S., *Peasant Intellectuals: History and Anthropology in north Eastern Tanzania* (Madison, Wis., 1990).

FITZGERALD, W. W. A., *Travels in the Coastlands of British East Africa and the Islands of Zanzibar and Pemba: their Agriculture and General Characteristics* (London, 1970 (first 1898)).

FREEMAN-GRENVILLE, G. S. P., *Select Documents of the East African Coast* (Oxford, 1962).

—— 'The Coast, 1498–1840', in R. Oliver and G. Mathews (eds.), *The History of East Africa* (Oxford, 1963), 129–68.

—— *Mombasa Martyrs of 1631* (London, 1980).

GALLAGHER, J. T. (ed.), *East African Culture History* (Syracuse, NY, 1976).

GLASSMAN, J., 'Social Rebellion and Swahili Culture: The Response to German Conquest of the Northern Mrima, 1888–1890', Ph.D. thesis (Wisconsin, 1988).

GOMM, R., 'Bargaining from Weakness: Spirit Possession in the South Kenya Coast', *Man*, n.s. 10 (1975), 530–43.

GRAY, J. M., 'Rezende's Description of Mombasa in 1634', *TNR* 23 (1947), 2–28.

—— *The British in Mombasa, 1824–1826* (London, 1957).

GRIFFITH, J. B., 'Glimpses of a Nyika Tribe (Waduruma)', *JRAI* 65 (1935), 267–95.

GUILLAIN, C., *Documents sur l'histoire, la géographie et le commerce de l'Afrique Orientale* (Paris, 1857).

GUYER, J. (ed.), *Feeding African Cities: Studies in Regional Social History* (London, 1987).

HAMILTON, R. W., 'Land Tenure among the Bantu Wanyika of East Africa', *JAS* 20 (1920), 13–18.

HARRIES, L., 'Swahili Traditions of Mombasa', *Afrika und Uebersee*, 43 (1959), 82–105.

—— 'The Founding of Rabai: A Swahili Chronicle by Mwidani bin Mwidad', *Swahili*, 31 (1961), 141–9.

—— *Swahili Poetry* (Oxford, 1962).

HARTWIG, G., 'Changing Forms of Servitude among the Kerebe of Tanzania', in S. Miers and I Kopytoff (eds.), *Slavery in Africa: Historical and Anthropological Perspectives* (Madison, Wis., 1977), 261–85.

HERLEHY, T., 'Ties that Bind: Palm Wine and Blood Brotherhood on the Kenya Coast during the Nineteenth Century', *IJAHS* 17 (1984), 285–308.

—— and MORTON, R. F., 'A Coastal Ex-Slave Community in the Regional and Colonial Economy of Kenya: The Wamisheni of Rabai, 1880–1963', in S. Miers and R. Roberts (eds.), *The End of Slavery in Africa* (Madison, Wis., 1988), 254–81.

HICHENS, W., 'Liyongo the Spearlord', typescript in SOAS library, London, MS 20500.

HINNEBUSCH, T., 'The Shungwaya Hypothesis: A Linguistic Reappraisal', in J. T. Gallagher (ed.), *East African Culture History*, (Syracuse, NY, 1976), 1–42.

HOBLEY, C. W., 'Some Native Problems in East Africa', *JAS* 17 (1922–3), 287–301.

—— *Kenya: From Chartered Company to Crown Colony: Thirty Years of Exploration and Administration in British East Africa* (London, 1929).

HODGES, G., *The Carrier Corps: Military Labour in the East African Campaign, 1914–1918* (London and New York, 1986).

HORTON, M. C., 'Early Settlement on the Northern Kenya Coast', Ph.D. thesis (Cambridge, 1984).

HUTTON, J. (ed.), *Urban Challenge in East Africa* (Nairobi, 1970).

ILIFFE, J., 'A History of the Dock-workers of Dar es Salaam', *TNR* 71 (1970), 119–48.

—— *A Modern History of Tanganyika* (Cambridge, 1979).

JANMOHAMED, K., 'African Labourers in Mombasa, c.1895–1940', in B. A. Ogot (ed.), *Economic and Social History of East Africa* (Nairobi, 1976), 156–79.

—— 'A History of Mombasa, c.1895–1939; Some Aspects of

Economic and Social Life in an East African Port Town under
Colonial Rule', Ph.D. thesis (Northwestern, 1977).

JOHNSON, D. A., and ANDERSON, D. M. (eds.), *The Ecology of Survival:
Case Studies from North-East African History* (London and Boulder,
Col., 1988).

JOHNSTONE, H. B., 'Notes on the Customs of the Tribes Occupying
Mombasa Subdistrict, British East Africa', *JRAI* 32 (1902), 263–
72.

KAYAMBA, H. M. T., 'Notes on the Wadigo', *TNR* 23 (1947), 80–96.

KENYA, *Kenya Colonial Report for 1929* (London, 1930).

—— *Mombasa Town Planning Scheme* (Nairobi, 1926).

—— *Native Affairs Department Annual Report, 1925* (Nairobi, 1926).

—— *Native Affairs Department Annual Report, 1928* (Nairobi, 1929).

—— *Native Affairs Department Annual Report, 1929* (Nairobi, 1930).

—— *Native Labour Commission, 1912–1913: Evidence and Report* (Nairobi,
1913).

KINDY, H., *Life and Politics in Mombasa* (Nairobi, 1972).

KIRKMAN, J. S., *Men and Monuments on the East African Coast* (London,
1964).

KIRO, S., 'The History of the Zigua Tribe', *TNR* 34 (1953), 70–4.

KITCHING, G., *Class and Economic Change in Kenya: The Making of an
African Petite Bourgeoisie, 1905–1970* (London and New Haven, Conn.,
1980).

KNAPPERT, J., *Four Centuries of Swahili Verse* (London, 1979).

KOFFSKY, P., 'The History of Takaungu, East Africa, 1830–1895',
Ph.D. thesis (Wisconsin, 1977).

KRAPF, J. L., *Travels and Missionary Labours during an Eighteen Years'
Residence in Eastern Africa* (London, 1968 (first 1860)).

—— *A Dictionary of the Suahili Language, Compiled by the Reverend Dr.
J. L. Krapf* (London, 1882).

LAMBERT, H. E., 'The Arab Community and the Twelve Tribes of
Mombasa', in G. Wilson (ed.), 'The Social Survey of Mombasa',
typescript in KNA library, 81–92.

LONSDALE, J., and BERMAN, B., 'Coping with the Contradictions: The
Development of the Colonial State in Kenya, 1895–1914', *JAH* 20
(1979), 487–505.

McDERMOTT, P. L., *British East Africa or IBEA. A History of the Formation and Work of the Imperial British East Africa Company* (London,
1895).

McEVOY, F. D., 'Understanding Ethnic Realities among the Grebo
and Kru peoples of West Africa', *Africa*, 47 (1977), 62–79.

McKAY, W. F., 'A Pre-Colonial History of the Southern Kenya Coast',
Ph.D. thesis (Boston, Mass., 1975).

MAMBO, R. M., 'Nascent Political Activities among the Mijikenda of

Kenya's Coast during the Colonial Era', *Trans-African Journal of History*, 16 (1987), 92–120.

MARTIN, J., 'Krumen "Down the Coast": Liberian Migrants on the West African Coast in the Nineteenth and Early Twentieth Centuries', *IJAHS* 18 (1985), 400–23.

MAW, J., and PARKIN, D. (eds.), *Swahili Language and Society* (Vienna, 1985).

MAZRUI, AL-AMIN, 'The History of the Mazrui Clan', typescript in Fort Jesus Library, Mombasa.

MIERS, S., and KOPYTOFF, I. (eds.), *Slavery in Africa: Historical and Anthropological Perspectives* (Wisconsin, 1977).

—— and ROBERTS, R. (eds.), *The End of Slavery in Africa* (Madison, Wis., 1988).

MITCHELL, J. C., *The Kalela Dance: Aspects of Social Relationships among Urban Africans in Northern Rhodesia* (Manchester, 1956).

—— 'The Concept and Use of Social Networks', in J. C. Mitchell (ed.), *Social networks*, 1–50.

—— (ed.), *Social Networks in Urban Situations* (Manchester, 1969).

MORTON, R. F., 'The Shungwaya Myth of Mijikenda Origins: A Problem of Late Nineteenth-Century Kenya Coastal Historiography', *IJAHS* 5 (1972), 397–423.

—— 'Slaves, Freedmen and Fugitives on the Kenya Coast, 1873–1907', Ph.D. thesis (Syracuse, NY, 1976).

—— 'New Evidence Regarding the Shungwaya Myth of Mijikenda Origins', *IJAHS* 10 (1977), 628–43.

MUMBA, M. K., *The Wrath of Koma* (Nairobi, 1987).

MUNRO, J. F., 'British Rubber Companies in East Africa before the First World War', *JAH* 24 (1983), 369–79.

—— 'Shipping Subsidies and Railway Guarantees: William Mackinnon, Eastern Africa and the Indian Ocean, 1860–1893', *JAH* 28 (1987), 207–30.

MUTORO, H. W., 'The Spatial Distribution of the Mijikenda *Kaya* Settlements on the Hinterland Kenya Coast', *Trans-African Journal of History*, 14 (1985), 78–100.

—— 'An Archaeological Study of the Mijikenda *Kaya* Settlements on Hinterland Kenya Coast', Ph.D. thesis (UCLA, 1987).

NEW, C., *Life, Wanderings and Labours in Eastern Africa* (London, 1971) (first 1877)).

NICHOLLS, C. S., *The Swahili Coast: Politics, Diplomacy and Trade on the East African Littoral, 1798–1856* (London, 1971).

NORDEN, H., *Black and White in East Africa* (London, 1924).

O'CONNOR, A., *The African City* (London, Melbourne, Sydney, 1983).

OGOT, B. A. (ed.), *Zamani: A Survey of East African History* (Nairobi, 1974).

—— (ed.), *Economic and Social History of East Africa* (Nairobi, 1976).

OLIVER, R., and MATHEWS, G. (eds.), *The History of East Africa* (Oxford, 1963).

ONSELEN, C. van, *Studies in the Economic and Social History of the Witwatersrand*, i and ii (Harlow and New York, 1982).

OWEN, W. F. W., *Narrative of Voyages to Explore the Shores of Africa, Arabia and Madagascar, Performed in HM Ships Leven and Barracouta* (London, 1833).

PARKIN, D., *Town and Country in East and Central Africa* (Oxford, 1975).

—— 'Being and Selfhood among Intermediary Swahili', in J. Maw and D. Parkin (eds.), *Swahili Language and Society* (Vienna, 1985), 247–60.

—— 'Swahili Mijikenda: Facing Both Ways in Coastal Kenya', *Africa*, 59 (1989), 161–76.

POUWELS, R., 'Sheikh al-Amin b. Ali Mazrui and Islamic Modernism in East Africa, 1875–1947', *International Journal of Middle Eastern Studies*, 13 (1981), 329–45.

—— *Horn and Crescent: Cultural Change and Traditional Islam on the East African Coast, 800–1900* (Cambridge, 1987).

PRINS, A. H. J., *Coastal Tribes of the North-Eastern Bantu* (London, 1951).

—— *The Swahili-Speaking Peoples of Zanzibar and the East African Coast* (London, 1967).

RANGER, T. O., *Dance and Society in Eastern Africa, 1890–1970: The Beni Ngoma* (London, 1975).

—— 'Missionaries, Migrants and Manyika: The Invention of Ethnicity in Zimbabwe', in L. Vail (ed.), *The Creation of Tribalism in Southern Africa* (London and Berkeley, Calif., 1989), 118–50.

ROBERTS, A. D., *A History of the Bemba* (London, 1973).

SALIM, A. I., *The Swahili-Speaking Peoples of the Kenya Coast, 1895–1963* (Nairobi, 1973).

—— 'The Elusive Mswahili: Some Reflections on his Culture and Identity', in J. Maw and D. Parkin (eds.), *Swahili Language and Society* (Vienna, 1985), 215–27.

—— *State Formation in Eastern Africa* (London and Nairobi, 1986).

SASSOON, H., 'Excavations on the Site of Early Mombasa', *Azania*, 15 (1980), 1–42.

SHERIFF, A., *Slaves, Spices and Ivory in Zanzibar: The Integration of an East African Commercial Empire into the World Economy, 1770–1873* (London, Nairobi, Dar, Athens, Oh., 1987).

SPEAR, T. T., 'Traditional Myths and Historians' Myths: Variations on the Singwaya Theme of Mijikenda Origins', *HIA* 1 (1974), 67–84.

—— *The Kaya Complex: The History of the Mijikenda Peoples to 1900* (Nairobi, 1978).

SPEAR, T. T., *Kenya's Past: an Introduction to Historical Method in Africa* (Nairobi, 1981).

—— 'Oral Tradition: Whose History?', *HIA* 8 (1981), 165–81.

—— *Traditions of Origin and their Interpretation: The Mijikenda of Kenya* (Athens, Oh., 1982).

SPERLING, D. C., 'The Growth of Islam among the Mijikenda of the Kenya Coast', Ph.D. thesis (London, 1988).

STEDMAN JONES, G., *Outcast London: A Study of the Relationship between Classes in Victorian Society* (Oxford, 1971).

STEERE, E., *Swahili Tales* (London, 1870).

STICHTER, S., *Migrant Labour in Kenya: Capitalism and African Response* (London, 1982).

—— *Migrant Labourers* (Cambridge, 1985).

STIGAND, C., *The Land of Zinj* (London, 1966 (first 1913)).

STRANDES, J., *The Portuguese Period in East Africa* (Nairobi, 1961).

STREN, R., 'A Survey of Lower Income Areas in Mombasa', in J. Hutton (ed.), *Urban Challenge in East Africa* (Nairobi, 1970), 97–115.

STROBEL, M., *Muslim Women in Mombasa, 1890–1975* (New Haven, Conn., 1979).

SUTTON, J. E. G., 'Dar es Salaam: A Sketch of a Hundred Years', *TNR* 71 (1970), 1–19.

SWANSON, M. W., 'The Sanitation Syndrome: Bubonic Plague and Urban Native Policy in the Cape Colony, 1900–1909', *JAH* 18 (1977), 387–419.

SWANTZ, L., 'The Zaramo of Dar es Salaam: A Study of Continuity and Change', *TNR* 71 (1970), 157–64.

VAIL, L. (ed.), *The Creation of Tribalism in Southern Africa* (London and Berkeley, Calif., 1989).

VANSINA, J., *Oral Tradition as History* (Madison, Wis. 1985).

WALLER, R., 'Emutai: Crisis and Response in Maasailand, 1883–1902', in D. A. Johnson and D. M. Anderson (eds.), *The Ecology of Survival: Case Studies from North-East African History* (London and Boulder, Col., 1988), 73–112.

WALSH, M., 'Mijikenda Origins: A Review of the Evidence', typescript in BIEA library, Nairobi.

WATTS, M., 'Brittle Trade: A Political Economy of Food Supply in Kano', in J. Guyer (ed.), *Feeding African Cities: Studies in Regional Social History* (London, 1987), 55–111.

WERNER, A., 'The Bantu Coast Tribes of the East African Protectorate', *JRAI* 45 (1915), 326–54.

—— 'A Swahili History of Pate', *JAS* 14 (1914–15), 148–61, 278–97, 392–413.

WESTCOTT, N, 'The East African Sisal Industry, 1929–1940: The

Marketing of a Colonial Commodity during Depression and War', *JAH* 25 (1984), 445–61.

WILLIS, J., '"And So They Called a Kiva": Histories of a War', *Azania*, 25 (1990), 79–85.

—— 'Thieves, Drunkards and Vagrants: Defining Crime in Colonial Mombasa', in D. M. Anderson and D. Killingray (eds.), *Policing the Empire: Government, Authority and Control, 1830–1940* (Manchester, 1991), 219–35.

—— 'The Makings of a Tribe: Bondei Identities and History', *JAH* (forthcoming).

WILSON, G., 'The Social Survey of Mombasa' (1957), typescript in KNA library.

WOLPE, H., 'Capitalism and Cheap Labour Power in South Africa: From Segregation to Apartheid', *Economy and Society*, 1 (1972), 425–67.

YOUNGHUSBAND, E., *Glimpses of East Africa and Zanzibar* (London, 1910).

Glossary

Thalatha Taifa	Three Tribes ⎱ who together make up the
Tissia Taifa	Nine Tribes ⎰ Twelve Tribes of Mombasa
Kilifi	the largest of the Nine Tribes
Wakilifi	Members of Kilifi
Kilindini	the largest of the Three Tribes
Wakilindini	members of Kilindini
beni	dance society (also *gwaride*)
buibui	Muslim woman's garment
gwaride	see *beni*
jamaa	friend, associate
kambi	Mijikenda elder(s)
kaya	sacred site of the Mijikenda
kibarua	casual labour
kipande	Native Registration Certificate
kubo	chief
liwali	governor
makuti	palm thatch
mama wa kumwosha	woman who instructs a girl at puberty
marinda	skirt worn by Mijikenda women
mjomba	mother's brother, sister's child
mudir	Arab district official
ndugu	relative
nyere	uninitiated Mijikenda men
serangi, serahangi	leader of a work-gang
shamba	cultivated land
Shihiri	a recent migrant from the Hadhramaut
tajiri	wealthy person, patron
tembo	palm-wine
tindal	leader of part of a work-gang
wajomba	plural of *mjomba*
washenzi	savages, uncivilized people
zumbe	chief

Index